THE NEW BOOK OF KNOWLEDGE ANNUAL

1979

HIGHLIGHTING EVENTS OF 1978

THE NEW BOOK OF KNOWLEDGE ANNUAL

THE YOUNG PEOPLE'S BOOK OF THE YEAR

Grolier

INCORPORATED
DANBURY, CONNECTICUT

ISBN 0-7172-0610-6
The Library of Congress Catalog Card Number: 79-26807

5

CONTENTS

CONTRIBUTORS

ALEXANDER, George
Science writer, *The Los Angeles Times;* President, National Association of Science Writers (1977–79)
THE BEES ARE COMING

ASIMOV, Isaac
Associate Professor of Biochemistry, Boston University School of Medicine; author, *Light; Today and Tomorrow and . . .; Science Past—Science Future*
NEW USES OF LASERS

BERTRAND, Gerard A.
Chief, International Affairs, U.S. Fish and Wildlife Service
CONSERVATION

BULL, John
American Museum of Natural History
PELICANS

CRONKITE, Walter
CBS News Correspondent
THE YEAR IN REVIEW

DOMOFF, Daniel J.
Consulting Editor, Educational Developmental Laboratories, McGraw-Hill Book Company
THE WEALTH OF THE ANTARCTIC
THE IRON AGE COMMUNITY
YOUTH IN THE THEATER

FERGUSON, Melba M.
Girl Scouts of the U.S.A.
GIRL SCOUTS AND GIRL GUIDES

FRENCH, Bevan M.
Program Chief, Extraterrestrial Materials Research Program, National Aeronautics and Space Administration, Washington, D.C.; author, *The Moon Book; Mars: the Viking Discoveries; What's New on the Moon?*
CATCH A FALLING STAR
SPACE BRIEFS

GOLDBERG, Hy
Co-ordinator of sports information, NBC Sports
SPORTS, 1978

GOLDSMITH, Harry
Former patent counsel
TOYING AROUND WITH AN IDEA

GRIMM, Michele and Tom
Writers and photographers; authors, *The Basic Book of Photography; Hitchhiker's Handbook; My Brown Bag; Twisters; Florida; What Is a Seal?*
FRISBEE-CATCHING CANINES

HAHN, Charless
Stamp Editor, *Chicago Sun-Times*
STAMP COLLECTING

HARP, Sybil C.
Editor, *Creative Crafts* magazine; *The Miniature Magazine;* member, Hobby Industry Association of America
DISCOVERING CRAFTS

HELLMAN, Hal
Author, *Transportation in the World of the Future*
TRANSPORTATION OF THE FUTURE

JENNER, Bruce
Athlete; winner of the decathlon at the 1976 Olympic Games
Highlight article in READY, SET—RUN!

KURTZ, Henry I.
Associate Editor, *Human Nature* magazine; author, *John and Sebastian Cabot; Captain John Smith*
OLD FORT WILLIAM
CAPTAIN JAMES COOK: A GREAT EXPLORER
FERRY TO FREEDOM

MISHLER, Clifford
Publisher, *Numismatic News; World Coin News; Coins* magazine
COIN COLLECTING

MORRISON, Louise D.
The Harpeth Hall School, Nashville, Tennessee
WHAT DO YOU SEE IN THIS PICTURE?

PAYTON, Carolyn R.
Director, Peace Corps
PEACE CORPS

PRICE, Harvey
Chief Scout Executive, Boy Scouts of America
BOY SCOUTS

SHAW, Arnold
Author, *52nd St.: The Street of Jazz; The Rockin' 50s; The Rock Revolution*
THE MUSIC SCENE

SKODNICK, Ruth
Statistician
INTERNATIONAL STATISTICAL SUPPLEMENT

SMITH, Don Jay
Educational writer, American Telephone and Telegraph
A CELEBRATION FOR JOHN BUNYAN

SPERLING, Susan Kelz
Author, *Poplollies and Bellibones: A Celebration of Lost Words*
DON'T GLOP YOUR BELLYTIMBER!

STODDARD, Alexandra
Designer, Alexandra Stoddard Incorporated; author, *A Child's Place; Style for Living*
DECORATING YOUR OWN ROOM

TESAR, Jenny
Sponsoring Editor, *Gateways to Science*
THE RETURN OF THE WINDMILL
MYSTERIOUS HAPPENINGS
THE TOWER OF LONDON

UDALL, Morris K.
Chairman, Committee on Interior and Insular Affairs, U.S. House of Representatives
ENERGY SUPPLY

VICTOR, John
President, Program Design, Inc.
COMPUTERS FOR YOUR HOME
ROBOTS: COMPUTERS IN FANCY PACKAGES

WHITE, JoAnn
Dog breeder and professional handler
SHOWING A TOP DOG

WOLF, William
Film critic, *Cue* magazine
CHARLIE CHAPLIN

THE WORLD IN 1978

One of the most important events of 1978 was the Middle East peace talks sponsored by U.S. President Jimmy Carter. Israel's Menahem Begin and Egypt's Anwar el-Sadat agreed to the framework for a peace treaty between the two countries. Later in the year, the two Middle East leaders won the Nobel peace prize for their efforts.

THE YEAR IN REVIEW

Momentous changes occurred on the world scene in 1978. The United States and China announced that they would establish diplomatic relations, ending 30 years of hostility. The United States and the Soviet Union moved closer to a nuclear-arms limitation treaty. And Egypt and Israel edged closer to a peace treaty.

CHANGES AROUND THE WORLD. Perhaps the most important developments took place in China. Long isolated from the world, this nation of almost a billion people has reversed its course. China has begun a program to modernize its economy, and to do this it is seeking Western economic and technological help. It formed new ties with Japan and other Western countries. And in December, China and the United States announced the start of diplomatic relations.

The Soviet Union, long at odds with China, was alarmed by China's budding friendship with the United States. This may have been partly responsible for last-minute problems with a new Strategic Arms Limitation Treaty (SALT II) being negotiated between the Soviet Union and the United States. By late 1978, after six years of negotiations, agreement on a new treaty seemed imminent. Then, after the U.S.–China announcement, delays occurred. But chances seemed good that SALT II would be completed early in 1979.

Meanwhile, the Soviet Union could point to new alliances of its own. It signed a 25-year trade pact with West Germany. Pro-Soviet governments took office in Afghanistan and Yemen (Aden). In Ethiopia, Soviet assistance was crucial in helping government forces defeat rebel groups. By year's end it was apparent that the Soviet Union had become the dominant military power in the Horn of Africa and in the Indian Ocean.

There were changes elsewhere in Africa, too. In Rhodesia, Ian Smith, leader of the white minority government, agreed to share power with three moderate blacks. However, this arrangement was rejected by guerrilla groups because most power in Rhodesia would remain in white hands for at least another decade.

Israel and Egypt moved another step closer to peace. In September, U.S. President Jimmy Carter invited Israeli and Egyptian leaders to the presidential retreat, Camp David, for intensive negotiations. After thirteen days, Israel's Menahem Begin and Egypt's Anwar el-Sadat agreed to a framework for peace and a December 17 deadline for signing a peace treaty. The conference was hailed as a diplomatic triumph for Carter. But as 1978 ended, negotiations were deadlocked and peace was still pending.

In Iran, the year began with violence as religious groups attempted to depose Shah Mohammed Reza Pahlavi, ruler of the nation for more than 37 years. The religious leaders and their followers, all traditional Muslims, objected to the rapid economic and social changes that had been instituted by the Shah. They were offended by such Western influences as movie theaters, liquor stores, and night clubs. They also said the Shah's rule was corrupt and oppressive. By the end of 1978, opposition to the Shah was widespread throughout the country, and the continuing violence had brought the nation—and its rich oil wells—to a standstill. As a result, the Shah asked a longtime opponent to form a civilian government. Many nations watched the developments closely. Some depend on Iran for a large portion of their oil; others wondered if a radical change of government would end Iran's alliance with the West.

Violence of another sort occurred in the jungles of Guyana. More than 900 members of an American religious group called the Peoples Temple died as the result of an apparent mass suicide and murder. The mass death was ordered by the group's leader, the Reverend Jim Jones, who told his followers that they were going to be killed by enemies.

The tragedy of the "boat people" has become a concern around the world. In 1978, thousands of Vietnamese fled Vietnam and a regime they considered repressive. The people crowded onto small fishing boats and headed out to sea. Many drowned at sea when the fragile boats overturned. Those who were rescued or who managed to reach other Asiatic lands found that no one wanted more Vietnamese refugees. Finally, a number of Western nations agreed to increase their quotas for Vietnamese immigrants.

CHANGES IN THE UNITED STATES. Inflation—that is, rising prices—was the country's number-one topic of conversation and also its number-one problem. Californians fed up with ever-rising property taxes began a tax revolt, which quickly spread across the country. Voters approved propositions that would set spending and tax limits on local and state governments. Leaders of the movement proposed an amendment to the U.S. Constitution that would cap federal spending. But whether cuts could be made without hurting police and fire protection, schools, and other services that Americans have come to expect remained to be seen.

The value of the dollar dropped drastically against other currencies. For American consumers, this meant higher prices on imported goods. For American workers, it meant a better market for their goods, both in the United States and overseas. The fact that the United States imports much of its petroleum was at least partially responsible for the fall of the dollar. In November, Carter's moves to fight inflation led to a rise in the dollar's value. However, both the dollar and the U.S. economy face a difficult 1979. One problem: OPEC, a group of oil-exporting nations, announced that it would increase oil prices 14.5 percent in 1979.

Carter's standings in the polls hit a low in midsummer, then bounced back up after the Camp David meeting. But debate continued on some of Carter's foreign-policy decisions, such as the Panama Canal Treaty and recognition of China, as well as on plans to limit inflation and budget deficits by holding down government spending.

A YEAR OF ACHIEVEMENT AND HOPE. 1978 was a year that saw new achievements in science, sports, and other human endeavors. Soviet cosmonauts set new space endurance records. Three men crossed the Atlantic in a balloon. A Japanese adventurer traveled by dog sled to the North Pole. The world's first test-tube baby was born in England. Muhammed Ali lost, then regained, his boxing title. Teenager Steve Cauthen rode Affirmed to racing's Triple Crown. And the New York Yankees came from behind to win the World Series.

Catholicism also held the spotlight in 1978, both with sadness and with joy. In August, Pope Paul VI died. His successor, John Paul I, died after only 33 days in office. Then, for the first time in 455 years, a non-Italian was elected pope. Athletic, good-humored, and outgoing, Pope John Paul II—a former Polish cardinal—quickly won the confidence and the hearts of the world's 700,000,000 Catholics.

Pope John Paul II's outspoken support for religious freedom and human rights brought new hope to Catholics, particularly those in Communist-ruled Eastern Europe. Similarly, Chinese Government statements favoring freedom of speech and democracy brought new hope to the Chinese people. In many nations around the world, freedom and human rights won important victories in 1978. As the year ended, people everywhere looked at their alliances—local, national, and international—and hoped these would ensure freedom, peace, and prosperity.

WALTER CRONKITE

6 President Jimmy Carter returned to Washington after a nine-day, seven-nation tour. The journey included visits to Poland, India, Iran, Saudi Arabia, Egypt, France, and NATO headquarters in Belgium. Four issues dominated Carter's talks with foreign leaders: the Middle East, human rights, the spread of nuclear weapons, and Western defense.

11 Two Soviet cosmonauts docked their Soyuz spacecraft to the Salyut 6 space station. They joined two other cosmonauts who had docked with the station in late 1977. This was the first time that two spacecraft had docked with a space station at the same time. It was an important step toward the establishment of a permanent space station, since it showed that the Soviet Union could change crews and keep the station supplied with food.

13 Senator Hubert H. Humphrey (Democrat from Minnesota) died at the age of 66. Humphrey—"the happy Warrior"—entered the Senate in 1949 and became a dominant figure in U.S. politics. From 1965 through 1968 he was vice-president of the United States. After an unsuccessful presidential race against Richard M. Nixon, Humphrey returned to the Senate in 1970.

A political cartoon showing Menahem Begin and Anwar el-Sadat after the suspension of Egyptian-Israeli peace talks.

A Canadian specialist handles radioactive debris from a Soviet satellite that malfunctioned, re-entered Earth's atmosphere, and broke up.

18 Anwar el-Sadat, president of Egypt, ordered his foreign minister to return from Israel, thereby suspending the Egyptian-Israeli peace talks. Disagreement between the two countries centered on the issues of Palestinian self-determination and the return of Arab territories occupied by Israel since 1967.

24 The first nuclear-related space crisis occurred when Cosmos 954, an unmanned Soviet spy satellite, re-entered Earth's atmosphere and broke up. The incident took place over a remote area in Canada's Northwest Territories. Canadian and U.S. scientists found some radioactive remains of the satellite and its nuclear reactor. But it is believed that no people were harmed by the accident.

FEBRUARY

8 The northeastern United States began to dig out from one of the worst snowstorms of the century. Heavy snow accumulations paralyzed traffic and brought business activity to a standstill. Winds and high tides caused great damage in coastal areas. This was the latest of several blizzards that had battered much of North America since the beginning of the year.

18 In Cyprus, two Palestinian gunmen killed the editor of Egypt's leading newspaper. With fifteen hostages, the gunmen then took off in a Cyprus Airways plane. But they were forced to return to Cyprus the next day because other nations refused to allow the plane to land. As Cypriot officials negotiated with the gunmen, Egyptian commandos arrived and attacked the plane. The gunmen surrendered. At the same time, Cypriot troops opened fire on the Egyptians, who had not received Cypriot permission for the attack. Fifteen Egyptians were killed. As a result of the incident, Egyptian President Anwar el-Sadat broke relations with Cyprus.

In one of the worst snowstorms to hit New York City, people take to skiing on city streets.

In Cyprus, Palestinian gunmen herd fifteen hostages onto a bus headed for the airport.

21 The U.S. Supreme Court, by refusing to hear an appeal, gave the oil industry the right to drill for oil and natural gas off the coast of New Jersey. No one knows how much oil and gas lie in this underwater area. (Exploratory drilling began in March, the first drilling to occur off the U.S. east coast.)

24 In China, the People's Political and Consultative Conference met for the first time since 1964. Among those present were leaders of minority groups, including the spiritual leader of Tibet. This appeared to be an attempt by Chinese leaders to improve relations with minorities, intellectuals, and overseas Chinese. Two days later, China's legislature, the National People's Congress, began a ten-day session. A ten-year plan for rapid economic growth and improved living standards was approved. Also approved was a new constitution that gives citizens many rights they hadn't had for more than twenty years, including the right to be defended in a trial.

4   A severe rainstorm caused mudslides and widespread flooding in southern California and northern Mexico. At least 25 people died as a result of the storm, which also caused extensive property damage. Almost 30 inches (760 millimeters) of rain fell on southern California in a series of storms during the 1977–78 winter. This ended a two-year drought and enabled towns to end water-rationing programs.

15   Citing a need to "root out [Palestinian] terrorist bases," Israeli troops entered Lebanon and took control of the southern part of the country. The invasion followed a Palestinian raid into Israel on March 11, in which more than 30 Israelis were killed. (On March 19, the United Nations called for Israeli withdrawal from Lebanon and agreed to send a U.N. peace force to the area to try to prevent further "hostile activities of any kind.")

The worst oil spill in history greatly harmed the animal life off the coast of France.

Coal miners returned to work in March, ending a 112-day strike.

16 Two Soviet cosmonauts returned to Earth after 96 days in space aboard the space station Salyut 6. This was the longest mission ever in the history of space flight. A highlight of the mission was the March 3 docking of Soyuz 28, which carried a Soviet colonel and a Czech pilot. The Czech became the first person in space from a country other than the Soviet Union or the United States.

16 In Rome, terrorists belonging to a group called the Red Brigades kidnapped Aldo Moro after killing his five bodyguards. Moro, one of Italy's most important political leaders, was premier five times. This was the latest in a series of attacks by Red Brigades members against politicians, judges, businessmen, and other important Italians. (On May 9, Moro was found murdered, in Rome.)

17 The supertanker *Amoco Cadiz* ran aground and broke in two off the coast of France. Its cargo—some 200,000 tons of crude oil—leaked into the sea, causing the worst oil spill in history.

27 Members of the United Mine Workers union began to return to work. This ended a 112-day strike, the longest walkout of coal miners in U.S. history.

APRIL

2 The Reverend Mary Michael Simpson, an American Episcopal priest, became the first ordained woman to preach in London's Westminster Abbey. In her sermon, she urged the Church of England to ordain women as priests. The Church of England and the American Episcopal Church belong to the Anglican Communion, a worldwide community of churches.

3 President Carter ended a seven-day trip that included stops in Brazil, Nigeria, and Liberia. The African visits were the first by an American president to black Africa. Carter told the Nigerians that his administration would work for majority rule in southern Africa.

6 A bill that raises the age at which most U.S. workers must retire, from 65 to 70 years, was signed into law by President Carter. The new law, effective January 1, 1979, does not affect voluntary early retirement plans.

17 U.S. General Lucius D. Clay died at the age of 80. He commanded the U.S. forces in Europe after World War II. He also organized the airlift that saved the people of Berlin during the Communist land blockade of that city in 1948 and 1949.

U.S. President Carter and family in Nigeria.

Will Geer, TV's "Grandpa Walton," died at the age of 76.

18 The U.S. Senate ratified a treaty that will give Panama complete control of the Panama Canal by the year 2000. A month earlier, the Senate had approved a treaty guaranteeing the neutrality of the canal.

22 Will Geer died at the age of 76. The American actor's career spanned six decades. In recent years he was best known for his portrayal of the grandfather in the TV serial "The Waltons."

27 A military junta seized power in Afghanistan, killing President Mohammed Daud Khan and members of his family and staff. The new government said the country would be nonaligned and independent.

30 Japanese explorer Naomi Uemura became the first person to reach the North Pole alone by dog sled. His trip across the frozen Arctic Ocean covered 600 miles (965 kilometers) and took 54 days.

1 The Soviet composer Aram Khachaturian died at the age of 74. He wrote many symphonies, concertos, film scores, and other compositions, using the folk music of his native Armenia as inspiration. The *Saber Dance,* his best-known piece, is popular around the world.

12 The U.S. Department of Commerce announced that hurricanes would be given both male and female names. For example, the second Pacific hurricane of 1978 will be named Hurricane Bud—not Hurricane Betsy or Barbara. This ends a 25-year-old practice of naming all tropical storms after women, which had been criticized by feminist organizations.

15 The U.S. Department of Agriculture ordered meat packers to greatly reduce the amount of nitrates in bacon. Nitrates have been used for hundreds of years to preserve bacon and to give it a reddish color. However, when bacon is cooked, the nitrates change to nitrosamines. In recent years, research has shown that nitrosamines can cause cancer in animals and so may also cause cancer in human beings. Instead of nitrates, other chemicals will be used to preserve bacon.

The Soviet composer Aram Khachaturian, who died in May.

Long lines form outside a casino in Atlantic City, New Jersey, where gambling became allowed for the first time.

24 Britain's Princess Margaret and her husband, the Earl of Snowdon, were divorced, ending eighteen years of marriage. This was the first time in 450 years that a member of the immediate royal family was divorced.

26 Antonio Guzmán was declared the winner of the Dominican Republic's presidential election, which had been held on May 16. He defeated Joaquín Balaguer, who had been president for twelve years. (On August 16, Guzmán became president. This was the first time in the nation's history that power peacefully passed between two constitutionally elected governments.)

26 Legal casino gambling began in Atlantic City, New Jersey. The seaside city thus became the second place in the United States where such gambling is allowed (Nevada has had legal gambling since 1931). New Jersey residents hope that the casinos will create new jobs and will encourage investment in the area. Tax revenues from the casinos may reach $35,000,000 a year by 1985 and will be used to help the poor and the elderly.

JUNE

8 Naomi James of Britain set a new record for sailing around the world. She completed the solo voyage in 272 days. This was two days faster than the previous record, set by Sir Francis Chichester in 1967. During the voyage aboard her sloop, *Express Crusader,* James set another record: the longest nonstop sail by a woman. This was the 14,000-mile (22,530-kilometer) trip from Capetown to the Falkland Islands.

9 It was announced that the Mormon Church would begin to admit black men to its priesthood. The 148-year-old church, otherwise known as the Church of Jesus Christ of Latter-Day Saints, had previously excluded black members from this assignment. Priesthood is a major part of the Mormon religion. All males are expected to become priests at the age of 12.

15 A U.S. Supreme Court ruling confirmed the strength of the Endangered Species Act. The court ruled that work on a $120,000,000 dam project in Tennessee must stop because, once completed, the dam would wipe out a fish called the snail darter. After the decision, the head of the Tennessee Valley Authority announced that the dam would be redesigned to protect the snail darter's environment.

Naomi James stands on her sloop after having set a world record for sailing around the world.

The bomb explosion in the Palace of Versailles caused great damage to many art objects.

26 A bomb planted by terrorists exploded in the Palace of Versailles. The palace, located southwest of Paris, is one of France's most historic buildings. It houses many beautiful furnishings and art treasures. The explosion caused heavy damage to a number of rooms, as well as to paintings, statues, and other objects.

28 The U.S. Supreme Court ruled against rigid racial quotas in college admissions. But it also ruled that minorities may receive special considerations. The decision, considered the most important ruling on civil rights since school segregation was outlawed in 1954, came in what is known as the Bakke case. Allan Bakke had brought suit against the University of California after being denied admission to its Medical College. The college had set aside sixteen of its entrance places for minorities. The court said that the college's quota system was unconstitutional because it was rigidly biased against white applicants like Bakke. But the court also said that flexible "affirmative action" programs, which give certain advantages to groups that have been discriminated against in the past, are allowable.

7 The U.S. Naval Observatory announced that astronomer James W. Christy had discovered a moon in orbit around Pluto. This is the first satellite known to orbit Pluto, which is believed to be the outermost planet in the solar system.

7 The Solomon Islands became an independent nation. Located east of Australia and New Guinea, the Solomons had been under British rule for 85 years. Peter Kenilorea became the country's first prime minister.

17 A two-day economic meeting of leaders from seven Western nations ended in Bonn, West Germany. The heads of the governments of Britain, Canada, France, Italy, Japan, the United States, and West Germany agreed to try to lower world unemployment without increasing inflation. The United States was criticized because it had not enacted an energy policy and had not reduced oil imports. High energy consumption by the United States is viewed by the other nations as a major threat to world stability.

The leaders of seven Western nations in Bonn, West Germany, for an important economic meeting.

The birth of the first "test-tube" baby makes the headlines of a British newspaper.

21   In a military coup, Juan Pereda Asbún became Bolivia's new president. On July 9, elections had been held in Bolivia for the first time since military rule began in 1966. According to the official tally, Pereda had more than 50 percent of the votes for president. However, the National Electoral Court voided the results, calling them fraudulent. Pereda then led a rebellion that forced President Hugo Banzer Suárez to resign and hand over the reins of office.

25   Medical history was made when a 31-year-old woman gave birth to the world's first "test-tube" baby. The baby, a girl named Louise, is the child of John and Lesley Brown of Bristol, England. She was conceived in a laboratory, from an egg taken from Mrs. Brown's body and from sperm taken from Mr. Brown. Two and a half days later, the fertilized egg was implanted in Mrs. Brown's uterus. From then on, the pregnancy proceeded normally. The success of the procedure offers hope to many women who have problems conceiving children.

6 Pope Paul VI died of a heart attack at the age of 80. Leader of the Roman Catholic Church since 1963, Pope Paul was known as the "Pilgrim Pope" because of his many visits to countries around the world. (On August 26, the church's Sacred College of Cardinals elected Cardinal Albino Luciani of Venice to be Pope. Luciani took the name John Paul I.)

6 Edward Durell Stone, one of America's most important architects, died at the age of 76.

14 Texaco Inc. announced that natural gas had been found at a drill site in the Atlantic Ocean, some 100 miles (160 kilometers) east of New Jersey. This was the first proof that natural gas, and perhaps petroleum, lie beneath the Atlantic off the eastern U.S. coast.

Edward Durell Stone, architect of the General Motors Building, died.

Jomo Kenyatta, president of Kenya for 15 years, died.

20 In Abadan, Iran, a fire swept through a movie theater, killing 430 people. This was the worst incident in a wave of violence that began in late 1977. Government officials blamed Muslim extremists for the fire. Conservative Muslims have opposed many of the government's liberalization policies, saying that they were contrary to the teachings of the Koran, the holy book of the Muslim religion. Movie theaters are considered sinful by conservative Muslims.

22 Jomo Kenyatta, president of Kenya, died. He was in his late 80's. Kenyatta was the nation's leader in its struggle for independence from Britain. When independence was won in 1963, Kenyatta became the first president. He helped Kenya become one of Africa's most stable and prosperous nations.

26 Charles Boyer, the French-born actor whose career spanned more than 60 years, died at the age of 79.

13 What may be the largest uranium ore deposit in the world was found in northwest Saskatchewan, Canada. The deposit lies far below a very deep lake, which will make recovery of the ore difficult. Uranium is used in nuclear weapons and as a fuel in nuclear reactors that produce electricity.

16 A powerful earthquake struck northeast Iran. About 25,000 people were killed, and some 40 villages were almost completely destroyed.

17 Middle East summit talks, which had begun September 6, ended with unexpected success. The meeting was sponsored by U.S. President Jimmy Carter and held at Camp David, the presidential retreat in Maryland. Israel's Menahem Begin and Egypt's Anwar el-Sadat agreed to the framework for a peace treaty between the two countries. The agreement was strongly criticized by the Soviet Union and most Arab nations, four of which broke relations with Egypt.

Menahem Begin, Jimmy Carter, and Anwar el-Sadat participated in Middle East summit talks in the United States.

Ventriloquist Edgar Bergen (pictured with his puppet Charlie McCarthy) died.

20 John Vorster, prime minister of South Africa since 1966, unexpectedly resigned. (On September 28, members of the ruling National Party elected Defense Minister Pieter Willem Botha to replace Vorster. Both men are strong advocates of South Africa's racial policy of apartheid, or separation of the races.)

25 A jetliner and a single-engine plane collided in the skies over San Diego, California, killing 144 people, including a number of people on the ground. It was the worst such air accident in U.S. history.

28 Pope John Paul I died of a heart attack at the age of 65. He had been pope only 33 days, the shortest reign of a pope in 373 years.

30 Edgar Bergen, America's best-known ventriloquist, died at the age of 75. Bergen's most famous puppet was Charlie McCarthy, a wisecracking city boy who wore a monocle.

OCTOBER

6   The U.S. Congress extended the time limit for ratification of the Equal Rights Amendment. The new deadline is June 30, 1982. By that date, 38 states must approve the proposed amendment to the Constitution.

11   Aristides Royo was elected president of Panama by the nation's congress. At 38, he is the youngest president in Panamanian history.

15   Irene Miller and Vera Komarkova became the first women ever to scale Annapurna. Annapurna is in the Himalayas and is the 10th highest mountain in the world. Miller and Komarkova were part of an American expedition. The group consisted of ten women who ranged in age from 18 to 50. It was the first American group to reach the mountain's top and only the fourth group ever to conquer the difficult peak.

Vera Komarkova (*left*) and Irene Miller (*right*)—shown with two Sherpa guides—became the first women to scale Annapurna, the tenth highest mountain in the world.

15 Dan Dailey, the American actor, died at the age of 62. He was best known as a song-and-dance man in film musicals of the 1940's and 1950's.

16 Karol Wojtyla, the Cardinal Archbishop of Cracow, Poland, was elected pope of the Roman Catholic Church. He took the name John Paul II. It was the first time in 455 years that a non-Italian was chosen pope.

23 A Treaty of Peace and Understanding between China and Japan went into effect. Documents ratifying the treaty were exchanged between leaders of the two nations at ceremonies in Tokyo, Japan. It is hoped that the treaty will improve political, economic, and scientific relations between China and Japan, and also contribute to peace and stability in the entire Asiatic region.

THE 1978 NOBEL PRIZES

Chemistry: Peter Mitchell of Britain, for his theory of bioenergetics. The theory explains how living cells store and transfer energy.

Economics: Herbert Simon of the United States, for his work on how complex economic organizations, such as multinational companies, make business decisions.

Literature: Isaac Bashevis Singer of the United States, for his "impassioned narrative art which, with roots in a Polish-Jewish cultural tradition, brings universal human conditions to life." Singer, a short-story writer and novelist, writes almost entirely in Yiddish, the language of central European Jews.

Peace: President Anwar el-Sadat of Egypt and Prime Minister Menahem Begin of Israel, for their peacemaking efforts in the Middle East.

Physics: Arno A. Penzias and Robert W. Wilson of the United States and Piotr L. Kapitsa of the Soviet Union shared the prize. Penzias and Wilson were honored for their discovery of background radiation in the universe. This helped support the "big bang" theory of how the universe was created. Kapitsa was honored for his work in low-temperature physics.

Physiology or Medicine: Daniel Nathans and Hamilton O. Smith of the United States and Werner Arber of Switzerland, for their work in genetics. Arber discovered enzymes that are able to cut genetic material. Nathans and Smith showed how these enzymes could be used to re-assemble genetic material in new ways.

NOVEMBER

1 Uganda announced that its troops had occupied 700 square miles (1,820 square kilometers) of territory in neighboring Tanzania. (Tanzania mobilized troops and by late November had driven the Ugandans out.)

2 The longest space flight ever ended. Soviet cosmonauts Vladimir Kovalenok and Alexander Ivanchenkov returned to Earth after 139 days, 14 hours, and 48 minutes aboard the Salyut 6 space station.

3 Dominica, an island in the eastern Caribbean, became an independent republic, ending almost 200 years of rule by Britain.

6 Military rule was imposed in Iran by the nation's ruler, Shah Mohammed Reza Pahlavi. Since the beginning of 1978, Iran had been swept with antigovernment demonstrations in which more than 1,000 people died. The Shah hoped that military rule would restore calm. However, opposition leaders called for new strikes and more demonstrations in an effort to oust the Shah.

7 In U.S. elections, the Republicans made modest gains but the Democrats retained control of Congress. The results in the House of Representatives—276 Democrats, 159 Republicans. In the Senate—59 Democrats, 41 Republicans.

7 Gene Tunney, the American heavyweight boxing champion from 1926 to 1928, died at the age of 80.

8 Norman Rockwell, the American artist known for his paintings of small-town America, died at the age of 84.

15 Margaret Mead, the noted American anthropologist and author, died at the age of 76.

18 In Guyana, more than 900 people died in an apparent mass murder and suicide. They were Americans who were members of the Peoples Temple, a religious cult led by Reverend Jim Jones. The Temple, based in San Francisco, had an agricultural community in northwestern Guyana. The horror started when U.S. Congressman Leo J. Ryan and others visited the commu-

Freedom from Want, by Norman Rockwell. The artist, who died at the age of 84, was well known for his paintings of small-town life.

nity to investigate charges of brainwashing and brutality. As Ryan and those with him began to leave the commune, a group of Temple members opened fire, killing Ryan and four others. Meanwhile, Jones summoned everyone in the community to a meeting at which he told them, "We must die with dignity." A drink containing cyanide was prepared. Except for a few members who escaped, all took the drink, either willingly or by force. In the days that followed, many investigations into the tragedy and into the life of the Peoples Temple were begun.

24 The Bolivian Army, led by General David Padilla Arancibia, staged a coup. This ended the four-month-old government of Air Force General Juan Pereda Asbún, who had seized power in a coup on July 21.

DECEMBER

7   Masayoshi Ohira was elected premier of Japan. He replaces Takeo Fukuda, premier since 1976.

8   Golda Meir, prime minister of Israel from 1969 to 1974, died at the age of 80.

15   The United States and the People's Republic of China announced that they would establish diplomatic relations on January 1, 1979. There have been two Chinese governments since 1949, when the Communists came to power and set up the People's Republic on the mainland. Their opponents, the Nationalists, set up a second government on the island of Taiwan. The United States and other nations supported the Nationalists. But, over the years, more and more countries began to recognize the Communist government. U.S. relations with the Communists improved during the 1970's. By establishing diplomatic relations, the United States would recognize the Communist government as China's only legal government. And it would end diplomatic relations with the Nationalists.

Golda Meir, prime minister of Israel from 1969 to 1974, died.

Deputy Prime Minister Teng Hsiao-ping, China's key policy maker, helped establish diplomatic relations between China and the United States.

17 The Organization of Petroleum Exporting Countries (OPEC) announced that it would raise petroleum prices 14.5 percent by the end of 1979. Countries such as the United States, which import large amounts of petroleum, expressed fear that the price hike would increase inflation and disrupt the world economy.

23 Argentina and Chile agreed to accept a peace envoy from Pope John Paul II to mediate a dispute between the two nations. At issue is who owns three islands at the Atlantic entrance to the Beagle Channel, at the southern tip of South America.

27 Houari Boumedienne, president of Algeria since 1965, died at the age of 51.

THE EQUAL RIGHTS AMENDMENT

In the late 1800's and early 1900's, many women paraded and demonstrated for the right to vote. They were booed or laughed at, and some were arrested. But they continued to fight. And finally, in 1920, they were successful—they won the right to vote.

Today, many women are again parading and demonstrating for their rights. They are focusing their efforts on the Equal Rights Amendment, or ERA. This is a proposed amendment to the U.S. Constitution. It states: "Equality of rights under the law shall not be denied or abridged by the United States or any state on account of sex."

In other words, people could not be discriminated against because of their sex. Men and women would have equal rights.

The ERA seems simple enough. But it is controversial—it has caused argument and debate ever since it was first introduced in Congress, in 1923. Almost 50 years passed before Congress approved it in 1972. But to become part of the Constitution, it must also be approved, or ratified, by legislatures of 38 states. By the end of 1978, thirty-five states had done so, although four had then voted to withdraw their approval. And people continued to argue for and against the amendment.

According to a 1978 poll, 58 percent of Americans are for ERA; 31 percent are against it; the remaining 11 percent are undecided. Why is the ERA so controversial?

People who oppose the ERA say it isn't necessary. They say that the amendment wouldn't give women any rights they don't already have. But supporters say that the laws giving equal rights can be changed. The ERA would be permanent. And they say it would strengthen laws that are sometimes ignored. For example, some laws require equal pay for equal work, but in practice men often earn more than women.

Opponents call the ERA "antifamily" and say it would destroy traditional American values. Supporters disagree. Judy Carter, President Jimmy Carter's daughter-in-law, says: "ERA does not require that any personal habits be changed. It simply guaran-

At the turn of the century, women marched to win the right to vote . . .

National Rally for Equal Rights

. . . while today, many women are marching to support the Equal Rights Amendment.

tees a woman the same legal rights as a man if she needs them."

Opponents say the ERA would mean that husbands would no longer financially support their wives. Phyllis Schlafly, a leading opponent, says: "The [present] law protects a woman's right to be a full-time wife and mother, her right *not* to take a job outside the home, her right to care for her own baby in her own home while being financially supported by her husband. ERA would remove this sole obligation from the husband and make the wife *equally* responsible . . . to provide 50 percent of the financial support of her family."

Supporters say the ERA would not affect relationships within a marriage—these would continue to be worked out by husband and wife. But in case of a divorce, they say, there would be a fairer sharing of property acquired during a marriage. And both parents would have an equal right to be awarded custody of children. "The *best* parent . . . would be considered," says Professor Laura Sager of New York University. And, she adds, husbands would have to support former wives only if the women could not support themselves. In many cases, the women need financial support and the ex-husbands have the ability to provide this support. But, says Sager, "take a couple who get divorced . . . with equal pay prospects. Why should the man have to [support] her?"

The ERA would also prohibit discrimination by the military. Among other changes, this would mean that women would be eligible for combat duty during wartime. Phyllis Schlafly says: "Foxholes are bad enough for men, but they certainly are not the place for women." The League of Women Voters disagrees: "The fact is that true equality does require that all persons accept the duties and responsibilities as well as the rights of citizenship."

Under ERA, men and women could not be treated differently by the law. Today, in many ways, they are treated differently. For example, in some states girls can marry at 16 without their parents' permission, but boys must wait until they are 18. In some states, women cannot take a job in which they have to lift heavy weights—even though at home they may lift young children who weigh more. Some state laws say that female workers should be given longer rest periods than male workers. Opponents of the ERA say such laws are fair because they take into account differences between men and women. Supporters say the laws are unfair to both sexes.

In 1978, Congress decided that once a state had ratified the amendment, it could not change its vote. And Congress extended the deadline for approval of the ERA from March, 1979, to June, 1982. Will the ERA be approved by then? Do *you* think it should be approved?

SOUTHERN AFRICA

Southern Africa, where the days of white rule seemed to be numbered, dominated the African news in 1978. For several years all eyes have been on Rhodesia and South Africa, the last two white-ruled African nations. People wondered how much longer relatively small numbers of white people could deny the large black populations the vote, civil rights, and a full share in the economic life of the two countries.

▶RHODESIA

For six years a small guerrilla war had been plaguing Rhodesia. This war was being waged by black nationalists whose goal was to topple the white government of Ian Smith—a government that had always refused to give full voting and other civil rights to Rhodesia's 6,500,000 blacks.

In the mid 1970's, Britain and the United States put pressure on Smith to move his country toward majority rule. If he would do this, perhaps the war might be stopped and the safety of the small white population (about 250,000 people) might be ensured.

What complicated matters was that there were five important black nationalist leaders. Two of these, Joshua Nkomo and Robert Mugabe, were the militants whose troops were waging the war. These leaders and their troops received arms and support from the Soviet Union and Cuba. In 1977, Nkomo and Mugabe combined their efforts, calling themselves the Patriotic Front. Because these leaders would not guarantee the safety of the whites if they came to power, Ian Smith did not want to deal with them.

Instead, Smith agreed to share power with the three moderate nationalist leaders: Bishop Abel Muzorewa, Reverend Ndabaningi Sithole, and Senator Jeremiah Chirau. The four leaders formed an interim government, and Smith promised to hold elections for black majority rule in December, 1978. But there was a flaw: none of the moderates had much influence with the guerilla troops. Even if they came to full power, the civil war would probably still rage on.

In October, 1978, Ian Smith and the Reverend Sithole traveled to the United States to try to gain support for their interim government. While there, they offered to attend an "all-parties conference," at which the five black nationalist leaders would try to find a way to share power together. However, even while Smith and Sithole were making this offer, Rhodesian forces were making the heaviest air strikes of the war on Nkomo's guerrilla camps in Zambia. The raids, which were in retaliation for attacks the guerrillas had carried out in Rhodesia, enraged the Zambians and the Patriotic Front and ended conference plans.

As the end of 1978 approached, the ground war in Rhodesia spread, the amount of the country under martial law reached 65 percent, and an increasing number of whites made plans to leave. And Ian Smith announced that in view of the stepped-up warfare, the elections leading to majority rule would have to be postponed. Still, there was one ray of light: the Smith regime promised to set aside laws discriminating against blacks in housing, hospitals, and schools.

▶SOUTH AFRICA

The big story involving South Africa in 1978 had to do with mineral-rich South-West Africa (also called Namibia), a former German colony that borders South Africa on the west. South Africa has governed the territory, which is vast in area, since the end of World War I. For many years, the United Nations has been urging South Africa to grant independence to South-West Africa. But South Africa refused.

What stopped South Africa from agreeing was the powerful South-West Africa People's Organization (SWAPO). SWAPO is a political party led by Communist guerrillas, and it is South Africa's enemy. South Africa feared that in U.N.-run elections, SWAPO (which claims to represent about half the people in the territory) would come to power. Then all good relations between South-West Africa and South Africa would end. And, since SWAPO is supplied with Soviet and Cuban arms, South Africa also feared future attacks from a well-armed and hostile neighbor on its western border.

However, in April, 1978, John Vorster, South Africa's prime minister, surprised the world by agreeing (under pressure from several Western nations) to a plan for a U.N.-supervised election in South-West Africa. This plan called for free elections in late 1978, the presence of U.N. troops in the territory during the elections and for a while afterward, and the withdrawal of South African troops.

In the summer of 1978, the plan hit a snag when the United Nations demanded that Walvis Bay, a deepwater port, be considered part of the territory. Walvis Bay had always been an enclave surrounded by the territory but belonging legally to South Africa's Cape Province. (An enclave is a small "island" of land surrounded by foreign territory.) Vorster opposed the demand for Walvis Bay. In September, he announced he could no longer support the plan.

Vorster unexpectedly resigned as prime minister in September. But his successor, Pieter W. Botha, held much the same views.

Both favored an "internal settlement." By that they meant a South African-supervised election, to take place in December. SWAPO promised to boycott this election because U.N. supervisors would not be on hand. The election would choose leaders from black and white parties friendly to South Africa—and SWAPO would not be represented in the new 50-member assembly.

As positions hardened, SWAPO's allies in Angola, to the north, massed troops near the territory's border. And South Africa built up troops along its own border. But despite the threat of a boycott, 80 percent of the territory's registered voters cast ballots in the December election. Most supported candidates backed by tribal leaders.

The United Nations declared the election void and called for a second vote, under U.N. rules. South Africa answered that it would hold U.N.-supervised elections in 1979. Negotiations to resolve differences between SWAPO and South Africa continued.

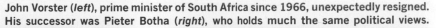

John Vorster (*left*), prime minister of South Africa since 1966, unexpectedly resigned. His successor was Pieter Botha (*right*), who holds much the same political views.

EUROCOMMUNISM

Eurocommunism is a political idea that began to flower in the mid-1970's but seemed to be wilting by the end of 1978. Since Eurocommunism is far from dead, however, it is a good idea to understand what it means.

The first Communist country was the Soviet Union, formed in 1917. Today, most of the other Communist countries follow the instructions of the Soviet Communist Party. These countries are dictatorships ruled by one party (the Communist Party). They disapprove of free elections and the free competition of many differing political parties. Most important, they approve of violent revolution as a way to bring Communism to power.

"Eurocommunism" is a word formed from the words "Europe" and "Communism." It stands for what claims to be a new kind of Communism that has been growing in Italy, France, and Spain. These countries are democracies. But each of them has a large and important Communist party that takes part in the life of the country. These Communist parties compete in elections and often win seats in the parliament (the governing assembly).

The Eurocommunists want to make political gains in non-Communist countries. But rather than trying to overthrow their governments, they say they will work for gradual change, co-operate in elections, and accept the existence of many political parties.

This is a big change, and people in both the Western democracies and in the Soviet bloc have been concerned about it. Some people in the democracies suspect that the new Eurocommunist parties might only be pretending to accept democratic ways. They

Voting in France: many people thought the Communists would make political gains, but they didn't.

worry that once a Eurocommunist party becomes part of the government of a democracy, its members might someday become the elected rulers of the country. Then the Communist rulers might decide to go right back to the typical Soviet Communist way of governing. And overnight, what had once been a democracy might very well find itself a dictatorship.

The Soviet Union and its closest Communist allies fear something quite different. They are afraid the Eurocommunist parties might veer too far away from the Soviet Communist pattern. They might be softened by the ways of the Western democracies and become too much like them.

▶EUROCOMMUNISM LOSES GROUND

By early 1978, the Spanish Communist Party had lost much of its importance because it had done very badly in the 1977 elections. So the Italian and French Communist parties were the ones to watch. Most people believed they would gain many votes in the 1978 elections and in both cases be asked to join the government, with members holding cabinet posts. It did not happen, for peculiar reasons.

Italy. In Italy the Communists are very numerous. They help the moderate party—the Christian Democrats—to govern the country under a deal worked out between them. In 1978 the Communists hoped to hold their first cabinet posts in the government. But the kidnapping and murder of Christian Democrat leader Aldo Moro put the Communists in a bad light.

Aldo Moro was not killed by Communists, however. In fact, the Communists condemned the killing and worked to try to find the criminals. Moro was killed by the Red Brigades, a terrorist group that had originally followed Communist teachings. But people associated the Red Brigades with the Communists, and so the Communists failed to make big gains in the election that followed the murder.

France. In France the Communist Party is not as large as the one in Italy. But it has been allied with the Socialists for several years. Together they are called "the Left." They form the major political threat to the ruling parties of the "Center-Right."

In Italy, the murder of Aldo Moro by the Red Brigades hurt the Communists at election time.

The Communists and Socialists had worked out a joint economic policy, and it formed the platform they were running on for the 1978 elections. But some months before the elections, the Communist leader, Georges Marchais, withdrew his support from the joint policy. Instead, he offered a hard-line, old-style Communist policy. The joint program collapsed, and the Left went down to defeat in the election. After the defeat, Marchais blamed the Socialists and seemed ready to break up the alliance. Some people wondered whether Moscow had ordered the break.

No one knows what will happen in France and Italy in the future. The Eurocommunists may soon gain more votes—and power—again. Or the suspicions of people who fear even the "softest" kind of Communism may continue to slow their progress.

THREE HOLY MEN

Saint Peter, the apostle of Christ, was the first pope. In the twenty centuries since Peter, 263 men have succeeded to his throne as leader of the Roman Catholic Church. In 1978 the world's 700,000,000 Catholics saw three men serve as *il papa* (Italian for "pope"): Paul VI, John Paul I, and John Paul II. Each of these three holy men, in his own way, well maintained the faith by which the Catholic Church has endured since the time of Saint Peter.

▶ **PAUL VI**

On August 6, 1978, the sad news was announced in Rome: *Il papa e morto*—"The pope is dead." Eighty-year-old Paul VI, who had been pope for 15 years, had died during the evening.

Born Giovanni Montini, Paul VI had been elected the 262nd pope in 1963, following the death of Pope John XXIII. He chose Paul as his papal name in honor of Christ's apostle Paul, who had carried the message of Christianity throughout the Mediterranean world. Like the apostle whose name he bore, Paul VI was a traveler—and he became known as the Pilgrim Pope. He was the first pope since 1809 to travel outside of Italy and he was also the first pope to board an airplane. He went to the Holy Land, to India, to New York City, to the Far East, to Africa, to South America. All his journeys were to promote world peace and understanding. During his reign, he made closer ties between the Roman Catholic Church and other Christian churches, such as the Anglican and the Eastern Orthodox. He also improved relationships between Catholicism and some major non-Christian religions: Judaism, Hinduism, Islam.

Paul VI led the Church during a time of great change. He presided over the Second Vatican Council, at which many aspects of worship were modernized. For example, Catholic masses are no longer conducted in

Paul VI: the Pilgrim Pope.

44

John Paul I: a short, popular reign.

Latin, but rather in the language of the congregation. Also, Catholics had for centuries abstained from eating meat on Fridays as an act of penance. But after the Second Vatican Council, "meatless Fridays" were no longer required of Catholics.

On most matters of Catholic doctrine, however, Paul VI insisted on retaining the original teachings of the Church. His 1968 message, "Of Human Life," reaffirmed the Church's position against birth control. Paul also maintained that only men may become Catholic priests, and he insisted on the tradition of priestly celibacy (the idea that the Catholic clergy may not marry).

Paul VI will be remembered as the man who stood before the United Nations General Assembly and said, "Never again war!" He will be remembered for his having wept when he saw the world's poor. And he will be remembered as a pope who held the Church together during a period of change.

▶ THE WHITE SMOKE

When a pope dies, how is the new pope elected? The world's cardinals, the "princes" of the Church, gather at the Vatican, which is the residence of the pope and the center of the Roman Catholic religion. Hidden away from the outside world, they cast ballots until one cardinal receives at least a two-thirds majority. At times, the election process has gone on for weeks, months, or even years. But after the death of Paul VI, the cardinals chose quickly, electing Albino Cardinal Luciani on the first day of voting. The traditional signal, white smoke rising from a chimney on the Vatican roof, told the world that the Church once again had a leader.

▶ JOHN PAUL I

It was a break in tradition. For the first time in history, a pope chose two names. He called himself John Paul I, naming himself after the two popes who had immediately preceded him. In choosing two names, he was telling the world that he would continue the work of those who had gone before him.

John Paul I was a modest man. Rather than a formal coronation as pope, he wanted a simple inaugural mass. Rather than be carried on a portable throne as other popes had been, John Paul I chose to walk. These, too, were significant breaks in tradition. John Paul I was showing that as pope he would live and act simply and remain close to his followers. He was thought of as a "pastoral pope," one who ministers directly to the needs of his "flock." And people loved him for it. Because of his joy and good humor, he was called the Smiling Pope.

John Paul II: the first non-Italian pope in more than 450 years.

Though in some ways untraditional, John Paul I was in other ways a conservative man. He insisted that Catholics maintain faith in the religious doctrines that had sustained the Church for centuries. He also believed that it was the duty of the Church to help the poor. But as a traditional churchman, he did not feel it was the duty of the Church to take part in political movements.

Sadly, the reign of John Paul I was very short. This man, who had touched so many with his smile and his simplicity, died only 33 days after his election, at the age of 65. For the second time in two months, the world's Catholics said good-bye to their pope. And once again, the cardinals came together to choose a successor.

The greatest break in tradition was yet to come.

▶JOHN PAUL II

When the white smoke rose above the Vatican on October 16, the news flashed around the world. For the first time in more than 450 years, the cardinals had elected a non-Italian pope. He was 58-year-old Karol Cardinal Wojtyla, from Poland.

Out of love for the two popes who had gone before him, he too chose the name John Paul.

The background of John Paul II may be very important in his reign as pope. Poland is a Communist country. Perhaps John Paul's election as pope is a sign that the Catholic Church will now seek better relations with the Communist world, even though as a cardinal, John Paul had criticized the Polish Communist government.

During World War II, the future pope worked against the Nazis in Poland. Since the war, he has had to live under Communist rule. He knows personally what it means to fight for human rights, and one of his first speeches as pope emphasized his concern for oppressed people.

John Paul II is athletic, intellectual, and good-humored. Like Paul VI and John Paul I, he is faithfully committed to the fundamental teachings of the Roman Catholic Church. He has lived with suffering, and many Catholics believe John Paul II will demonstrate the Christian ideal of the suffering servant of all humanity. The reign of the 264th pope has begun hopefully.

THE TAX REVOLT

The tax revolt of 1978—what was it, and how did it happen? It all began in California. Many people there were very angry about the high taxes they were paying on their homes. They protested by putting signs on their lawns and bumper stickers on their cars. Then, in June, they went to the polls and passed Proposition 13. This amendment to the state constitution cut property taxes by more than half and limited future increases in property taxes.

The message of the California voters was clear, and it swiftly spread across the country. Taxes of all kinds had kept going up, and some people said they couldn't afford to pay them. And many people felt that, while they were paying more, they were getting less from their government. Because public officials had not cut spending and reduced waste on their own, the California taxpayers showed that they could force government to spend less by giving it less money. In the November elections, thirteen other states also voted to limit government spending.

State and local officials—and some taxpayers, too—began to worry. They felt that reduced government spending would lead to cutbacks in such important services as school programs, police and fire protection, and aid to the poor, the elderly, and the handicapped. And many government workers could lose their jobs.

Still, many people hoped that the passage of Proposition 13 would encourage officials at all levels to make sensible cuts in their budgets. And almost all politicians running for office in 1978 promised that they would cut spending.

By the end of the year, the effects of the tax revolt were still unclear. Government spending had been rising at the rate of over 10 percent a year. People felt the pinch and wanted taxes lowered—but at what price? Were they willing to accept reduced government services in return? Voters were demonstrating that they had the power to change things they didn't like, but it was not clear what changes they really wanted.

"Enough is enough!"

THE BOAT PEOPLE

In late summer, 1978, a British ship neared a small boat in the South China Sea. The British captain was shocked by what he saw: the tiny boat was filled with people, most so weak as to be near death. They were Vietnamese refugees—35 adults and 19 children—who, seeking freedom, had fled their country in a leaky, old boat. They were lucky to be rescued by the British crew. In a few more days these refugees would certainly have died, just as 20 on the boat had already died. And just as thousands of other Vietnamese "boat people" had died—from starvation, exposure, and drowning in a wide, cruel sea.

▶ESCAPE BY SEA

In 1975, the Vietnam War had finally ended. The Communist North Vietnamese had won, and they took over South Vietnam. But many people in the South could not, or would not, live under Communist rule. Some had fought against the Communists during the war. Others had been part of the South Vietnamese Government and were afraid the Communists would jail them or kill them. Still others couldn't abide the food shortages that plagued the country. So they fled Vietnam, some trying to escape by land, and others, the boat people, by sea.

The only available boats, however, were small fishing boats that had never been meant for ocean voyages. Month by month, thousands of refugees secretly boarded these tiny, unsafe craft, hoping to find more welcoming lands. But many never reached their destinations. It has been estimated that more than 50 percent of the boat people have died at sea. The waves and the weather were too much for the frail wooden boats. The boats broke up, the people drowned—if they had not already died of hunger and cold.

But many of the refugees could have been rescued. Drifting for days in the Gulf of Siam or the South China Sea, they often came upon freighters. Waving frantically, the Vietnamese appealed to be rescued. But unlike the British ship that saved 54 people from certain death, the freighters ignored the pleas of the boat people and left them to die at sea.

There is a traditional law of the sea. It says that ships must always rescue those in distress, even sailors from sinking enemy battleships. What caused the freighters to break this traditional law? Many nearby non-Communist nations—Thailand, Malaysia, Japan, the Philippines, Indonesia, Hong Kong, Singapore, South Korea, Taiwan, Australia—do not want any more Vietnamese refugees. They feel they are already overburdened with refugees. When freighters carrying refugees have reached these countries, they have often been refused permission to unload their cargo. This is because the countries are afraid they will have to take the refugees along with the cargo. As a result, many freighters have stopped rescuing boat people. Some ship captains will give food and water to the refugees, but they will not take them aboard.

▶SOME REACH LAND

Not all the boat people must depend on the mercy of passing freighters. Some do reach land. But the countries they reach often turn them away and send them back out to sea. Some boat people are beset by robbers and murderers. And some boat people only reach crowded, dirty refugee camps. Although Thailand and Malaysia want no more refugees, these countries have set up refugee camps. Here, the boat people jam together in skimpy huts, subsist on meager rations, and await resettlement, often in France or the United States.

Since 1975, over 170,000 refugees from Indochina (Vietnam, Laos, and Cambodia) have settled in the United States. More than 40,000 have settled in France. Smaller numbers are living in Canada, Australia, and Malaysia.

▶A SPECIAL RESPONSIBILITY

In July, 1978, U.S. President Jimmy Carter responded to the increasing numbers of refugees. He ordered all American ships to pick up boat people, and he stated that these refugees could resettle in the United States if they could not find homes elsewhere. In giving this order, President Carter was hoping that other nations would no longer turn away American ships that carried Vietnamese refugees. If the countries could be sure that the United States would accept responsibility for the boat people, then perhaps the countries wouldn't be so reluctant to care for them temporarily.

President Carter's order would of course increase the number of refugees in the United States. But many Americans believe that the United States has a special responsibility to admit refugees from Indochina. It was, after all, the Vietnam War that created the refugee problem in the first place.

What happened to the 35 adults and 19 children picked up by the British ship? In September, 1978, they arrived in Singapore and were placed under the care of the United Nations high commissioner for refugees. Perhaps their future, and that of thousands of other boat people, will be happier than their past.

Many South Vietnamese fled their country in small, unsafe fishing boats not meant for ocean voyages.

THE ANIMAL WORLD

Because of its coloring, this tiger almost blends into its surroundings. This is animal camouflage, and it helps an animal to protect itself from enemies.

ANIMALS IN THE NEWS

Dinosaurs ruled the earth for 165,000,000 years. It has long been believed that they were cold-blooded, inactive animals—like snakes and other reptiles. But recently, a group of scientists presented strong evidence that dinosaurs were actually warm-blooded —like people and other mammals. They say that the way dinosaurs were built indicates that they had high blood pressure and were swift and active animals. But there is still much controversy about the question.

Have you ever seen a fish with headlights under its eyes? This rare, deepwater fish is the *Kryptophanaron alfredi,* also called the flashlight fish. The fish uses its lights to protect itself by blinding its enemies and to attract other fish for food. It can "turn off" its lights by drawing a layer of skin over them. In 1978, six of these fish were found in the Caribbean.

This tiny water creature——a Socorro isopod——has been around for 130,000,000 years. Less than $\frac{2}{5}$ inch (10 millimeters) in length, the isopod looks something like a sow bug or pull bug. It swims on its back, waving all 14 legs as it glides along in the water. About 2,500 Socorro isopods are known to exist. All live in a drainage pond connecting two hot springs near the Socorro Mountains in central New Mexico. In 1978, the Socorro isopod became the first crustacean to be placed on the U.S. Government's list of endangered species.

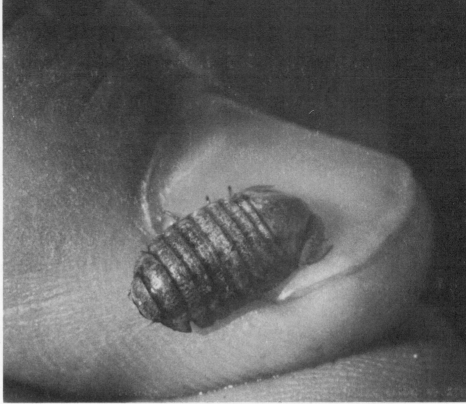

In 1978, Champion Cede Higgens became the first Yorkshire terrier to be chosen best in show at the Westminster Kennel Club show. This show is considered to be the "super bowl" of American dogdom. The tiny dog with the long flowing coat had already been a winner of 31 other best-in-show awards.

Male Princess Parrotfish

SALTY PETS

"I bought some spotted sweetlips," said Barbara.

"My parents gave me a blackbar soldier," said Jimmy.

"I want a whitespotted puffer and a Moorish idol or two," said Kim.

It's hard to tell, but these children are talking about fish. They have a hobby that has suddenly become very popular. They have saltwater aquariums and are raising fish that are as colorful in appearance as they are in name.

Saltwater aquariums, as the name tells you, are ones that contain salt water, like that in oceans. Only ocean fish can live in these aquariums.

There are many different kinds of ocean fish. Some are very big. Others are tiny. Some swim in deep water, never coming near the shore. Others live among the coral reefs in shallow, tropical waters. Some are peaceful. Others often fight. Some are very choosy about food. Others can adapt to many different diets. Which are best for an aquarium?

Most people choose fish that live among the coral reefs. Coral reef fish are generally small, some only an inch (2.5 centimeters) or so in length. Most are less than a foot (30 centimeters) long.

Some of the coral reef fish are shades of gray, brown, or white. They quietly blend into their rock and sand surroundings. Others are the most colorful fish in the world.

Some fish are easier to raise in aquariums than others. Damselfish are recommended for beginning hobbyists. These are attractive fish and usually do not cost very much money. However, most damselfish have strong territorial instincts. That is, each one chooses an area and calls it home. It quickly attacks another member of its species that invades its "property." An exception is the damselfish known as sergeant major or prison fish. This yellow-and-black striped fish likes to move about in groups, or schools.

Most clownfish are also easy to raise. So are triggerfish, but they are fighters—one in a tank is enough!

If you would like to start a saltwater aquarium, talk to people who work in aquarium shops and pet stores. They will tell you how much it will cost to set up an aquarium and show you some of the fish you can raise. And they will explain how to keep the aquarium clean and the fish healthy.

Keeping a saltwater aquarium isn't as easy as keeping a freshwater one. But once you get the hang of it, you will receive a great deal of pleasure from the hobby. You will learn a lot about the lives and habits of saltwater fish. And you, too, will talk about sweetlips and Moorish idols.

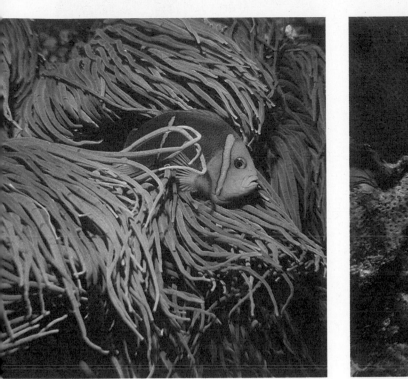

Clownfish

Blackbar Soldierfish

Whitespotted Puffer

Masked Butterflyfish

ASTOUNDING CASTLES OF CLAY

Have you ever heard of termites building houses instead of eating them? Well, if you were to take a trip to the plains of eastern Africa, you would see giant mounds, or earthen "castles," that have been built by termites no bigger than ants. Some of the castles stand 20 to 30 feet (6 to 9 meters) tall, and weigh as much as two or three huge elephants. Each castle is the home of millions of termites.

Actually, the termites live in underground chambers and use the towering mound as a ventilation system, or air-conditioning unit.

The tiny African termites, most of them totally blind, construct their astounding air-conditioning systems because they are sensitive to extreme heat. By building high "chimneys" filled with holes, they can regulate the airflow and the temperature of their homes. Each giant mound consists of a maze of tunnels, walkways, and arches. Cool air circulates throughout this maze and is directed to the chambers below. If the air is very hot, worker termites dig for water and squirt it on the inner walls, thus cooling their home.

Most of the termites in a castle colony are worker termites. They are the ones that build the castles. Their saliva acts like cement when it is mixed with the soil. Inside their earthern dwelling, the workers raise fungus gardens to provide food for the entire colony. The fungus helps the termites to digest wood, the most popular termite dish. Workers feed the digested wood to soldier termites, which are not able to feed themselves. The workers also take care of their queen.

This termite is in a fungus garden, below the towering clay castle. Termites eat the fungus, which helps them to digest wood.

The gigantic queen is the most important termite in the colony because of her ability to lay eggs.

Permanently sealed deep inside the clay castle, the fertile king and egg-laying queen remain in a termite royal chamber. The king is bigger than his workers. But it is the queen that receives all the attention. Four inches (10 centimeters) long and as thick as a hot dog, the gigantic queen dwarfs all the other termites.

Why is the queen so important to the termite society? The reason is her egg-laying ability. A termite queen can lay up to 30,000 eggs a day. The eggs are then stored in special chambers, or nurseries, until they hatch. The queen lays eggs regularly to replace termites that have been destroyed by weather or by enemies.

Termites are constantly threatened by many different enemies. The aardvark, with its long sticky tongue, is able to scoop up thousands of termites in one mouthful. And ants, one of their most feared enemies, can burrow deep into the mound and kill even the king and queen.

Soldier termites protect the society. These soldiers are sterile females with very large heads and powerful jaws. When attacked by invading ants, the soldiers can block a tunnel and kill their enemies. Soldier termites rarely venture outside, where they would be unable to defend themselves or to protect their queen.

The castles of clay that dot the African countryside may look like ruins of a past civilization. But they are the homes of a fascinating society—a society of termites that builds houses instead of eating them.

ADOPT AN ANIMAL

"Please Don't Feed the Animals."

You see that disappointing sign in just about every zoo you go to. If you bring a pocketful of peanuts for the elephant, you usually have to eat them yourself.

But what's this? A new sign! And this one says, "Please *Do* Feed the Animals."

That's right. Many zoos are beginning to ask people to feed their animals. But instead of asking you to reach into your pocket for peanuts, the zoos would rather you reached in for money.

Like everyone else, zoos have been faced with budget problems. The cost of animal food, in particular, has gone way up. So some zoos have come up with a solution to the problem: ask people to "adopt" an animal. An animal lover could choose his or her favorite animal, pay its food bills for the year, and become the animal's "foster parent." As a foster parent, you may not take "your" animal out for a stroll, but you do receive the joy of helping the animal.

The first zoo to try the "adopt-an-animal" program was the Columbus, Ohio, zoo. Other zoos, such as the Brookfield Zoo near Chicago, also have successful programs. Often, an individual person or a family will adopt an animal. Sometimes a class in a school—or the whole school—will raise the money to adopt an animal.

What does it cost to adopt a zoo animal? That depends on the animal. It takes only $10 to feed an Australian flying squirrel for one year. But it takes $2,000 to buy enough fish for a dolphin's yearly fill. Between these two extremes you would pay $25 for a hedgehog and $50 for a medium-size snake. A llama will chomp down $100 worth of grain and grasses, and a leopard will lick its chops over $400 worth of meat. A tiger may cost you $800, a gorilla about $1,000, and a hippopotamus about $1,500.

So if you'd like to become a "zoo parent," please do feed the animals—but not with popcorn and peanuts. Make it cash instead!

SHOWING A TOP DOG

Dog showing has become a major sport, involving hundreds of thousands of exhibitors and their dogs. And the top dog show is the Westminster Kennel Club show, held every year in New York City. One of the competitions at Westminster is for young people only—the junior showmanship finals.

In 1978, more than 70 youngsters competed in this event. After two days of competition, the field was narrowed to eight finalists. In front of applauding crowds, they posed and gaited their dogs as the tension mounted. Finally, the national junior handler champion was chosen—13-year-old Sondra Peterson of San Diego, California.

Many young people have learned that showing dogs is a fascinating and challenging art. It isn't all ribbons and trophies—it involves a lot of hard work. The judges at a dog show form an opinion on the basis of what they see. So a good handler must be able to pose and move the dog to show it to its best advantage. It is the handler's ability that is judged in junior showmanship. Being able to handle a dog smoothly and calmly amid all the noise and tension of a dog show requires a great deal of practice for both the dog and the young handler.

Junior handlers often get their first experience at match shows, which are informal and inexpensive training grounds for exhibitors and dogs. They then move on to point shows, where dogs can earn points toward championship titles. Along the way, the young handlers learn how to pose and gait their dogs, and how to condition and groom them to have them looking their best.

Junior showmanship competition is usually divided by age into classes for boys and girls 10 to 12 and 13 to 16 years old. Entrants compete in different classes based on their records of achievement. All the dogs must be purebred and owned or co-owned by their handlers. Through a special program, dogs are sometimes donated by breeders to encourage young people in the sport of showing dogs.

Junior showmanship is more than excitement and prizes. It teaches good sportsmanship. Lasting friendships are often made among those who meet at ringside or through a nationwide pen pal program. And many top breeders, judges, exhibitors, and groomers in the dog show world got their start in junior showmanship. Perhaps the world of dog shows is waiting for you!

JO ANN WHITE
Dog breeder and professional handler

WHO'S HIDING?

Can you find the hidden animals in the pictures on these pages? Why are they hard to see?

When animals blend into their surroundings, it is known as animal camouflage. Camouflage helps an animal protect itself from enemies. It also helps an animal catch prey—the camouflaged animal can sneak up before the prey realizes it is there.

Camouflage usually has to do with color. When the colors of an animal are nearly the same as the colors of its surroundings, the animal becomes difficult to see. Consider the polar bear. It spends much of its time on large pieces of floating ice. It tries to catch and kill seals for food. Because the polar bear is white and blends in with the ice, it can sneak up on the seals. Imagine how much harder if would be for the polar bear to catch seals if it were brown or green.

Animals that live in northern lands often have two coats. In summer, weasels, snow hares, and Arctic foxes have brown hair. As summer ends, they shed the brown hair and grow white coats.

Flounders and some other flatfish can change their appearance to blend with sand, mud, or pebbles. This is done by enlarging or shrinking color spots in the skin. On a pale, sandy ocean floor, the flounder will be pale. If it moves to a spotted, pebbled area, it too will become spotted. Squids, octopuses, and certain shrimps and frogs can also change color quickly.

Some animals practice a form of camouflage called mimicry. This means pretending they are something else. There is a mantis in Malaysia that looks like a pink and white orchid. Insects searching for nectar suddenly find themselves under attack. At the same time, birds and lizards that would like to eat the mantis don't see it. They only see an "orchid."

There are tree-dwelling geckos that look like bark, and chameleons that look like dried leaves. The viceroy butterfly fools its enemies by looking like a monarch butterfly. The monarch butterfly tastes awful, and animals that have eaten one or two avoid it—and anything that looks like it.

The young mule deer blends into the forest floor. If it senses danger, it will remain absolutely still so that its enemies won't see it.

The spotted scorpionfish is almost invisible in the coral reef where it lives. This fish is also protected by very sharp spines.

In winter, the ptarmigan is almost completely white and nearly disappears in the snow. In summer, this same ptarmigan has speckled brown feathers that help it blend with the rocks of the tundra.

61

The coyote's yellowish brown coat blends in with the grasses. Rabbits and mice won't see it slowly coming closer until it is too late to escape.

Weasels that live in Canada and the northern United States are pure white in winter. This helps them hide from animals that want to catch them.

This geometrid moth caterpillar hopes its enemies will think it is a twig. By staying very still and keeping its body at a certain angle, it looks like part of the tree. This kind of camouflage is called mimicry.

The varying hare, or snowshoe rabbit, is another animal that changes coats with the seasons. In summer, it disappears into the grasses. In winter, it is pure white except for the tips of its ears.

This cricket frog is nearly invisible in the stream. Its brownish coloring and warty skin make it look just like a bunch of pebbles in the water—until an unsuspecting insect wanders by.

THE HALL OF REPTILES AND AMPHIBIANS

Did you know that:

• People eat pythons more often than pythons eat people.

• Many lizards can shed their tails, probably to escape danger. The broken-off tail continues to snap and jump, diverting the enemy while the lizard runs away.

• In Colombia, Chocó Indians use substances from the skins of certain frogs to make poison for their blowgun darts.

These are some of the things you can learn in the new Hall of Reptiles and Amphibians, at the American Museum of Natural History in New York City. None of the animals are alive there. But they are nearly perfectly re-created. For example, there is a Burmese python made of plastic. A real Burmese python, which is a very rare snake, was drugged and covered with plaster for about twenty minutes. This was the first time that a plaster mold was made from a living snake. After the plaster was removed and the snake awoke, it was given to a nearby zoo. The plaster mold was then used to make a plastic model of the snake. The model was carefully painted, scale by scale.

The hall has many displays that show how reptiles and amphibians look, and live, in their natural habitats. Komodo dragons (the largest lizards in the world) are shown devouring a dead wild boar. A huge loggerhead turtle skeleton hangs from the ceiling of its exhibit case, as if swimming through the ocean. A female leatherback turtle is shown laying eggs in a nest on a Florida beach.

Within many of the displays, there are "mini-exhibits." These explain the biology of reptiles and amphibians. They show how the animals move, eat, reproduce, use en-

Eye to eye: A youngster looks at a cobra, one of the world's most poisonous snakes. Nearby, there is an exhibit that explains how to treat snake bites.

Lunch time: This exhibit (*above*) shows the natural habitat of Komodo dragons. These animals live in Indonesia where, as you can see, they may feed on wild boar.

Anatomy lesson: This exhibit (*right*) shows how reptiles are built. At the far left is a python skeleton. Look at all the ribs it has!

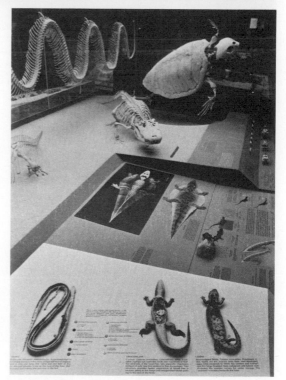

ergy, and ward off enemies. There is a caiman (a relative of the alligator) eating a frog—and a frog eating an insect. There is a salamander with gills, a snake with legs, and a flying frog.

Other exhibits describe the role that reptiles and amphibians play in human lives. Did you know that European exploration of the Americas would not have been possible without the green turtle? This animal was killed to provide fresh meat for explorers, who otherwise would not have had enough food for the long voyage across the Atlantic.

Reptiles and amphibians are among the most colorful and varied animals in the world. Visit the new hall, and you will learn all about their world.

WHY ANIMALS FIGHT

Nobody likes fighting, except maybe bullies, boxers, and hockey players. Fighting upsets people. It causes bloody noses and black eyes, and it really doesn't solve any problems.

Fighting isn't good for animals either. When two animals of the same species fight, it is a waste of their time and energy. It keeps them from being on guard for predators. And it could leave them weak and crippled.

But animals of the same species often need to show who has the right to living space, food, or mates. How do they do it without fighting?

One way is to use the Big Noise. Tiny shrews may stand face to face and scream their heads off at each other. The one who screams the loudest wins a living space called a territory.

Another way is the Terrible Tooth Show. Baboons and wolves curl their lips, screw up their faces, and show their long canine teeth. The ones who can put on the meanest and nastiest looks become the leaders of the rest of the group.

Still another way is the Big Body Bluff. Owls spread their wings and fluff out all their feathers. This makes them look twice their real size. Cats stand sideways and lift the hair on their backs to look big and mean. Praying mantises rear up and wave their strong front legs while showing off their colorful wings.

Whatever way they use, animals usually can show who's boss or who should own a territory. And most do it without losing a single hair or feather.

For some animals, though, bluffs don't always work. Then the animals may come

Zebra stallions will kick and bite each other.

Bull elks lock antlers and push and shove.

66

Bears stand up, growl, and swipe at each other.

Fighting Siberian tigers may really be playing.

into contact or fight. But even then the rule usually is "Don't hurt anybody!" To show who's boss of the herd, two bull elks may stand head to head, lock antlers, and push and shove. The weaker gives up; the stronger gets the most mates.

Brown bears may fight over the best fishing spot. They stand up, growl loudly, and swipe each other with their powerful paws. The weaker bear usually runs off before either gets hurt. Zebra stallions will kick and bite to see who gets to lead the herd and to mate with the mares. Again, the weaker fighter knows when to give up.

Most animal fights are between two males. But females may also fight, or a male may fight with a female. Many times, though, a male and a female may appear to be fighting when they actually are not.

Before mating, red foxes stand on their hind legs and hug each other with their front legs. All the while they hold their mouths wide open. And a pair of yellow-billed storks flap their wings and hit their bills together. They have taken movements that male storks use in fighting and have turned them into a love dance.

So why do animals fight? It's a way they decide, when bluffing fails, who can mate and raise strong, healthy babies. It's a way they decide who gets a territory and the food to be found there. And it's a way they decide who is strong and brave enough to lead and defend the group. For animals, fighting is usually a harmless contest that leads to peace.

GERRY BISHOP
Ranger Rick's Nature Magazine

THE BEES ARE COMING

One of the common sounds of summer is the hum of honeybees as they flit about the garden. These gentle insects have always been thought of as nature's helpers. They carry pollen from bloom to bloom, making the flowers develop into fruit. Bees make honey, too—that delicious natural food. Of course we know that bees can sting, but they usually do that only when disturbed. And a person will usually suffer stings from only a bee or two.

All this is true of the type of honeybee living in North America and Europe. These bees are called European bees. But in South America another type of honeybee, originally from Africa, is making many people nervous. It is not gentle. In fact, its nickname has become "the killer bee." And this bee is moving toward North America.

But let's take a closer look at this killer bee and the stories that have sprung up about it.

▶ THE AFRICAN BEE

We'll begin in Africa, where William Lyon, a bee specialist, had a frightening encounter with the killer bees. The young American was working in the eastern African country of Kenya several years ago when a Kenyan woman came to him for help. She owned a house that she wanted to rent out, but could not do so because a large colony of African honeybees had moved into one of the walls. No one, of course, wanted to live under the same roof with a great many bees. Would Lyon help her get rid of them?

Lyon agreed to help her and went, with an assistant, to her house. He knew that this particular kind of bee could mean trouble. But his assistant, who was less familiar with the bees, abruptly yanked a board off the side of the house. Thousands of bees sprang from their nest and began stinging everyone and everything in sight.

The villagers fled in all directions. But the bees continued to chase them, stinging men, women, children, and animals. The bees even entered other village huts and attacked the people they found there. No one was safe, not even Lyon and his helper in their beekeeper suits. These special suits have snug-fitting cuffs around the ankles and wrists to prevent bees from getting inside, and there is a bonnet with a veil to protect the face and neck. Beekeepers usually wear these suits whenever they handle bees. But the suits didn't do much for Lyon and his assistant. The bees were able to wriggle under the edges of the veils.

It was a horrible experience. But Lyon finally brought the bees under control by going back to his laboratory, picking up backpacks of insecticide, returning to the village, and spraying them.

It is incidents like this that have earned this little honeybee the name of "killer bee." Some writers have even gone so far as to declare that the bees have a natural hatred for human beings because humans have been raiding the insects' hives and taking their honey for thousands of years.

Scientists say that explanations like this are nonsense. People have always taken the honey from all kinds of honeybees—why should the African kind be the only one to have this intense hatred?

The more likely reason for the African bee's alarming fierceness is to be found in its genes, the tiny biochemical units of heredity we all carry.

The African bee's genes probably make it a tough little fighter. And because it is a tough little fighter, it has been able to defend itself and its hive against other creatures that would prey upon it—creatures like army ants, armadillos, wasps, and, of course, people. By defending itself, the bee has survived.

The African bee is also very sensitive to disturbances of any kind, and it responds with great vigor. When a human acts this way, we say that the person has a "quick temper" or a "short fuse."

Scientists are pretty sure that when any bee stings something, it releases into the air a biochemical substance called a *pheromone*. Pheromones, which have a chemical property that bees recognize, are, in effect, messages. Insects use them to communicate with one another. And so when the first few bees in a hive are disturbed and attack the offending party—whether it be a cow, a column of ants, or a human—their stinging sends out alarm calls to the other bees in the hive. The alarms summon the other bees to the defense of the hive.

When an African hive is disturbed, large numbers of bees give chase. So the alarm process snowballs: more bees mean more stings. More stings mean the release of more pheromones. More pheromones mean more bees called into action. More bees, more stings. And so on.

"Fool around with ordinary honeybees," said one specialist, "and you may get ten or fifteen stings as you escape. But fool around with these African bees, and you may get several hundred stings before you can finally get away from them."

It is the large amount of venom that hundreds of bees inject into a victim that makes them such a hazard to other creatures. The venom itself is basically no different from that of other types of honeybees.

▶THE AFRICAN BEE REACHES SOUTH AMERICA

Back in 1956, government scientists in Brazil decided to import some African bees.

The Brazilians knew that the African bee was a fierce insect, but they also knew that it was a hard worker and an excellent producer of top-quality honey.

The plan was to crossbreed the African bees with the gentle European bees kept by Brazilian beekeepers and farmers. The scientists hoped the crossbreeding would produce a bee that would be easy to handle but would also fly far and wide in search of food. This searching, known as foraging, is very important in agriculture because the bees carry pollen for different fruit crops as they fly from blossom to blossom. This process, called pollination, enables plants to bear fruit.

But the Brazilians never got the chance to carry out their plan. A beekeeper accidentally released most of the queen bees into the wild. And their descendants (called Africanized bees) have been spreading across South America ever since. Today the bee can be found throughout Brazil, Uruguay, Argentina, Venezuela, and parts of Colombia and French Guiana. And it is these bees that are heading for North America.

What has happened as the bees have spread out over wider and wider areas? Have they caused widespread death and de-

Africanized honeybees look very much the same as European honeybees. Here, two Africanized bees are exchanging food (honey).

An Africanized bee collects water from water plants. The water will be brought back to the hive, where it will cool the colony by evaporation.

struction? Apparently not. There have been a number of reported cases of humans dying as a result of massive stinging by colonies of Africanized bees, but only one or two are considered to be true stories.

Several groups of American bee experts have visited South America in the past few years to get a firsthand look at the Africanized bee. They have found out some interesting things.

First of all, not all Africanized bees are equally vicious. Although all these bees (which look nearly the same as the European honeybees most people are familiar with) must be treated carefully, it does seem that only some of them are likely to go on stinging rampages. This difference between one group and another tells scientists that the reason for the bees' behavior must be in their genes.

Secondly, experiences with the bee in southern Brazil, Uruguay, and Argentina show that its ferocity can be brought under control. In those regions, there were large populations of gentle European honeybees. The Africanized bees that invaded those countries mated with the resident bees. The offspring of these matings were very much like what the Brazilian scientists had had in mind when they imported African bees: hard-working, productive honeybees.

Whenever beekeepers or farmers in those southern areas found a colony of bees whose fierceness had not been lessened by crossbreeding with more gentle local bees, they either removed the queen bee from the hive and destroyed her (since only the queen lays eggs) or destroyed the entire colony.

There are well-established bee populations in Costa Rica and other parts of Central America and in Mexico, and crossbreeding with these should help soften the Africanized bee's fierce nature. Vicious colonies or vicious queens will have to be spotted and destroyed.

One thing is clear, say the experts: the bee will never be brought under control by insecticides. Any poison that kills bad bees will also kill good bees. But by carefully planned breeding programs and by the destruction of ferocious individual bees, the Africanized bee may become a welcome guest to North America when it arrives here—probably sometime in the early 1990's.

GEORGE ALEXANDER
Science Writer
The Los Angeles Times

FRISBEE-CATCHING CANINES

The Frisbee whirls through the air. A player named Dink springs into action. He catches the disc before his feet hit the ground. What accuracy! What a dog!

Dink is a lucky dog, too. Jim Strickler saw him in a Pittsburgh dog pound and took him home as a pet. His new owner also taught Dink to catch a Frisbee.

Dink learned to run after the flying disc, leap into the air to grab it with his teeth, and then bring the Frisbee back to his master. He became so good at catching and fetching Frisbees that Jim entered him in a few contests. And Dink kept winning.

Then, after only eighteen months of training, Dink made the finals of the 1978 World K-9 Frisbee Championship. This canine contest was held in the Rose Bowl stadium in Pasadena, California, as part of the fifth annual World Frisbee Championships.

Three other dogs also reached the finals, which were seen by 50,000 people. Ashley Whippet, who had been the world champ for three straight years, ended up in second place. Toke came in third; and Ivey Lee, fourth. Dink placed first—becoming the world's greatest Frisbee-catching canine. Dink was awarded a $1,000 savings bond and all the dog food he could eat for one year.

No one knows Dink's age or breed, but his owner/trainer thinks one of the dog's parents must have been a Labrador retriever. "Dink just loves to chase Frisbees and bring them back to me," says Jim. The day Dink won the championship, his happy owner gave him a big steak for dinner!

Any dog can compete for Dink's title as the world champ. Preliminary catch-and-fetch tournaments, sponsored by park and recreation departments, are held during the summer in more than 500 cities across the United States. Nine regional winners are chosen, and they compete for the honor of performing at the world Frisbee finals in the Rose Bowl.

Dink—the 1978 World Frisbee Champ—with his proud owner, Jim Strickler.

72

In the all-important finals, the dogs perform one at a time and are awarded points by the judges. During two minutes of catch-and-fetch competition, a point is given each time a dog catches a Frisbee thrown by its master at least 45 feet (13.7 meters). If a catch is made with all four paws off the ground, the dog gets an extra point. The dogs are also allowed three minutes of freestyle performance. They are judged on their style and agility in catching and returning the plastic discs.

A little booklet has been written about how to teach your dog to catch a flying Frisbee. To receive a free copy of this booklet, write to:

Gaines Dog Research Center
250 North Street
White Plains, New York 10625

For information about local K-9 catch-and-fetch contests, write to:

Lander and Associates
5430 Van Nuys Boulevard
Van Nuys, California 91401

MICHELE AND TOM GRIMM
Authors, *What Is a Seal?*

Former world champion, Ashley Whippet.

This catch made with four paws in the air earned Dink an extra point.

WORLD OF SCIENCE

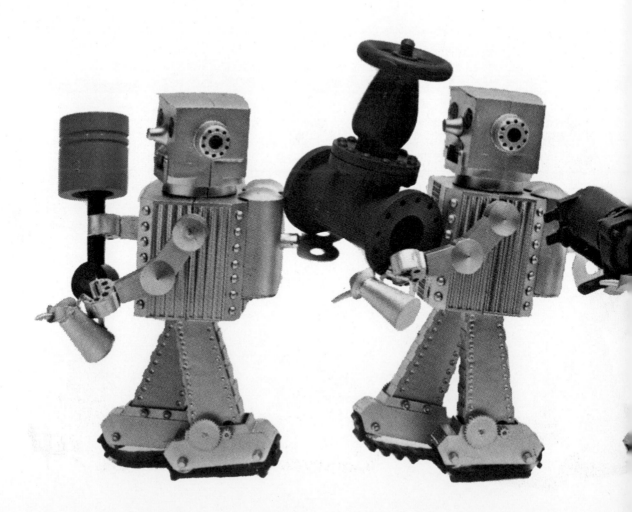

Robots, which are really computers in fancy packages, do many things to help people.

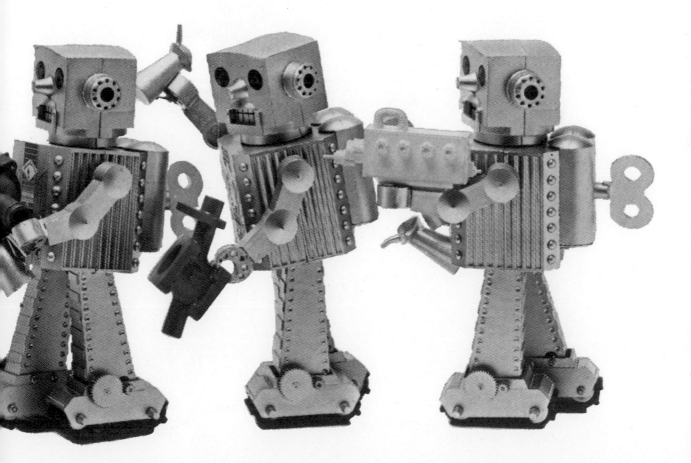

TRANSPORTATION OF THE FUTURE

On his way into the kitchen, Andrew Wilson touched the button marked "Car" on the electronic communications panel in his living room. By the time he had finished breakfast, a rented Electra-car, delivered automatically from the town depot, was waiting for him at his front door.

Andrew slid into the sleek two-seater, inserted his All-Credit card (which acted as both ignition key and accounting agent), stepped on the accelerator, and was on his way.

A short drive brought him to the automated electronic highway. As he approached the entrance to the highway, he punched out his destination on a computer console located on the car's dashboard. This beamed his destination, plus the car code, to the highway control computer. His car radio came on.

"I see," said Highway Control, "that you are going to the Long Distance Transportation Terminal in New York City. Your distance to the terminal is twenty-eight miles, or forty-five kilometers. The trip this morning will take seventeen minutes. Please switch to automatic now."

Andrew Wilson flicked the proper switch and relaxed. "Now for an important decision," he chuckled. "Shall I read, sleep, or watch the news on television?"

Feeling the car slow down, Andrew opened his eyes. His car radio came on again and a gentle voice said, "Mr. Wilson, you are approaching the terminal. We hope you enjoyed your ride."

Andrew shook himself slightly and mumbled, "So soon?" He checked the map displayed on his cathode-ray tube. Sure enough, the little white dot showed that he was entering the midtown New York City area.

Soon the Electra-car came to a smooth halt in the basement of the giant Long Distance Terminal. Andrew got out, punched the "Park" button, and watched the car glide away, to be used by someone else. He mused, "I think I read somewhere that people had to park their own cars a hundred years ago. Seems hard to believe."

A few steps brought him to a moving floor called a glidewalk. He stepped on and a female voice sounded in his ear: "Welcome, traveler, to the first *fully integrated public transportation system on earth*. Where are you bound?"

"Area 303, San Francisco, California."

"You have a choice of the hypersonic transport plane, which takes one hour, or the gravity-vacuum tube, which takes about two hours."

"I'd like to take the tube."

"Then kindly place your All-Credit card in the slot at your right. It will be magnetically encoded and given right back to you. We wish you a pleasant trip."

A vision of transportation in the world of tomorrow.

That was quite a vision of the future, wasn't it? You may not believe this, but the part of the vision that will be the most difficult to achieve is "the first fully integrated public transportation system on earth."

Today a person taking a trip may start in an automobile, and use a bus system, a subway line, a railroad, an airline, or perhaps a ship for the second and third legs of the journey. It is unusual for the employees of one of these systems to know even the schedules and prices of the other systems.

Strangely enough, there is much better co-ordination in cargo, or freight, transport than there is in passenger transportation. Freight can be packed into large sealed containers, picked up by a truck, transferred to a railroad, then moved onto a ship, and never be unpacked until the containers reach their destination. This process is called "containerization," and it has brought about a small revolution in the freight transportation field.

Perhaps someday in the future the basic passenger vehicle will be a sort of box or cabin. These streamlined boxes (which one scientist calls "cartridges") could be designed as part of a total transportation sys-

tem. At the start of a long trip, the traveler would drive a car with foldaway controls to a terminal. The car (with its wheels retracted) would then be hooked into the system and would be transferred from ground to sea and air on larger carriers, with the vehicle serving as a stateroom all through the trip. At the end of the journey, the vehicle's foldaway controls would be re-activated, and it would become a car once again.

▶ THE FUTURE OF THE AUTOMOBILE

Of course, such a system as the one just described probably lies many years in the future. In the meantime a big decision will have to be made in a number of the world's major countries: Can the automobile be permitted to remain the chief means of passenger transportation? The automobile and the superhighway may well be the finest transportation system known. Nearly everyone wants to own a car. It is comfortable and private, and is the only kind of vehicle that can conveniently carry a passenger door to door.

But the automobile has brought many troubles with it. It pollutes the air, has many safety problems, and eats up valuable

THE TRAVELING CARTRIDGE

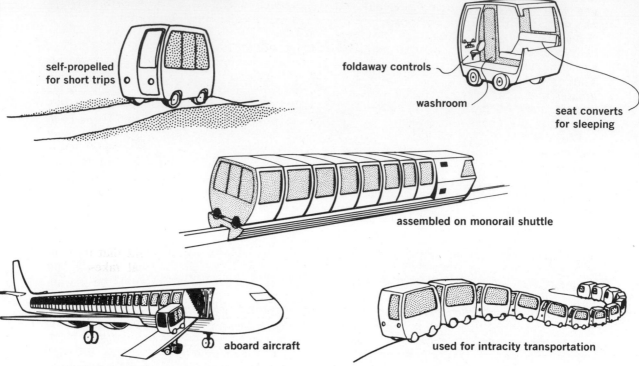

self-propelled for short trips

foldaway controls

washroom

seat converts for sleeping

assembled on monorail shuttle

aboard aircraft

used for intracity transportation

land—for parking lots as well as roads. And there are just too many automobiles.

Equally worrisome is the fuel problem. Today supplies of crude oil (from which gasoline is made) are dependent on political conditions in the oil-producing countries. And at some time in the future, the world may run out of oil completely——for automobiles or for anything else. So substitutes for oil and gasoline must be found.

One alternative is to "grow" fuel. In parts of oil-short Brazil, alcohol is already being added to gasoline. The alcohol is produced from sugarcane, sweet potatoes, manioc, and other starchy crops that can be grown rapidly. If enough of this alcohol can be produced, it may one day replace gasoline. It is actually a superior fuel——it gives slightly better mileage and burns more cleanly.

The electric car would also be a good substitute, if a satisfactory energy-storage method could be found. At present, electric batteries are very heavy. And motors run by electric batteries do not provide the power of the gasoline engine. Batteries must be recharged about every 60 miles (100 km).

▶PRIVATE AND PUBLIC TRANSPORTATION

The success of the automobile has had an unfortunate effect on types of public transportation such as buses and trains: they are being used less and less. With less income, the systems deteriorate and provide poor service, which only turns more riders away.

Attempts are being made to change this. New rapid-transit (subway) systems are being built, and some older railroad lines are being upgraded. Modern, air-conditioned buses and special bus lanes have also helped. But a new approach, some new thinking, is needed. Some combination of public and private transportation has to be worked out.

Combining the public and private systems requires a major redesign of both, which will not happen soon. But some work along these lines has already been done. One proposed vehicle is the Urbmobile.

The Urbmobile, an electric car, would be driven in the usual way for short, local trips. But for longer distances the car would travel on steel rails. This steel "guideway" would be much like a railroad track. In fact, the car would have two sets of wheels—one with rubber tires for the highway and one with steel rims for the guideway.

Because these cars would be electronically controlled on the guideway, more cars could be used than on regular highways. They could also travel faster and with greater safety, since (1) the tracks would be protected and (2) most accidents are caused by drivers' mistakes in judgment.

Whether it is the Urbmobile or some similar model that finally goes into use, these cars would surely be lighter than today's cars—mainly to save energy. And because long trips would be taken on the public system (the track), the reasons people give for needing big, heavy, powerful cars (comfort, safety, holding the road at high speed) would no longer be valid.

Another step along the road to combined systems might be automated highways. As in the road/rail system described above, you would drive your own car on short trips. But for longer trips you would drive onto automated highways, where the vehicle would be electronically controlled for speed and direction.

▶MAKING PUBLIC TRANSPORT COMPETITIVE

Another way of making public transportation more attractive is to change the basic idea of carrying people in large groups. A new approach, called "demand activated transport" or "personal rapid transit," is rather like a horizontal elevator. Small, individual cars would be used for each person or group traveling together to the same place. As the riders entered the vehicle, they would punch out their destination on a control board. The main computer would route the car through the system's many branches nonstop. If one entered a station and no cars were available, pushing a button would bring the nearest empty one. It would be practically the same as pushing a button to call an elevator.

Simple versions of these systems already exist. The "people mover" is similar to personal rapid transit in that driverless cars are used. But they operate along a fixed route and make a specific number of stops along the way, like a subway. Such a system is in operation at the Dallas/Fort Worth airport.

The more advanced systems can be programmed to skip stops where customers are not being picked up or delivered.

▶VTOL AND STOL

As population increases, and as metropolitan areas run into each other to become megalopolises, roads and even guideways will become further clogged. One alternative for "medium distance" travel is flying from city center to city center. Air travel is now the one form of public transportation that is as popular as the automobile. But because modern commercial aircraft are large, noise and space problems force airports to be built well outside of cities. When travel time to and from the airports is taken into account, the time saved by flying may evaporate.

For a while it was thought that helicopters, which are true vertical take-off and landing (VTOL) aircraft, would be the answer to intercity travel. They have the advantage of needing little space to take off and land, and so can set down with ease on such places as lawns and the tops of buildings. But helicopters are too noisy for regular service in cities, and they are expensive to build and operate. If quiet, efficient

The Urbmobile, an electric car, could be driven in both the usual way and on steel rails like a railroad car, as shown below.

This "people mover," a driverless system, is in use at the Dallas/Fort Worth airport.

VTOL's were developed, roof-top landing pads could be located right in downtown areas. (There was one operating on top of the Pan Am Building in New York City for several years that provided direct connections with outlying airports. But because of noise and safety problems, it is no longer in use.)

A compromise has been found in the STOL (short take-off and landing) airplane, which is a medium-size passenger aircraft built for quiet operation and the ability to land on and take off from very short runways. Airports for this kind of aircraft can therefore be built at the edge of cities, rather than way out in the suburbs.

▶LONG-DISTANCE TRAVEL

For future long-distance travel, much depends on supplies of energy. Pollution is an important issue too. The experience of the supersonic transport (SST), which the United States stopped developing, and which Britain and France are having trouble selling, is an example. The British/French SST can travel twice as fast as other commercial aircraft. But it is noisy and tends to pollute the air more than subsonic aircraft do.

If these problems can be solved, we may see these aircraft flying in greater numbers. We may even see the next step, hypersonic aircraft. (The word "hypersonic" refers to something able to travel five or more times the speed of sound.) And a dazzling concept this is—for now we are talking of speeds of about 4,000 miles (6,500 kilometers) an hour through the upper atmosphere. But even in the upper atmosphere, there is some air resistance to movement. The faster something moves, the more resistance it encounters. Hypersonic aircraft would thus need more fuel than the supersonic.

High-Speed Ground Transportation. It is possible that really high-speed travel in the future will not be in the air at all, but through tubes on or under the ground. One exciting concept is a gravity-vacuum system. The vehicles would fit into the tubes like pistons. With a vacuum (empty space) in front of the vehicle, and air behind it, the vehicle would be propelled (pushed) forward. It could reach extremely high speeds, for there would be no air resistance.

And an additional, and free, source of power would be used—gravity. Imagine a pendulum (such as a stone tied to a string) pulled to one side and let go. It will "fall" to the lowest point, continue on through it, and stop at a point opposite where it started. Now imagine that a tunnel has been dug between two cities in a similar form. Once the train was permitted to start rolling, gravity

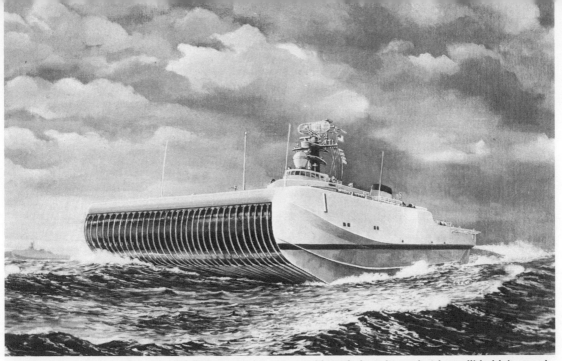

An SES would ride on a cushion of air and travel at incredibly high speeds.

alone would pull it along at ever-increasing speed until it reached the bottom point. After that, momentum would keep it going.

An advantage of tube travel is safety. The passages through vacuum tubes would have to be well-protected guideways, and collisions with other traffic would be impossible. Moreover, the system would never be affected by the weather.

Sea Travel. Safety is also behind some new ideas in over-the-ocean freight transport. Water transportation has been used for thousands of years, of course. But during almost all that time, the vessels have ridden on the water's surface. Rough seas and high winds have caused many a shipwreck. They have also been responsible, at least in part, for many of the oil spills of recent years.

Nuclear-powered submarines may be the future carriers of freight. A giant 300,000-ton submarine oil tanker has already been proposed. Submarines can travel as fast or faster than most surface craft. Future submarines may be able to reach speeds of 90 miles (150 kilometers) an hour and more.

People are probably not going to want to travel by submarine—certainly not for pleasure. But two other kinds of craft make a revival of ocean travel a real possibility. One of these, the air-cushion vehicle (ACV), operates a given distance above the surface of

the water, on a cushion of air. Air-cushion vehicles, called hovercraft, are already in use in a regular ferry service between England and France. They cross the choppy English Channel in 30 minutes, at a speed of about 75 miles (120 kilometers) an hour.

Still larger and faster craft of this type are being designed. To distinguish them from ACV's, they are named "surface effect ships" (SES's). Planners in the U.S. Navy imagine an SES as big as an aircraft carrier, traveling at a top speed of 155 miles (250 kilometers) an hour. Such a ship could cross the Atlantic Ocean in less than a day, or one fifth the time now required by the fastest liner. The SES also would use much less energy per passenger than an airplane uses—combining the advantages of luxury, comfort, efficiency, and speed in transoceanic travel. Sounds good, doesn't it?

On the other hand, it may be that the best and most farsighted planning of all will require us to return to basics. We may have to redesign our living and working areas, bringing them closer together. That will enable us to cut down on motorized transport and depend more on the most reliable means of transportation on earth—our legs.

HAL HELLMAN
Author, *Transportation in the World of the Future*

IT'S A GREEN, GREEN WORLD

Would you like to run through a corn-field? See a rice paddy? Touch a banana tree? Would you like to do all three within minutes of one another?

Corn grows in Kansas, rice in Japan, bananas in Central America. And—all three grow in New York City, in a beautiful glass building. The building is the conservatory of The New York Botanical Garden. The conservatory originally opened in 1901. Over the years, however, it fell into disrepair. Glass broke, metal rusted, and the building could no longer be used for growing many beautiful and interesting plants. Several years ago the Botanical Garden received a gift of $5,000,000 to restore the conservatory. The building was fixed up, and in 1978 it again was opened to the public.

One of the most popular areas in the conservatory is the *Greenmuse,* which is filled with exhibits planned especially for children. The opening exhibit was called the "Greenworld Grocery Store." More than 40 living food crops were displayed. There were rows of tall corn plants. There were rice plants growing in a huge tub filled with water. There were banana plants and bean plants and even an avocado tree. Each plant

had a sign giving visitors a clue to its name. One sign said, "I am red or green, sweet or hot, and even though I have the same name I am not friends with the salt shaker." Can you guess what this plant was? It was the pepper plant!

The main purpose of this exhibit was to tell city girls and boys where the foods we eat come from. They discovered, for example, that spaghetti is not "born" in a grocery store or a factory. Nor is spaghetti the "stem of a plant that grows in Italy." Rather, it is made from flour, which comes from the seeds of wheat plants.

Other exhibits in the conservatory tell about the roles that plants play in our lives: They are sources of oxygen and of fibers for clothes. They have provided, with their great beauty and variety, inspiration for art and music. And they have been a source of pure enjoyment throughout history.

In the *Tropical House,* plant fossils, some 250,000,000 years old, appear beside their living counterparts. It is easy to see the similarities between the ancient and the modern plants. Visitors learn about a plant's environment, too. In the *American Desert House,* it is warm and very dry, and the soil is very sandy. More than 100 different types of desert plants are displayed, but the star is a towering, 100-year-old saguaro cactus.

Nearby is the *Fern Forest*—also warm but very, very humid, with soil that contains little sand. The forest is filled with ferns from all over the world. There are giant ferns and small mosquito ferns. There are ferns in pools, on limestone, on dry cliffs and wet banks. To make it easy for visitors to view all these interesting plants, there is a "skywalk" in the forest. From the top of the walk people can look down on a waterfall, a pool, and even a simulated volcanic crater.

And there are still other displays. They range from mosses and mushrooms in the underground *Green Tunnel,* to a grove of tall palm trees beneath the conservatory's soaring central dome. There's even a topiary garden, where plants have been shaped into fanciful animal forms.

You can touch almost all the displays in the conservatory. But please, don't feed the animals!

From the skywalk, visitors can look down on the variety of plants in the lush *Fern Forest.*

There are more than 100 different kinds of desert plants in the *American Desert House.*

CATCH A FALLING STAR

Have you ever wanted to hold a star in your hand?

Some scientists are doing just that right now. They are probing deeply into the secrets of a piece of rock that fell to Earth from outer space. This space material is called the Allende meteorite. It is already famous as a storehouse of ancient data about how the sun and the planets were formed 4,500,000,000 (billion) years ago. Recently scientists have discovered that Allende contains something more: substances that came out of other stars before our solar system was even formed.

Until the early morning of February 9, 1969, Allende was a nameless piece of cosmic rock, one of billions that circle the sun like miniature planets. On that morning the rock plunged into our atmosphere. Had Allende been the size of a pea or a golf ball, it would have burned up completely, making a brief "shooting star" across the night sky. But Allende weighed tons. Its passage through the air produced a giant fireball that lit up the night sky over northern Mexico. It even shed light as far away as Texas and New Mexico in the United States. As the light died, there were thunderous explosions as the meteorite broke up in the air. Then came the pattering sound of thousands of meteorite fragments striking fields and deserts in northern Mexico.

Allende quickly became one of the most-studied meteorites in history. Nearly two tons of fragments were collected from a stretch of land along the River Allende, for which the meteorite was named. Because there was so much material, many scientists could study the meteorite at the same time. And they did—many of them in laboratories set up to study the moon rocks that were to be brought back by Apollo 11 only a few months later.

Right away the scientists discovered something new in Allende: They found large white fragments that were made up of unusual minerals. And some of the minerals had never been found in meteorites before. These minerals were rich in such chemical elements as calcium, aluminum, and titanium, and they had been formed at very high temperatures. Scientists think that these white fragments were the very first solid matter to appear when the solar system itself began to form from a huge whirling cloud of hot dust and gas.

White fragments are scattered like pearls on the dark mass of a piece of the Allende meteorite. The fragments contain tiny bits of stars that lived before our solar system was even formed.

To have an actual record of the very beginning of the solar system was startling enough. But a few years later, scientists began to realize that those white fragments in Allende contained something even more exciting. Careful study showed that the oxygen in the fragments was slightly different from the oxygen found in other meteorites, moon rocks, and Earth materials. Allende contained too much of a kind of oxygen called oxygen-16.

Where had this extra oxygen-16 come from? Why hadn't it been mixed in with the normal oxygen that makes up other rocks and meteorites? Scientists began to believe that it must have come from some source outside the solar system. Perhaps the oxygen-16 had come from another star—possibly from a supernova that, in exploding, had sprayed its atoms into the dust cloud that was to become our own solar system. Trapped in the newly formed white fragments before it could be mixed or lost, some of this "extra" oxygen-16 was then caught up into the Allende meteorite and preserved for billions of years.

And there is an even more astonishing possibility. Maybe the exploding star ac-

tually caused our solar system to form by sending shock waves through the original dust cloud, causing it to swirl and condense—and eventually producing the planets and the sun.

Now there is a frenzy of study as scientists try to see more clearly into this dim time before the solar system was formed. Within the last couple of years, high-powered electron microscopes have given a first look at what may be the interstellar particles themselves. Inside some of the minerals from the Allende meteorite are tiny bits of matter less than a thousandth of an inch in size. These are made up of even tinier grains of minerals formed at high temperatures and of alloys of platinum and other rare metals. This is a kind of mixture that has never before been seen in our own solar system.

What will we find as we probe more deeply into Allende and other meteorites? The work is just beginning. It will be a long time before we understand these tiny pieces of stars—stars that flared and died before the sun was born.

DR. BEVAN M. FRENCH
Author, *The Moon Book*

85

It's sunrise and the beginning of a new day. Will it be sunny or cloudy?

WHAT WILL THE WEATHER BE?

"Everyone talks about the weather but nobody does anything about it," wrote *The Hartford* (Conn.) *Courant* in 1897. Since then, millions of people have quoted this famous saying. But it's not true! All around the world, scientists are busy studying and doing something about the weather—about the natural forces that bring rains and droughts, hailstones and sandstorms, tornadoes and hurricanes.

Many of these scientists are concerned with predicting, or forecasting, the weather. They want to be able to tell us what the weather will be like tomorrow, next week, and even a month from now. And many people rely on their work. Airlines need to know what flying conditions their pilots will encounter. Oil companies need to know how much fuel their customers will be using for the winter. Farmers need to be warned of freezing temperatures that could damage unprotected crops. Mountain resorts need to know if it will be a good winter for skiing.

▶WHAT IS "WEATHER"?

Weather can be defined as the condition and behavior of the atmosphere—the air that surrounds Earth. The atmosphere is very complicated and many processes take place in it. There are wind and temperature conditions, moisture and pollution levels, cloud coverage, and so on. All are related to one another. And atmospheric conditions in one part of the world can affect what happens halfway around the globe.

The air that surrounds our planet is constantly moving. Heat from the sun warms the air, especially near the equator. The warm air expands upward and, high above Earth's surface, moves toward the poles. Cool air moves toward the equator to take its place. Thus we have winds. Differences in temperature and the rotation of Earth itself cause winds to blow in many patterns. Masses of warm and cold air sometimes bump into each other. When this happens, a storm usually results.

Winds can carry moisture and pollutants with them, and they can be carried far away. Perhaps you have read of times when China exploded atomic bombs. Within a few days, radioactive fallout from these explosions was over Canada—carried there by winds. Also, sometimes a mass of air gets stuck and doesn't move for several days. When this happens, pollutants produced by cars and factories aren't carried away. The air becomes loaded with smoke and gases and becomes unhealthy to breathe.

Thus, to make accurate weather forecasts for your area, scientists need to know what is happening elsewhere in the world. They need to know in what direction the air is moving and how fast it is moving. They need to know how much moisture is in the air. They need to know how the atmosphere 20 miles (32 kilometers) above Earth will affect the weather in your backyard.

But weather predictions are not always accurate, even when the best information is available. For this reason, scientists are seeking better ways to forecast the weather.

▶NEW METHODS OF WEATHER PREDICTION

Computers are part of the newest method of forecasting weather. Scientists have developed mathematical equations that act as models of the atmosphere. Once scientists have specific facts about atmospheric conditions, they use computers to solve the complicated equations. The computers then forecast the weather for the following days. But this method of weather prediction is still in the experimental stage, and the equations need to be improved.

Since 1967, the Global Atmospheric Research Program (GARP) has been helping scientists learn about the atmosphere and develop better forecasting methods. The most recent GARP project began in late 1978, and it may help to improve the mathematical equations. It is called the First GARP Global Experiment. You'll probably be reading about it in newspapers and magazines. Some 140 countries are taking part in this one-year project, which will study the atmosphere and weather all around the planet. Even the surfaces of the oceans will be studied.

Thousands of scientists, engineers, and

A drawing of an environmental buoy. These carry instruments that measure air and sea conditions.

technicians are working on the Global Experiment. Information on atmospheric behavior and conditions is being gathered at ground stations and from the air and sea. Far above Earth, satellites are photographing cloud patterns. Some airplanes carry little black boxes that automatically record weather data, while other planes drop devices that record wind speed and direction over the ocean. Ships are sending weather balloons aloft twice a day and setting out hundreds of weather-watching buoys. The buoys and balloons carry instruments to gather information about the atmosphere.

All this new information is then fed into computers, which, in turn, should help to improve the mathematical models. Can very accurate mathematical models be made? How far ahead can weather be predicted? These are questions that GARP scientists hope to answer soon.

SPACE BRIEFS

In early 1978, the U.S. National Aeronautics and Space Administration (NASA) picked 35 men and women as astronauts for space shuttle flights in the 1980's. The shuttle, which is now being built, is a winged spaceship that is launched like a rocket and glides back to Earth like an airplane. It can be used again and again to carry astronauts and instruments into orbit around the Earth. And it can stay up for as long as a month at a time.

Only 15 of the new astronauts are pilots.

Six women, the first to be selected for space training, were among 35 new astronauts in 1978.

The other 20 are "mission specialists" who will carry out observations and experiments in orbit. The six women in the group are the first ever selected for space training. The new astronaut group includes astronomers, doctors, engineers, geologists, and physicists.

▶AND THE RUSSIANS GO 'ROUND AND 'ROUND

Cosmonauts from the Soviet Union dominated space in 1978, living for over a year in a huge Earth-orbiting space station called Salyut 6. (*Salyut* means "salute.") Crews of Soviet cosmonauts "drove to work"—from Earth into orbit—in spacecraft called *Soyuz* ("union") and returned to Earth the same way. The Salyut station can hold four cosmonauts at a time. By the end of 1978, 10 men had stayed in it for periods of from one week to almost five months. They had also compiled an impressive list of space records:

January 11. First "double docking" of two spacecraft at a space station. While Soyuz 26 was docked at one end of the Salyut space station, a new arrival, Soyuz 27, docked safely at the other end.

January 22. First resupply of a space station by a robot spacecraft. An unmanned spacecraft, Progress 1, flew to the Salyut and docked safely. It carried fuel, food, and supplies for the cosmonauts working aboard the space station.

March 3. First international crew in space. A Russian and a Czech traveled to Salyut and back in Soyuz 28. A second international crew, a Russian and a Pole, flew Soyuz 30 to dock with Salyut in June.

March 16. Longest stay in space. Two Soviet cosmonauts returned to Earth after living in Salyut for 96 days. This broke the record of 84 days, 1 hour, and 17 minutes set by the U.S. Skylab 4 astronauts in 1974.

November 2. Longest stay in space, breaking the March 16 record. Two other cosmonauts returned after living in Salyut for 139 days, 14 hours, and 48 minutes—almost five months.

The Soviet voyages seemed to have established Salyut 6 as the old science-fiction dream come true: a working space station.

Soviet cosmonauts Vladimir Kovalenok (*left*) and Alexander Ivanchenkov spent almost five months in space.

Cosmonauts arrive, live and work in the station for long periods of time, and then leave as other cosmonauts come to take their places. Salyut 6 can be resupplied by robot spacecraft and might be maintained for as long as five years.

▶THE SKYLAB IS FALLING

Space stations don't always stay where you leave them. During 1978, NASA was trying desperately to prevent the U.S. Skylab space station, uninhabited since 1974, from dropping lower and lower toward Earth's atmosphere. If Skylab dropped too low, it would enter the atmosphere and burn up, perhaps scattering pieces over a large area of Earth.

Why didn't Skylab stay put? Even at Skylab's height, there is still a tiny bit of atmosphere. This bit of atmosphere is enough to slow down an orbiting spacecraft in several years' time, making it fall back to Earth. The last astronauts left the "House in Space" in February, 1974. At that time,

NASA estimated that Skylab would remain safely in orbit until 1982 or 1983. There would be time enough for a space shuttle mission to visit the Skylab and boost it into a higher orbit. Then it could be preserved and used for years as a space station.

But the sun entered the picture. The sun's activity follows an 11-year cycle, and we are just approaching the peak of its activity. Unfortunately, the sun now seems a little more active than people thought it would be. It is putting out a little more energy than expected. And the Earth's atmosphere is being heated and has expanded more than expected. The upper fringes of the atmosphere reached out toward Skylab, and the slightly denser air started to drag the spacecraft down.

NASA did everything it could to save Skylab. The station was successfully "awakened" in January after a "sleep" of almost four years. Ground crews instructed Skylab's on-board computer to keep the small end of the station pointed forward as it

Skylab may enter Earth's atmosphere late in 1979.

They were trying to solve the mystery of a planet that should be like the Earth—but isn't. Venus is the closest planet to Earth. It is about Earth's size and weight. Before the Space Age, scientists thought Venus was a "twin" of Earth. But now we know that Venus has a thick atmosphere, 100 times as dense as Earth's. It is made of carbon dioxide and laced with clouds of sulfuric acid. The surface temperature on Venus is a scorching 900°F (480°C), hot enough to melt lead.

Why have two planets that seemed so similar turned out to be so different? Why do Venus and Earth have such different atmospheres? Is Venus a model of what the Earth might have been—or what it might become? These are the questions that the American and Soviet spacecraft hoped to answer.

The U.S. Pioneer Venus 1 went into orbit around Venus on December 4. It carries instruments that will study the Venusian atmosphere and map the rapid motions of its clouds for almost a year. The orbiter will actually dip into the upper part of the atmosphere to sample it directly. Pioneer Venus 2, following five days behind, was really five spacecraft in one. Before reaching Venus, it launched four missile-like probes. These probes plunged into the Venusian atmosphere and analyzed it on their way down toward the planet's surface. Two of the probes actually penetrated the entire atmosphere and survived to transmit data from the surface itself. One probe lasted for more than an hour.

While U.S. spacecraft probed the atmosphere, two Soviet spacecraft, Venera 11 and 12, arrived in late December to reach toward the searing surface itself. These two craft launched probes that made soft landings on the planet. One probe beamed information back to Earth for 110 minutes.

moved around Earth. This maneuvering reduced the atmospheric drag on Skylab so that it would stay in orbit a few months longer.

But the extra few months were not enough time to allow a shuttle mission to reach Skylab. And in any case, NASA could not be sure that a rescue mission would be successful. Skylab's power supply and control systems were beginning to wear out.

In December, NASA abandoned plans to save Skylab. And the space station was expected to enter the atmosphere in late 1979 or 1980, becoming a gigantic meteor complete with fiery tail.

▶A CLOSE LOOK AT EARTH'S "TWIN"

A fleet of American and Soviet spacecraft converged on Venus in December, 1978.

▶NEW MOONS

Planets like to have moons. Earth has one, Mars has two, and giant Jupiter has at least 13. Now we find that even Pluto, the tiny planet farthest from the sun, has a moon. Pluto is so far from the sun (40 times as far as Earth is) that the moon showed up only as a bulge in a picture of Pluto taken

U.S. Pioneer Venus 2 (*left*) sent four probes to Venus' atmosphere. Pioneer Venus I (*right*) orbited the planet.

by the U.S. Naval Observatory. The moon is apparently about one third the diameter of Pluto itself. It revolves around Pluto in about six days.

▶ONE PICTURE, TWO WORLDS

Our moon used to be far away. Now we are moving so far out into space that a camera can photograph both Earth and the moon at the same time. In 1978, a Voyager spacecraft bound for Jupiter looked back to take this picture of Earth and the moon from about 7,000,000 miles (11,660,000 kilometers) away. Earth, mottled with clouds, is the larger crescent; the moon is the smaller crescent above it.

The same cameras that showed us to ourselves are being aimed at unknown worlds. Voyagers 1 and 2, launched in 1977, are due to swing by giant Jupiter and ringed Saturn—giving us close looks at a dozen of their moons whose features we have never seen. Voyager 2 may go on to Uranus. It may even eventually reach distant Neptune (in 1989) before leaving the solar system forever. The Voyager travels will be the last great voyage of solar system discovery. When they are done, Pluto will be the only world yet unvisited by spacecraft.

DR. BEVAN M. FRENCH
Author, *The Moon Book*

A rare picture showing Earth and its moon—taken by a spacecraft far out in space.

KING PHILIP'S TOMB?

More than 2,000 years ago, a small kingdom called Macedon (located in what is now northern Greece) grew to become one of the great empires in history. During the reign of King Philip II (359 B.C. to 366 B.C.), Macedon joined with other Greek states and built a powerful army. Under Alexander the Great, Philip's son, the Macedonian army conquered most of the known world—from Spain to India.

Alexander died in 323 B.C., and his body was buried in Egypt. Philip had been assassinated thirteen years earlier, but his final resting place was unknown. Now a Greek archeologist claims to have found King Philip's tomb.

Late in 1977, a team of archeologists was digging up a burial mound on the outskirts of the small farming village of Vergina in northern Greece. There are many such mounds around Vergina, but this one was especially large. Seventeen feet (5 meters) below the ground, the diggers came upon a tomb with marble doors and a multicolored painting of a lion hunt on the front. Unlike many ancient tombs, this one had not been opened by thieves.

Inside the tomb, the diggers found a treasure chest of vases and goblets made of gold and silver. There was a complete set of princely armor fashioned out of bronze and trimmed with gold and ivory. But the most breathtaking find of all was a solid gold casket with legs in the form of lions' feet. On the lid was the bursting star symbol of the royal family of Macedon. The casket contained the bones and teeth of a man. A gold diadem (a type of crown) like the ones worn by Macedonian kings was also found in the tomb.

The archeologist who discovered the tomb, Manolis Andronikos, believes that the bones are those of King Philip. Various objects found in and around the tomb were of types made only between 350 and 320 B.C. These objects helped him to date the tomb. And the only king who had died on Macedonian soil during that period was Philip. The archeologist also found five small sculptured heads, carved out of ivory. Two bear a strong resemblance to portraits we already have of Philip and Alexander.

Not everyone is convinced that the tomb is the burial place of the Macedonian ruler. Some archeologists feel that more proof is needed. However, even if the tomb proves not to be that of King Philip, it is still a major archeological find. Said the archeologist who found it, "It will take years for us to study everything in the tomb, but in the end we will have a new understanding of the Macedonian world."

This is believed to be the tomb of King Philip, a great Macedonian ruler.

SOME VERY OLD FOOTPRINTS

How long have human beings lived on Earth? What did the first humans look like? Where did they live?

One scientist who has spent many years trying to answer these questions is Mary Leakey. She and her late husband, Louis Leakey, are famous because of the interesting archeological finds they made in what is now northern Tanzania in Africa. Their best-known finds occurred in the late 1950's and 1960's, in Olduvai Gorge. Among their finds were what are believed to be the oldest known humanlike fossils. The fossils are about 2,000,000 years old.

In recent years, Dr. Leakey has been working at Laetolil, about 30 miles (50 kilometers) from Olduvai Gorge. Here, the ground is made up of layers of volcanic ash and lava. These materials are excellent preservers of bones, tracks, and other remains of living things.

Early in 1978, Dr. Leakey announced an exciting discovery. In the volcanic ash, she found some footprints that are 3,500,000 years old. She said she was "75 percent sure" that they were made by a hominid (a humanlike creature). About 50 other experts also looked at the prints. They, too, said Dr. Leakey, believed that the prints were made by a hominid.

A track of five prints was found. They appear to be made by a two-legged animal, not by an animal that walked on all four limbs. In two prints, impressions of what seem to be the big toe can be seen.

The arrangement of the prints indicates that the creature probably moved very slowly and took very short steps. The average length of the prints is 6.1 inches (15.5 centimeters). If the tracks were indeed made by a hominid, the creature who made them was quite small—perhaps 4 feet (1.25 meters) tall. This is based on the estimate that the length of a human footprint is equal to 15 percent of the body's height.

It is not possible to tell anything else about the creature's appearance from the prints. To learn more, parts of the skeleton are needed. No such remains have been found in the area so far.

At Laetolil, Dr. Leakey also found the prints of many animals, including antelopes, giraffes, giant elephants, a saber-toothed cat, and other species that are now extinct. When these animals roamed the land 3,500,000 years ago, this spot at Laetolil was a watering hole. The animals came here to drink or to catch and kill other animals. Did humanlike creatures walk among the elephants and giraffes? Did they kneel beside the water to drink? Did they hide from the saber-toothed cats? What do you think?

These footprints may have been made 3,500,000 years ago by a humanlike creature.

NEW USES OF LASERS

The place: a far-off galaxy, thousands of light-years from Earth. The scene: famed Jedi knight Ben Kenobi and the evil Darth Vader parry and thrust in a duel to the death with laser light sabers. Meanwhile, the Death Star, a planet-size battle station, prepares to fight the rebel forces with a deadly array of laser guns.

This scene is from the epic space fantasy *Star Wars*. It is pure science fiction—or is it?

Scientists in the Soviet Union and the United States are already investigating ways to use lasers as weapons of war. They are, for example, trying to develop lasers that can destroy enemy missiles moments after they are launched.

Lasers will certainly be used by the military in the future. But right now they are being used to benefit humankind.

▶ WHAT IS A LASER?

The name "laser" is formed from the first letters of the words *l*ight *a*mplification by *s*imulated *e*mission of *r*adiation. This tells you that a laser is a device that amplifies, or

strengthens, light. It can take a weak beam of light and make it so strong that it can cut through steel and diamonds.

Laser light is unlike any other light we know. It does not spread out in all directions like sunlight or lamplight; it weakens only a little as it travels away from its source.

▶ LASERS AT WORK

Because the laser is so powerful, it is revolutionizing science and industry.

Medicine. Surgeons use lasers to repair detached retinas. The retina, the screen on which images fall, is "welded" back in place, restoring vision to the patient. Laser beams are also used to cut out cancerous tumors without harming the surrounding tissues.

Communications. Radio and television signals are normally carried from the transmitter to your home on long radio waves. Now, experimental systems that use laser beams to carry these signals are in operation. Laser light waves are only a millionth as long as radio waves. By using tiny light waves, you can send millions of times as many messages along the same path as you can by using long radio waves. The laser beam travels along strands of glass that are finer than hair. A cable of such glass fibers is no thicker than a match. Yet it can carry the equivalent of hundreds of books of information each second.

Metrology. The science of measurement has been greatly advanced by lasers. Laser light has been beamed to the moon and reflected back to Earth by special devices placed on the moon by astronauts. By measuring the time it takes for the reflected light to bounce back, scientists have measured the distance to the moon within an inch.

The use of lasers to measure distances is important on Earth, too—in predicting earthquakes. Scientists believe that there are a number of subtle changes that take place in the earth just before a quake. Lasers may help detect them in time to issue earthquake warnings. In places where earthquakes are common, for example, laser beams could be used to measure the distance between two hills. Sudden, tiny changes might be detected, indicating that the ground was stretching or compressing—that something might give way and that an earthquake would take place.

Three-dimensional images. In ordinary photography, light reflected from a scene is recorded on a flat piece of paper coated with chemicals. The result is a two-dimensional image. When laser beams are directed at the scene, the waves of laser light cross over the reflected waves of ordinary light, producing a three-dimensional pattern that can be recorded on a special film. If light is then passed through the film, the waves form again in the same pattern, reproducing a three-dimensional image. One day we may even have three-dimensional television, thanks to lasers.

Industry. Lasers are being used as cleaning devices. Laser beams can remove soot and grime from buildings without harming the stone, brick, or metal beneath. The device vaporizes the dirt, leaving no debris behind. Laser beams were used to clean Winchester Cathedral, in England, and parts of the Acropolis, in Athens, Greece.

High-intensity lasers are being used to drill holes through many materials—even diamonds, the hardest known substance. Laser drilling is quick and clean. And the material can be cut or shaped in any desired way by moving the laser beam. The beam's strength can be adjusted to cut textiles, leather, plastics, or even steel.

Energy. Perhaps the most important use of lasers will be in supplying energy. Oil is running out, and we will need alternate energy sources. One possibility is hydrogen fusion. When the tiny nuclei of heavy hydrogen atoms are squeezed together to form helium nuclei, immense amounts of energy are released.

A safe, practical way of producing hydrogen fusion has not been perfected. But lasers may help. Scientists are working on a technique that uses powerful laser beams to force the nuclei together. Someday, lasers may supply much of the world's energy.

ISAAC ASIMOV
Associate Professor of Biochemistry
Boston University School of Medicine

Laser beams can be used to clean statues without harming them.

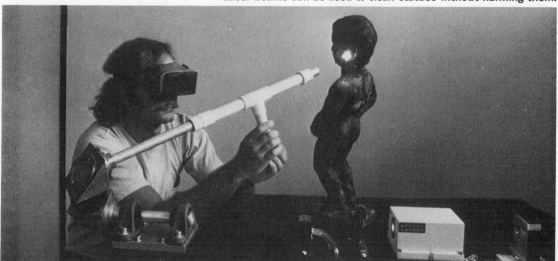

FLIGHTS OF FACT AND FANCY

Jules Verne, the "father of science fiction," was the author of stories that were enjoyed as fantasies at the time they were written. They told of events that were exciting but totally imaginary. At least, that's what most people who read them in the 19th century thought. But in 1978, the 150th anniversary of Verne's birth, it seemed as if he had written with a crystal ball set beside his inkwell. For as scientific knowledge grew, many of the fantastic things that Verne wrote about came true.

Jules Verne was born in Nantes, France, on February 8, 1828. He earned a degree in law but then decided to become a writer. He was fascinated by mechanical devices and had acquired a great deal of knowledge in both science and mathematics. Combining this knowledge with a lively imagination, Verne produced novels of adventure, such as *Journey to the Center of the Earth,* that were instantly popular. In fact, Verne's stories were so well liked that several thousand mourners attended his funeral in 1905.

Verne's novels are still popular—in part because of their uncanny ability to see into the future. And none of his novels described the future with greater accuracy than *From the Earth to the Moon.*

▶THE VISION THAT CAME TRUE

From the Earth to the Moon was written in 1865. But it's hard to believe that Verne wasn't looking ahead to the first actual moon landing, in 1969. The similarities between some of the events in the novel and the Apollo 11 mission are astounding.

To begin with, both spacecraft were piloted by three-man crews. Verne's travelers were not trained scientists—they were members of a gun club in Baltimore, Maryland, who wanted to claim the moon for the United States. But the site Verne had them choose for their launch into space was in Florida—only about 140 miles (225 kilometers) from the actual Apollo launch at Cape Canaveral.

Verne's spaceship was called the *Columbiad*; the command ship of the Apollo 11 mission was called the *Columbia*. The real and fictional capsules were also very much alike in size and shape. The cone-shaped spaceship that carried Verne's travelers is described as being 15 feet (4.5 meters) high and 9 feet (2.7 meters) in diameter. The Apollo command module, also cone-shaped, was a little over 10 feet (3 meters) high and less than 13 feet (4 meters) in diameter.

Through precise scientific calculations, Verne's capsule was aimed to meet the moon on its orbit around Earth. Such calculations must be equally perfect today. Verne wrote that it would take 97 hours, 13 minutes, and 20 seconds to reach the moon. In reality, the Apollo team made the trip in 103 hours and 30 minutes.

Jules Verne's spaceship looked remarkably like . . .

Verne's travelers were weightless in space, as were the Apollo 11 astronauts. And like their 20th-century counterparts, Verne's trio of "aeronauts" made careful observations of the moon's surface and photographs of what they saw.

There are still other similarities between the real story and the imagined one. In Verne's story, the state of Texas fought long and hard for the honor of being the site of the launch. And even though the launching of both ships took place in the state of Florida, Texas was the home of Apollo Mission Control in 1969.

Unlike the Apollo 11 astronauts, Verne's crew did not actually land on the moon. But the author did provide them with rockets to send them on a safe journey back to Earth. As a matter of fact, both journeys, real and fictional, ended with "splashdowns" in the Pacific Ocean. Both crews were recovered by American ships. And not surprisingly, both sets of space travelers returned as heroes to an admiring nation.

Of course, there were many aspects of true space travel that were unknown to Jules Verne in 1865. For example, while Verne understood the theory of propulsion, he shot his brave crew into space not with a launching rocket but with an immense cannon that was packed with hundreds of tons of guncotton, a high-power explosive. And Verne's travelers made their voyage with all the comforts of home—including two pet dogs. Instead of being secured in place for the flight, they sat on comfortable couches. They cooked solid food on gas stoves and drank fine wine. Jules Verne's guesses about space travel were truly amazing, but he still had a great deal to learn about the science of space.

▶VISIONS CLOSER TO EARTH

On August 17, 1978, the *Double Eagle II,* a hot-air balloon carrying three modern "aeronauts" from the United States, landed in a wheat field near Paris, France. This was the first successful trip across the Atlantic in a balloon. For more than a century, balloonists had tried and failed to make this trip. Some had even lost their lives in the effort.

As the world watched the adventure of *Double Eagle II,* many people recalled the

. . . the command module of the 1969 moon flight.

best-known balloonist of all—Phileas Fogg. Fogg is the central character in what is perhaps Jules Verne's most popular story, *Around the World in Eighty Days.* The story of Phileas Fogg, who accepts a bet to go around the world in 80 days and completes part of the trip in a hot-air balloon, has thrilled and amused generations of readers. Now the crew members of *Double Eagle II* have indicated that they may attempt to complete the entire trip in a balloon. But today it is believed that a balloon trip around the world would take only about 30 days.

The tales of Jules Verne were once thought to be entertaining stories and nothing more. But, whether beneath the sea or high up in the air, we may well see even more of Jules Verne's visions become reality.

THE WEALTH OF THE ANTARCTIC

A vast, frozen continent lies at the southernmost reaches of the world. Its name is Antarctica, and it is the coldest place on Earth. Almost all of Antarctica's more than 5,000,000 square miles (12,950,000 square kilometers) are covered with ice. A temperature of −127°F (−88°C) has been recorded at the South Pole.

Yet out of this frozen world may come the solution to one of the world's most serious problems: food shortages and starvation. This is because the seas around Antarctica are rich with fish. The question is, can the nations of the world agree on how to harvest the Antarctic's wonderful wealth?

▶JOURNEYS TO THE BOTTOM OF THE WORLD

Explorers were attracted to the Antarctic long before anyone suspected that its seas might solve the world's food problems. The English sea captain James Cook led two ships in a voyage toward the South Pole in the 1770's. He did not land on Antarctica, but his ships certainly entered the iceberg-filled Antarctic seas. An American sea captain, John Davis, is believed to have been the first to land on Antarctica, in 1821.

By the early part of the 20th century, many countries had sent explorers, including the United States, Russia, Britain, France, Australia, and Norway. And in 1911, the Norwegian Roald Amundsen became the first to reach the South Pole, the very "bottom of the world."

▶CO-OPERATION OR CONFLICT?

Throughout the 20th century, scientific research and further exploration have gone on in the Antarctic. The research has been conducted mostly by five nations: Belgium, Japan, South Africa, the United States, and the Soviet Union.

To some extent, the nations that have bases on Antarctica have co-operated with each other. During the International Geophysical Year (1957–58), twelve nations set up scientific research bases in the Antarctic.

There have, however, been disputes between some nations as to who should control portions of the Antarctic. Seven nations—Argentina, Australia, Britain, Chile, France, New Zealand, and Norway—have all claimed parts of the Antarctic continent as their own. And some of these nations are claiming the same land. This has led to problems. Who owns Antarctica? Should anyone? Or does the continent at the bottom of the world belong to everyone?

The Antarctic Treaty of 1959 tried to deal with some of these problems. This treaty, signed by the five researching nations and the seven land-claiming nations, stated that no land claim may be added to or subtracted from. The treaty also provided for co-operation between the nations. And it stated that the Antarctic regions would be open to explorers and researchers from all nations.

▶NATURAL RESOURCES

In the early 1960's, the world became aware of the huge fishing resources of the Antarctic seas. In particular, a shrimplike crustacean (shellfish) called krill abounds in those chilly southern waters. There is so much krill, in fact, that food scientists hope that krill may one day provide most of the world's protein.

There are other fish as well. Japanese and Soviet fishing boats have caught hundreds of thousands of tons of cod in recent years. Some experts believe that the Antarctic waters may soon produce 100,000,000 tons of fish a year. That amount would equal the yearly catch in the whole rest of the world!

But now the question of international co-operation comes up again. The "hungry" nations of the world will want, and need, a fair share of this huge protein supply. Yet it is the wealthier nations that are better able to harvest all that fish. If the world's nations cannot agree on Antarctic land claims, will they be able to agree on the distribution of fishing rights?

And there is another problem, one that is connected with krill fishing. This is the problem of the Antarctic environment. Many Antarctic animals—such as whales, penguins, seals, squid, and fish—depend upon krill for their food. If too much krill is caught for humans, will these other creatures die out?

Krill may one day provide most of the world's protein.

In addition to the fish supply, there are also valuable minerals and oil in the Antarctic. Only the highly industrialized countries are capable of extracting these riches from the earth. Again, the question—will the world's poorer nations be kept from sharing this Antarctic wealth?

▶THE CANBERRA CONFERENCE

In an attempt to answer some of these questions, a thirteen-nation conference was held in Canberra, Australia, in early 1978. The twelve signers of the 1959 treaty were joined by Poland.

The Canberra Conference concentrated mainly on the harvesting of the protein-rich krill. There were many disagreements among the nations. But they did agree to create a commission that would control krill fishing in the Antarctic waters. The commission would have the power to set up fishing quotas. Experts would examine the effect of krill fishing on the Antarctic environment.

The conference marked an important step toward international co-operation. However, there is still much to be worked out and more meetings were scheduled. And the old problem of the "ownership" of the Antarctic will not go away. It is especially hoped that the later conferences will not dissolve into an argument over a question that is as old as the human race: whose is it—yours, mine, or ours?

DANIEL J. DOMOFF
Consulting Editor
Educational Developmental Laboratories

BEACH PATTERNS

Waves rush to meet the shore, then retreat to the ocean deep. Each wave leaves its own pattern in the sand. It may last only until the next wave comes. One pattern is washed away, another takes its place.

In some places, the waves carry sands and other material from the ocean bottom up onto the beach. In other places or at other times, the waves carry sands away from the beaches. As a result, beaches are always changing. Some get wider, others get narrower. Some are decorated with shells and bits of coral, others have pebbles worn smooth by tumbling waters.

The wind also plays an important role in creating beach patterns. It picks up light grains of sand, leaving behind the heavier ones, which may be differently colored. The wind may carry the grains far away, even depositing them on other shores.

Wind and water often work together. In winter, when temperatures drop below freezing, water and sand may form solid blocks—rather like what would form if you filled an ice-cube tray with very wet sand. The wind attacks the blocks of sand, sculpting out soft spots, rounding edges, widening cracks.

If you walk along a beach, you can help the waves create interesting beach patterns. Place a shell or pebble in the sand. Watch what happens as the water flows over it and then retreats. Your object diverts the return flow of water, so that a pattern of diverging lines forms in the sand.

Next, look for the two most common patterns left by the water: ripples and swash marks. Ripples look like the surface of a piece of corrugated cardboard. In between the crests of the ridges are shallow depres-

This pattern was made by wind and waves, which removed the white sand faster than the heavier red sand.

This pattern was formed over many years by winds that carried sand from Africa to the Canary Islands.

sions. Often, the depressions glisten in the sunlight. This is due to tiny pieces of the mineral mica, which were left behind by the retreating waves.

Swash marks indicate the highest spot on the beach reached by waves. As a wave rushes up the beach, it carries sand, bits of plants, shells, and other material. When the wave reaches its highest point, it deposits this sediment, then recedes. The line formed by the sediment—the swash mark—is often concave. As the tide goes out, each wave moves a shorter distance up the beach than the previous wave. Thus it is that a pattern of concave lines is formed along a flat sandy beach.

All these different patterns can be photographed. Enlarged and mounted, the photographs make beautiful works of art that can be displayed in your home or given as gifts to friends. So the next time you walk along a beach, take along a camera and look for the patterns.

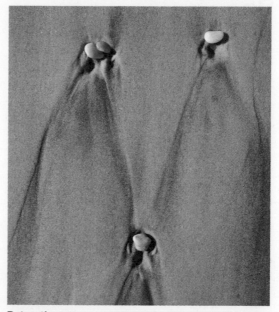

Retreating waves created this pattern of diverging lines in the sand around these pebbles.

In many places, waves deposit lovely shells and bits of coral on the beach. Each one of these remains of living things has its own interesting pattern.

COMPUTERS FOR YOUR HOME

Brian O'Conner hurried home from school. He wanted to try out his new "Star Wars" game on H.C., his family's home computer. He stopped at the front door and punched his code on a set of push buttons. H.C. unlocked the door. A voice greeted Brian from the computer terminal: "Brian, your mother will not be home until six. She left a snack for you in the oven." Then H.C. turned on the oven to heat the snack.

H.C. continued, "Your mother left you a shopping list, which I will type out for you. She would like you to do the shopping before the store closes."

Brian went over to the computer's printer, which was busy typing the list. OK, he thought, I'll get in a quick game of "Star Wars" before I go shopping. He loaded his game tape into the computer and began to play. A few minutes later the screen went blank and a message appeared on the screen—"It's getting late. You had better get to the store."

Brian took the list and hurried out of the house. H.C. turned off the lights and locked the door.

Does this story sound like science fiction? It's not. Everything that happened in the story can be done right now with a small, inexpensive computer. Maybe your family already has one.

Let's find out a little bit more about these amazing machines.

▶EARLY COMPUTERS

Computers have been around for many years. Twenty-five years ago the heart of a computer was a set of vacuum tubes. These tubes acted like dams—when they were "on," electricity could flow. When they were "off," electricity was stopped.

The first computer was called the Electronic Numerical Integrator and Calculator (ENIAC). ENIAC contained thousands of these vacuum tubes and miles of wire. The computer itself filled a huge room, and still another large room was needed for all the equipment that supplied power to the vacuum tubes. ENIAC used so much power that the lights in nearby areas dimmed when the computer was turned on.

ENIAC was incredibly fast. It could add numbers at speeds measured in thousandths of a second. Calculations that would have taken a person 100 years to do were performed in two hours. But ENIAC was finicky. The tubes burned out and had to be replaced. Just imagine trying to find a single burned-out tube in a room filled with thousands of tubes. It was a big job, and dozens of people were needed to keep ENIAC working.

Computers like ENIAC were very expensive to build and to maintain. Only large companies and research centers could afford them or find the room to keep them.

▶THE MICROCOMPUTER IS BORN

Today you can buy a computer in a department store or in a computer store. You can even order one from a mail order catalog. These computers are called microcomputers because they are quite small. A microcomputer looks like a portable typewriter. This keyboard is plugged into a TV and into a cassette tape recorder. The whole microcomputer system plugs into regular wall sockets and uses very little electricity. But as small as this computer is, it is faster

and more powerful than ENIAC was. It is even more reliable than ENIAC, which cost millions of dollars to build and run. The modern microcomputer costs no more than a good stereo or a fancy 10-speed bike.

How is this possible? Well, computers and other electronic devices have been getting smaller and better over the years. The old vacuum tubes that used to control the flow of electricity through the machine have been replaced with transistors, small crystals that don't burn out.

Scientists didn't stop when they invented the transistor. They continued to work, and soon they discovered that they could etch, or draw, tiny transistors onto thin wafers of silicon, a substance similar to glass. At first they etched a few transistors onto each wafer. Soon they were able to increase the number of transistors that could be etched onto a single wafer. By 1975, they were able to put what amounted to a whole ENIAC

These tiny chips, many much smaller than a postage stamp, are the heart of a microcomputer. Each chip can "store" thousands of bits of information.

computer on one wafer the size of a postage stamp! This wafer, called a chip, became the heart of the microcomputer.

▶WHAT CAN A MICROCOMPUTER DO?

The first, larger computers were used to make complicated mathematical calculations that would take too long for people to do with pencil and paper or even with a calculator. However, as time went by, designers learned how to do other things with computers. For example, numbers can be used to stand for letters, so that when numbers are typed into a computer, words are printed out. Many newspapers are now printed by computer. When you get advertising in the mail, the label was probably printed by a computer that has your name in its "memory."

A microcomputer, or home computer, can do nearly all the things that a business or scientific computer can do. You can type out words, numbers, and pictures that are displayed on a TV screen. If a printer is at-tached, the computer can write letters or fill out forms. With the addition of a simple electrical controller, it can turn on an oven or a sprinkler system. It can turn on the air conditioner if the temperature increases or turn down the thermostat at night. It can even be adapted to sense fires and "call" the fire department.

A microcomputer can also work like a private tutor. It can help you study for exams. It can give you practice in doing math problems, give you spelling quizzes, teach you algebra or a foreign language.

A microcomputer will also play games with you. It can play card games, checkers, or chess. There are now games that have been developed especially for the micro-computer. Many of these games involve "simulations." In a computer simulation, the computer imitates the way things happen in real life. "Lunar Lander" is a popular computer simulation game. The goal of the game is to land a rocket on the moon. One mistake and CRASH!

A microcomputer looks very much like a typewriter. It is plugged into a TV and into a cassette tape recorder.

Many people visit computer fairs to buy parts to build their own home computers.

COMPUTER TALK

Of course, a computer can't do any of these marvelous things until someone tells it what to do. No matter how sophisticated and advanced they are, computers can't think. A set of instructions, called a program, must be given to the computer. But the computer can only understand a complicated language called machine code. This machine code is just too difficult for the average home computer user to learn. So most small computers are equipped with something called an interpreter. With an interpreter, the computer can understand programs that look very much like English.

The most popular computer language is Beginners All-Purpose Instruction Code—called BASIC, for short. BASIC is quite easy to learn, and many children are proving to be good at writing computer programs in BASIC. A book called *101 BASIC Games* contains programs that were written by junior and senior high school students.

Programs that have already been written are available on cassettes. These cassettes can just be popped into the home computer system. The instructions on the cassette "tell" the computer what to do.

COMPUTER FAIRS

Computer fairs have become very popular and are being held in many cities. If you visit a computer fair, you can buy software (such as the latest cassette programs) and see and learn about hardware (the actual machines). And perhaps one day, in the not-too-distant future, you too will come home from school for a music lesson or a quick game of "Star Wars"—with your own home computer.

JOHN VICTOR
President, Program Design, Inc.

ROBOTS: COMPUTERS IN FANCY PACKAGES

The kinds of things that people do can be put into three basic groups. First, we do things that we enjoy or that will make us better people—such as taking piano lessons, studying for tests, and playing baseball. Second, we do things that need to be done but don't really make us better—such as mowing the grass, washing dishes, and taking out the garbage. Third, we do things that are dangerous or very difficult—such as handling dangerous chemicals and moving heavy machinery.

People have spent a long time trying to find substitutes for human labor that could do the boring, dangerous, and hard things that need to be done. We now have these substitutes for people. We call them robots. And the modern robot is really a computer in a fancy package.

Many people think that robots are a recent invention. This is not true. Robots

"The Young Writer," an amazing early automaton.

have been around for thousands of years. The first robots were actually automatons (aw-TOM-uh-tons). The ancient Egyptians were said to have built figures that could move their arms. Steam was used to make the arms move. In the 14th century the Arabs built an automaton that filled a wash basin with water and later emptied the dirty water when the user had finished washing. People continued to build automatons. And as they learned more about science—especially the science of mechanics—the machines became very sophisticated.

In 1774, Pierre Jacquet-Droz, a Swiss, built an automaton that was so amazing that people came from all over Europe to see it. It was called "The Young Writer," and it was the figure of a young boy sitting at a desk. He would pick up a pen, dip it into an inkwell, and write a message several lines long. People could not understand what was happening. They thought it was magic because they couldn't see the system of gears and pulleys that made the figure work. Jacquet-Droz was arrested and accused of being a sorcerer.

In 1817, the writer Mary Shelley came to Switzerland to see "The Young Writer." The automaton gave her an idea. In 1817 she wrote one of the most famous books ever written—*Frankenstein*. We all know the story of the mad scientist who built a man out of body parts. Dr. Frankenstein's monster was an artificial man. But Frankenstein's monster showed us what could happen when artifical life went wrong. This is the difference between a science fiction robot and a real robot. The real robot does only what it is made to do. It does not have a brain. It does not think.

Books and plays continued to be written about robots, but the word "robot" wasn't used until 1921. At that time a Czech playwright named Karel Capek wrote a play called *R.U.R.* In Capek's play, robots were mechanical men designed to take the place of real men working in factories. Men decided that the robots would work even better if they had emotions like real people—if they could love and hate and cry and hurt.

So these emotions were built into the robots. But, the plan backfired, and the robots took over. Their final act was to destroy all humans. The word "robot" comes from the Czech word *robota,* which means "work." Since 1921, "robot" has come to mean a machine that does the work of a person.

There have been many famous robots in the movies. Perhaps you know of the Tin Woodsman *(The Wizard of Oz),* Gort *(The Day the Earth Stood Still),* Artoo-Deetoo and See-Threepio *(Star Wars).*

Even though most of these robots are too fantastic to be real, there *are* real robots. And these robots can do wonderful things. In fact, Isaac Asimov, the famous scientist and science fiction writer, was so sure that robots would become a way of life that he developed the Three Laws of Robotics:

1. A robot must not injure a human being or through inaction allow a human being to come to harm.
2. A robot must obey the orders given it by human beings except where such orders would conflict with the First Law.
3. A robot must protect its own existence as long as such protection does not conflict with the First or Second Law.

▶MODERN ROBOTS HELP PEOPLE

Real-life robots do things that are helpful to people. Did you know that your family car may have been welded together by a robot? Have you ever made a phone call and gotten a recorded message? A telephone answering machine is a kind of robot.

Probably the most widely used robots in the world are the Unimates—industrial robots. A Unimate doesn't look like a TV robot. What you see is a large metal box that is about 5 feet (1.5 meters) square. This box contains the computer that controls the Unimate. A long, heavy "arm" with "fingers" at the end does the actual work.

Unimates are used in factories all over the world. They can put small pieces of metal together to make valves. They can move heavy machine parts from one place to another. They can pull hot metal out of furnaces. On an assembly line, a group of Unimates can weld the metal bodies of cars to the frames. A team of Unimates can make 450 welds in less than a minute. They

This robot can paint a ceiling, vacuum, answer the door, take telephone messages, and even "talk."

are all good welds, too. Some Unimates are still going strong after 65,000 hours of work. That's more than 30 years of man hours!

How would you like a job standing in the cold rain for eight hours, with cars and trucks zooming by? You probably wouldn't like it very much, but Silent Sam doesn't mind a bit. Silent Sam is another kind of robot that does useful work. He looks like a tall man. He wears work clothes and a hard hat, and he waves a red flag. But he isn't a man. If you get up really close you can see that Sam is made of plastic. Sam's job is traffic control. Operated by batteries, he can be placed right in the middle of a busy intersection or in the most dangerous spot on a construction site. He will direct the cars and trucks for 24 hours a day. His arms never get tired, and he doesn't get scared if a truck comes too close. Sam is popular with police departments, telephone crews, and highway construction companies.

Big Al is a brand-new robot, designed to guard banks. He is even taller than Silent Sam, weighs almost 700 pounds (318 kilograms), and is shaped like a cone! He doesn't wear a regular bank guard suit or carry a gun. But he is tough, and he is bulletproof. Here is how the people who build Big Al and his brothers describe how he works: "He has a humanlike voice. If you cross his path, he will demand identification. If you have the right ID, Al will let you past. If not, he calls "HALT." If you move more than 3 feet (90 centimeters), Al gives out a high-pitched scream that will make you think your head is going to explode. If you *still* don't stop, Al will grab you with his "hand" and hold you until the police arrive." By the way, his "hands" have a squeeze power of 1,000 pounds (453 kilograms). You can imagine that not too many bank robbers would want to take a chance if they knew that Big Al was around.

Unimate, Silent Sam, and Big Al are just a few of the robots designed to help make life easier for people. Have you read about any more? How about the Viking landers that searched for life on the planet Mars?

Would you like to build a robot? If you're handy, maybe you can. Jonathan Kaplan did it when he was only 11 years old. Now he's a teenager, and he's still building robots. His latest can do more than 200 tasks.

If you would like to try to build a robot, go to your local library or a computer store. They have books that will tell you how.

▶INSIDE A ROBOT

But before you start on your own robot, you must know what goes on inside those

Silent Sam is a robot that can direct traffic for 24 hours a day.

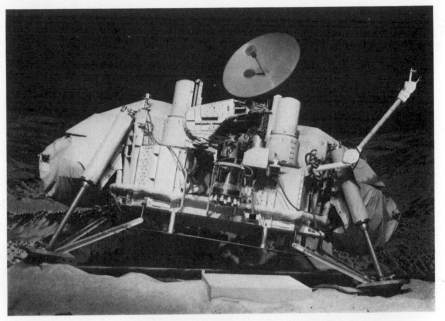

Many robots do not look like people. This Viking lander is a robot that searched for life on the planet Mars.

metal heads. A robot needs three basic parts. It needs mechanical devices to do the work. In simple robots these devices are usually gears and levers. More complicated robots have hydraulic systems. These are much like the devices that lift cars in garages. They operate by squeezing a fluid into a small space, creating a lot of force.

The second part that a robot needs is a sensor or a series of sensors. The sensors tell the robot what it is doing. Sensors may be as simple as "feelers" like those on an insect or as complicated as a TV camera.

Finally, the robot needs a "brain." Often the brain is a microcomputer. A human prepares a program that will tell the robot's mechanical devices what to do. The program is fed into the memory of the microcomputer. The microcomputer sends messages to the mechanical devices and thus makes the robot work. The sensors make sure that the robot is doing its job. They will inform the computer if anything goes wrong. If the robot is to do something different, a new program is written for the computer's memory.

So you can see that we really don't have to worry about robots taking over the world. They couldn't without the help of people.

JOHN VICTOR
President, Program Design, Inc.

Jonathan Kaplan builds robots. Would you like to?

Marconi, in 1896, with his first wireless receiver.

MARCONI'S WIRELESS RADIO

On a brisk winter day in 1903, on a hill-top in southwest England, the Italian inventor Guglielmo Marconi and several assistants huddled around a wireless radio receiver. They were listening to the dots and dashes of a Morse code message being beamed to them from a transmitter on Cape Cod in Massachusetts—2,000 miles (3,200 kilometers) across the Atlantic Ocean.

The message on that historic day—January 19—was from U.S. President Theodore Roosevelt. It was part of an exchange of greetings between the American president and Britain's King Edward VII. And it was the first two-way transatlantic communication using wireless telegraph (or radio).

That scientific triumph is still honored today. The work of Marconi, who is often called "the father of the wireless," set the stage for the radio and television of today.

In January, 1978, the 75th anniversary of Marconi's feat was commemorated with a re-enactment of the event—on that same hilltop at Poldhu, England. On hand were Marconi's widow and one of his daughters. There were also groups of schoolchildren to share in the excitement, which included a wireless greeting sent from President Jimmy Carter of the United States. And there were other messages, in many languages, from all over the world.

It was back in 1894 that Guglielmo Marconi, then a young man of 20, first became interested in the idea of using electromagnetic waves for communication. At that time, the telegraph was the only way to send messages long distances. But the telegraph required wires on land and an enormous number of underwater cables at sea.

How marvelous it would be, Marconi thought, if all those cables could be replaced by a wireless telegraph. It would be especially helpful to ships at sea trying to communicate with one another or with land stations. So he left his native Italy and went to England, where there was more shipping activity. In 1901, Marconi accomplished what many thought was impossible. He sent the first transatlantic wireless signal from his station in England to a receiving station in Newfoundland, Canada.

Some people had argued that it couldn't be done. They believed that radio waves could only move in a straight line. But Marconi proved that radio waves could bend to follow the curve of the earth's surface. That discovery led to the development of radio and television.

Marconi received many honors, including the Nobel prize in physics in 1909. When he died in 1937, he had earned a reputation as one of the world's great scientific pioneers.

SUN DAY

May 3, 1978, was a day of celebration. In many countries around the world people gathered to honor one of our most important friends: the sun.

It was Sun Day. At the United Nations, people welcomed the rising sun with songs and dances. In Denmark, people toured houses heated by solar energy. In Japan, people learned how to build a device to collect the sun's energy.

And in the United States, President Jimmy Carter said he would increase the amount of money the U.S. Government spends on solar research. "The question is no longer whether solar energy works. We know it works," said Carter. In fact, he said he plans to install a solar hot water heating system in the White House.

The President also talked of the advantages of solar energy. Unlike oil and coal, the sun's energy is not controlled by a small group of countries or companies. It is available to people everywhere. And the sun's energy, as Carter pointed out, "will not run out. It will not pollute our air or poison our waters. It is free from stench and smog. The sun's power needs only to be collected, stored, and used."

Sun Day was organized by Denis Hayes, an environmentalist. In 1970, he had organized Earth Day, which focused on pollution. "Earth Day emphasized a problem," said Hayes. "Sun Day emphasizes a solution."

Sun Day had three purposes:

1. To increase people's interest in and understanding of solar energy.
2. To increase government support of solar energy research and development.
3. To decrease our dependence on nuclear energy and on fuels such as coal and oil.

There are many ways to use the sun's energy. At present, it is used primarily to heat water and to heat and cool homes. Some 40,000 homes in the United States now have solar devices. By 1985 the number may reach 1,500,000.

Other buildings also use solar heating devices. A new fire station in Dallas, Texas, gets its heating, cooling, and hot-water needs supplied by 60 solar collectors on its roof. A public school swimming pool in San Antonio, Texas, is now heated by solar energy. And on Sun Day, the Anheuser-Busch brewing company introduced a solar device that heats the water used in making beer.

Robert Redford, the well-known actor, is an enthusiastic supporter of solar energy. Redford was one of the people who celebrated Sun Day at the United Nations. "The reason for Sun Day is to start making the solar dream a current reality," he told those who were gathered there. His dream is fast coming true, as more and more people are realizing that the sun is a very special friend.

THE RETURN OF THE WINDMILL

People are rediscovering the windmill. They are fixing up and using old windmills. They are building new ones that look very different from the older models. And in 1978, a small ranching town in northeastern New Mexico made the headlines because of its windmill. The town, Clayton, became the first community in the United States to have a windmill supply part of the public utility's electricity. (This is the electricity produced by a company, called a utility, for use by all the people in an area.)

Why this new interest in windmills? The answer is simple: the energy crisis. The world is running out of oil and coal, the fuels that now provide most of our energy. As supplies of oil and coal decrease, their costs go up ... and up. There is another problem with oil and coal—pollution. Burning them pollutes the air. Getting them out of the ground may cause water pollution and, in the case of coal, may leave the earth badly scarred and unusable for many years to come.

In contrast, wind is free; it doesn't cost anything. We will never run out of it, though there are periods when the wind doesn't blow. And wind power doesn't cause pollution. Thus, the windmill, which has been used for hundreds of years to pump water and grind grains, is now being redesigned and tested as a device to produce electricity.

▶HOW WINDMILLS WORK

A windmill has several important parts, but the part that catches your eye is the sails. There are many different kinds of sails. Some look like wooden shutters. Others are made of cloth. Still others have many-bladed metal fans. The Clayton windmill has two very long blades that look like an airplane propeller.

It is important that the sails be at the correct angle to the wind. Otherwise they will

The sails on this windmill in the Netherlands look like wooden shutters. There are still many working windmills in Holland.

Some sails are made of cloth, as on this windmill in Greece.

not turn or they will turn too fast. The person in charge of the windmill does this by turning, or winding, the mill. Depending on how the sails are attached to the mill, either the top or the entire windmill is turned.

The operation of a windmill is simple. The wind turns the sails, which turn the axle, or wind-shaft. As the axle turns, any machinery attached to its bottom end also turns.

The machinery may be a millstone used to grind corn, wheat, cocoa, pepper, or other substances. It may be a pump, used to bring up underground water. It may be a turbine, used to produce electricity.

▶WIND POWER

The wind has always interested people. The ancient Greeks believed there was a god who ruled the winds. They called him Aeolus. He kept the winds in a cave on an island. When he wanted to, he set them free to blow over the land. The rest of the time, he kept them locked up so they wouldn't cause storms or hurt people.

No one is certain who invented windmills, or even when they were invented. Many authorities believe they were invented in the Middle East. There is evidence that windmills existed in Persia (now Iran) in the 7th century. Genghis Khan, the 12th-century Mongol who conquered most of Asia, was responsible for introducing this kind of windmill to China.

The earliest evidence of windmills in Europe dates from the 12th century. These windmills were quite different from those in the Middle East. It is possible that the windmill was invented separately in these two areas of the world.

For almost 700 years, windmills were very common throughout Europe. A 1768 map of Liverpool, England, shows the locations of 27 mills. In Holland, some 9,000 windmills were operating at one time. The mills became a favorite subject of painters, including the Dutch artist Rembrandt.

The development of the steam engine in the 18th century resulted in a decline in the number of windmills. Windmills became less

113

Windmills were once very important in parts of the U.S. This one, with a metal-bladed sail, still exists in South Dakota.

profitable, especially when they couldn't grind flour finely enough to meet legal requirements. Today, working windmills can still be seen in many parts of Europe. But they are not as important as they once were.

The first windmills in North America were built by people who went there from Europe. The Dutch, for example, built many windmills in New Amsterdam, which is now New York City.

Eastern Long Island had many windmills. In the late 1880's, these attracted so many painters, with their easels and other materials, that some farmers complained that they could hardly get to their own barnyards. Some windmills on Long Island and in other parts of North America have now become tourist attractions.

Windmills were once very important in rural parts of the midwestern and western United States. In these places, there wasn't enough river water for people and animals. So windmills were built that pumped water from deep within the earth. More than 6,500,000 windmills were built in the United States between 1880 and 1930. They provided water for homes, farms, fire departments, and the locomotives of transcontinental trains. But these mills, even with modifications, could not produce very much electricity.

In the 1930's, the U.S. Government began building transmission lines to carry electricity to rural areas from power plants far away. This electricity was very cheap. It was used to run appliances in homes, to grind grain, and to pump water. As a result, most of the windmills fell into disrepair. That's just what had happened around Clayton, New Mexico. And as old timers watched the town's new windmill begin to turn, they told stories about the old mills and how they worked.

▶PROBLEMS TO BE SOLVED

Building a windmill that pumps water or grinds grain is not difficult. But building one that will change wind energy into electrical energy is still a challenge. Scientists and engineers are studying ways to solve the following problems:

A Steady Supply. The wind does not blow all the time. And it blows at different

Clayton, New Mexico, is the first U.S. community to have a "wind machine" supply part of its public utility's electricity.

speeds. If a building depended entirely on windmills for electricity, there would be times when the lights, television, freezer, and other electrical appliances wouldn't work.

At the present time, the best way to avoid this problem is to have both a windmill and a conventional generator. This is how the Clayton system works. Any electrical energy produced by the windmill goes into the utility's electric system. This automatically cuts down the amount of electricity produced by the system's oil-burning generator. When the wind doesn't blow, the oil-burning generator produces extra electricity so that the town's needs are met.

High Costs. Electricity produced from wind machines such as the one in Clayton now costs about three times as much as that generated from oil. The wind may be free, but the machinery needed to harness the wind is expensive.

Scientists expect the costs to come down as the size of the wind machines goes up. Other improvements in the machinery should also cut costs. In contrast, the cost of electricity from oil and coal is expected to continue to rise.

As Canadian Prime Minister Pierre Trudeau stated, "the era of cheap energy is behind us . . . . Conservation of energy must become a way of life—in our personal lives, and in commerce and industry. Our ingenuity must be invested in alternate energy sources and alternate technologies which are oil-conserving."

The wind can become an important alternate source of energy. Windmills will never be able to supply all our energy needs. But by using them to provide even 10 percent of our electricity, we would save billions of dollars now spent to buy oil from other countries. And windmills would help conserve the world's dwindling supply of oil.

JENNY TESAR
Sponsoring Editor, *Gateways to Science*

MYSTERIOUS HAPPENINGS

• Fifty people in a New York City skyscraper report seeing a silvery UFO hovering over a nearby park.

• Dozens of people in Virginia report seeing a huge water snake "with a head the size of a cantaloupe."

• Millions of people watch a woman on a popular television show predict what cards people will draw from a deck of cards.

More and more people are reporting all sorts of strange happenings. They say they have seen monsters and visitors from outer space. They tell about dreams that come true and about friends who are mind readers. They practice witchcraft and believe in horoscopes.

All these are things that scientists cannot explain—at least not yet. In general, scientists tell us to view these phenomena with caution. But they admit that there may be some truth in them.

Some scientists have formed an organization to investigate mysterious phenomena. It is called the Committee for the Scientific Investigation of Claims of the Paranormal (CSICP, for short). Let's look at some of the subjects they are studying.

▶UFO's

In 1908 a huge area in Siberia was destroyed. Trees were broken and crashed to the ground. There was a big fire and a lot of radiation. For many years, scientists puzzled over the cause of this mysterious event. The evidence indicates that the disaster was caused by something from space that crashed onto Earth. Scientists have suggested many possible answers: a comet, me-

Many mysterious things cannot be explained—such as this UFO, photographed in Zanesville, Ohio.

A scene from *Close Encounters of the Third Kind*. Movies such as this have increased interest in UFO's.

teorites, and so on. None of these answers fit all the evidence. Then in 1978, Felix Zigel, a well-known, respected Soviet astronomer, offered a new suggestion. He said, "The more we know of the . . . catastrophe, the more confirmation we find in the fact that the unidentified flying object that exploded over the forest in 1908 was an extraterrestrial probe."

It was good news to people who believe that creatures from outer space have visited—and are visiting—Earth. Of course, Zigel hasn't proved his idea. No one has ever proved that creatures from other parts of the universe have visited us. Nor has anyone ever disproved it.

An unidentified flying object, or UFO, is something in the sky that cannot be explained. It is something that behaves in an unusual way. Many things that appear in the sky seem to be unexplained or unusual. People may see a large, round, shiny object hovering far away over the ground and call it a UFO. But a meteorologist looking at the same object will realize that it is a weather balloon.

There has been an increase in interest in UFO's in recent years. Part of this is due to two very popular movies about creatures from outer space: *Star Wars* and *Close Encounters of the Third Kind*. But even before these movies came out, many people believed in UFO's. In the United States alone, more than 15,000,000 people say they have seen UFO's. Even President Jimmy Carter reported seeing one when he was governor of Georgia.

The reported shapes of UFO's are varied. Some people say they see UFO's that look like big round balls. Other UFO's form doughnuts. Others look like giant cigars or light bulbs. Still others look like footballs or rockets.

Many sightings can be easily explained. President Carter's UFO was actually the planet Venus—which is often very bright in the sky and so is often mistaken for a UFO. Weather balloons, rocket launchings, and airplane collisions are often mistaken for UFO's. So are night-flying birds that reflect light from the ground over which they are flying. Meteorites that leave a trail of light as they fall through the atmosphere have been mistaken for UFO's. So has an unusual kind of lightning called ball lightning. This consists of a mass of moving light about the size of a grapefruit. Often it explodes in midair.

The great majority of UFO's turn out to be IFO's (Identified Flying Objects). But perhaps 20 percent of the sightings cannot be explained. Several years ago, for example, a large, brightly lit UFO was seen in the air over Iran. According to the report of the sighting, a military fighter plane chased the UFO and came within 25 miles (40 kilo-

meters) of it. Suddenly, the UFO discharged an object that headed right toward the plane. The plane's pilot tried to fire a missile at the object. But at the very instant he tried to do this, his weapons-control panel went off and he lost all communications. Quickly, he put the plane into a dive to get out of the object's path. The object then returned to the UFO.

UFO's have been investigated by scientists everywhere. One major research program was called Project Blue Book. It was carried out by the U.S. Air Force over a period of 22 years. Finally, in 1968, the Air Force ended the study. Its conclusion: there was no scientific evidence to support the belief in visitors from outer space.

Many people who have studied UFO's agree with the Air Force's conclusion. And many disagree.

Alien or aluminum? Two young Ohioans, bedecked in aluminum foil and gas masks, look amazingly like this mysterious creature photographed by an Alabama policeman.

Astronomer J. Allen Hynek thinks "it's no longer possible to sweep away the whole subject. It reminds me of the days of Galileo, when he was trying to get people to look at sunspots. They would say that the sun is the visible symbol of God; God is perfect; therefore the sun is perfect; therefore spots can't exist; therefore there's no point in looking."

Hynek worked on Project Blue Book. He says that experts who worked on the project couldn't solve about 500 of the UFO cases. Today, Hynek is head of the Center for UFO Studies in Evanston, Illinois. (He was also the technical consultant for *Close Encounters of the Third Kind*.)

What does Hynek think UFO's are? "I don't give theories because I don't know *what* to believe," he says. "The only thing I'm sure of is that there's an intelligence connected with this. I don't know whether this intelligence is from very far off, or whether it is mataterrestrial—near us in the same way that TV pictures are right now passing through this room—or whether it will finally turn out to be from inner space, some strange manifestation of our own psychic energy. It could be coming from a parallel dimension or reality that's much closer than we could possibly imagine."

Philip J. Klass of CSICP believes that most UFO sightings are psychological. People read about them in newspapers, magazines, and books. They also hear about them on television. Says Klass: "If people think there are UFO's to be seen, they will go out and look for one."

Klass has investigated UFO reports for more than 12 years. "I have yet to find *one* that could not be explained," he says. "There's nothing I'd like better than to say that I'd finally found proof of a genuine UFO. It would be the greatest story in the history of journalism. So I'm not skeptical on principle, just on the evidence."

Herbert Blumer of the University of California also thinks UFO's are imagined rather than real. "When conditions are unsettled or when people are worried and unhappy about their lives, they tend to 'see things'," he says. "When people are uneasy, there is usually a rash of reports of the sudden appearance of strange objects."

▶MONSTERS

In the Scottish Highlands there is a long narrow lake named Loch Ness. This is the home of the legendary Loch Ness Monster—Nessie, for short. Nessie is reported to be 50 feet (15 meters) or more in length. It has a big body, a long neck, and a small head. It is a shy creature. Yet over the past 40 years, thousands of people have reported seeing it.

The Himalayas are home for Yeti—the famous abominable snowman. Yeti is thought to look like a cross between a man and an ape. It walks upright, has long hair covering most of its body, and leaves large footprints in the snow of the mountains.

Another apelike monster is Sasquatch, who is said to live in the Pacific Northwest. And in 1978, Chesapeake Bay on the east coast of the United States seemed to get a

Shy, timid Nessie has eluded scientific search parties, but thousands of people have reported seeing it.

Is this Sasquatch? The American version of the abominable snowman is said to live in the Pacific Northwest.

A woman dreams that a heavy chandelier will fall on her baby. She awakes, lifts the baby out of its crib, and takes it to her own bed. Two hours later, the chandelier falls from the ceiling and crashes into the crib.

Extrasensory perception, or ESP, is the ability to become aware of something—such as something that will happen—without using the known senses. In other words, ESP does not involve the senses of sight, sound, smell, touch, or taste.

There are four main kinds of ESP:

Telepathy is also called mind-reading. It is the apparent ability of two minds to communicate by some means other than the known senses. For example, a waitress gives a customer his order—before he orders it.

Clairvoyance is the apparent ability to perceive objects and events not present to the known senses. These objects and events may be removed in space or in time. For example, a dog goes and stands just inside the door several minutes before its mistress arrives home. It seems to know she will soon enter the door, even though she is still a block or two away.

Precognition is the apparent knowledge of a future event. The woman who dreamed of the falling chandelier had this ability.

Psychokinesis is the apparent ability to use the mind to control physical objects. One well-known person who claims to have this ability is Uri Geller. He claims he can use the power of his mind to move compass needles, bend keys, twist spoons, and start watches.

Often, the term "psychic phenomena" is used to describe different ESP events. ("Psychic" means having to do with the soul or mind.) Many people have investigated psychic phenomena. For example, CSICP investigated a girl who claimed she could predict what card a person would draw from a deck of cards. Although her television performance was impressive, she did poorly at the committee's laboratory. When she shuffled and dealt out the deck, she was very accurate. But when she did not shuffle or deal, she did even worse than mathematical chance would predict.

You can test your ESP ability by using special ESP cards. These are available in

new resident. Some 30 people reported seeing a long, ugly creature that has since been named Chessie. "I can't imagine anything like it in the world—it looked like a great big oversized snake," said one woman who saw it.

There is no real evidence that any of these creatures exist. Photographs that supposedly show some of them are not very clear. Some, in fact, seem to have been faked. Expeditions that have tried to find these monsters have not been successful.

Scientists believe that in many cases people actually see something. But they probably see ordinary animals—for example, a large bear in the Himalayas or some otters in Chesapeake Bay. Weather conditions may blur the image—and people's imaginations do the rest.

Do you have ESP? Try this experiment with a friend: Buy or make a set of ESP cards. Every three minutes or so your friend should pull a card from the deck and think about the symbol on the card. Write down what you think the symbol is. If you are right more than 25 percent of the time, you may have ESP.

many stores. Or you can make your own. There are 25 cards. Five have a circle on them. Five have a cross. Five have waves. Five have a square. And five have a star. Give the cards to a friend, who should mix them. You go into another room where you cannot see your friend. At set intervals—say every three minutes—your friend should pull one card out of the deck and think about the symbol on that card. You write down on a piece of paper what the symbol is.

Mathematical chance says you should be right 20 percent of the time, or one out of every five times. If you try this test many times and you seem to be right 25 percent or more of the time, you may have ESP.

People who believe in ESP think that everyone has this ability. But, they say, some people just don't know they have these powers. Others are afraid to admit they have ESP.

Many scientists believe there is some basis for ESP. But they would like to see more and better experiments carried out. This is not easy. Traditionally, scientific tests have been based on things that can be measured and observed. Many tests take place in a laboratory or involve hooking people up to machines. Such things tend to distract people who claim to have psychic powers.

Nonetheless, studies continue. At the same time, more and more people are believing in psychic phenomena. They believe because they've seen ESP in themselves or in people close to them.

In his book *The Occult,* Colin Wilson wrote: "In the past few centuries, science has made us aware that the universe is stranger and more interesting than our ancestors realized. It is an amusing thought that it may turn out stranger and more interesting than even the scientists are willing to admit."

Most scientists admit that this may happen. But, they say, the best way to learn about mysterious phenomena is to use logic and reason—the same tools that scientists have always used. To prove that UFO's and monsters and ESP exist, *scientific* evidence is needed.

JENNY TESAR
Sponsoring Editor, *Gateways to Science*

FUN TO MAKE AND DO

You can do all kinds of wonderful things with crayons—like this "black magic" crayon art.

STAMP COLLECTING

Stamp collecting, the "hobby of kings and king of hobbies," continued its great popularity in 1978. More people than ever before took an active interest in this exciting hobby, and an even greater number of stamps was issued.

▶ANNIVERSARY ISSUES

One event commemorated by many countries was the 200th anniversary of the discoveries made by Captain James Cook, the great English explorer. Canada issued two stamps to celebrate Cook's exploration and map chartings of its Atlantic and Pacific coasts. The United States issued two stamps commemorating Cook's discovery of Hawaii. The Cook Islands, discovered by Captain Cook in 1773, issued a set of three extra-large stamps that also celebrated the discovery of Hawaii. And a number of other countries and territories in the Pacific marked Captain Cook's explorations with commemorative stamps in 1978.

In 1977, an important anniversary for stamp collectors had been the Silver Jubilee (25th anniversary) of Queen Elizabeth II's accession to the throne. In 1978, many countries celebrated the 25th anniversary of her actual coronation. Britain came out with a commemorative set showing the symbols of royalty that were associated with the coronation ceremony in 1953—the gilded State Coach, St. Edward's Crown, the gold Orb, and the Imperial State Crown.

Italy issued a special aerogramme (an airmail letter/envelope) to note the 50th anniversary of the voyage of the dirigible *Italia* to the North Pole. Later in 1978 the commander of the expedition, Umberto Nobile, died. He had lived to be in his 90's.

▶ANIMALS ON STAMPS

Canada released a most attractive stamp in its series for endangered wildlife. It shows the peregrine falcon, one of the fastest of all birds, perched on a rocky coast. It has been estimated that this bird can dive at speeds of more than 200 miles (320 kilometers) an hour. As it issued the stamp, Canada announced that for the first time a per-egrine falcon that had been raised in captivity and then set free had mated in the wild and borne young.

The United States issued a special souvenir sheet to honor the Canadian International Philatelic Exposition (CAPEX 78), held in Toronto. The eight-stamp sheet depicts animals that live along the U.S.-Canadian border, the longest unguarded border in the world. The stamps show a blue jay, a Canada goose, a mallard duck, a cardinal, a raccoon, a red fox, a chipmunk, and a moose. This was the first such U.S. souvenir sheet honoring a foreign stamp exhibition.

The United States also issued a block of four commemoratives in its wildlife conservation series. Pictured are the great gray owl, the saw-whet owl, the barred owl, and the great horned owl, all found in North America.

Britain issued a series of four stamps in honor of its favorite animal, the horse. First publicly unveiled by Princess Anne, the stamps show horses ranging in size from the large and powerful Shire horse to the tiny Shetland pony.

▶CHANGES IN U.S. STAMPS

In the United States there was a particularly interesting issue in 1978—stamps that had no denomination but only the symbol "A" on them. These stamps were prepared a few years ago when a rate change seemed likely. But a decision on the new rate was made in time to allow new stamps to be printed with the correct denomination. The "A" stamps were placed in storage. Then in 1978 the Postal Service expected its first class, single letter rate to be raised to 16 cents, and it prepared a large quantity of 16-cent stamps. But the Service was only allowed an increase to the 15-cent rate, and there weren't enough 15-cent stamps on hand when the new rate went into effect. So the stored "A" stamps (worth 15 cents) were released until more stamps could be printed with a 15-cent denomination.

A great many 15-cent stamps were then quickly produced. They include a depiction of the Fort McHenry flag that inspired

1978 STAMPS
FROM AROUND
THE WORLD

A TOPICAL COLLECTION OF MUSICAL INSTRUMENTS

Francis Scott Key to write "The Star-Spangled Banner"; a very attractive 15-cent stamp showing two prize-winning American roses; and the first commemorative issued in the 15-cent denomination, honoring the field of photography.

The United States conducted an interesting experiment early in the year—the release of a miniature stamp, about three quarters of the size of a normal stamp, in the 13-cent denomination. The stamp has an Indian Head Penny as its design, and there were 600 stamps to a full sheet, compared to 400 full-size stamps per sheet. The Postal Service believes it can save money on its regular issues with smaller stamps. But the final decision is yet to be made.

▶OTHER STAMPS FROM AROUND THE WORLD

Britain continued to enchant stamp collectors throughout the world by drawing upon and illustrating its long history. One very popular 1978 issue was a series depicting four royal castles and palaces.

Japanese stamps that are issued annually for the mailing of New Year's cards featured a toy horse in 1978. Since 1953, the Japanese New Year's stamps have shown local toys or handicrafts that are created at different spots in Japan. These have usually represented the Oriental twelve-year animal zodiac cycle. Taiwan and North and South Korea also issued stamps in celebration of the Oriental Year of the Horse.

A particularly lovely U.S. issue was a block of four commemoratives containing segments of an American quilt done in a "basket" design. The quilted basket design on each stamp is positioned diagonally, with the handles pointed toward the center of the block. A diamond shape emerges from the area where the basket handles meet.

The United States also issued a block of vividly colored commemorative stamps featuring four forms of American dance—ballet, theater, folk, and modern dancing. As in the quilt commemoratives, the designs (in this case, figures of dancers) were positioned diagonally on the stamps.

In 1978, Argentina was the host country for the World Cup soccer championship. Soccer is the world's most popular sport and more soccer stamps have been issued throughout the years than for any other sport. Argentina issued special stamps for the 1978 competition. One set shows cities where matches took place, and another set has interesting representations of players from different countries. When Argentina won the championship, it issued special stamps marking the win. Many other countries also issued stamps for the championship competition and for the winner.

Illustrating the beauty of nature, Algeria issued an especially lovely set of four stamps. Each stamp in the series shows the flowers of a fruit tree in glorious bloom.

The United Nations issued a set of four stamps of different denominations on the theme of world peace. Each shows an original work of art by artists from the United States, Italy, West Germany, and Japan.

The United Nations and many individual countries also issued stamps in celebration of what they thought was the total elimination of smallpox. But in August two cases of smallpox were discovered in England. The cases were thought to have been caused by mishandling of the virus in a laboratory.

The highly popular Europa series, issued each year by the member nations in the Conference of European Postal and Telecommunication Administrations, featured monuments as its 1978 theme. Buildings such as cathedrals, town halls, and castles reflect each country's pride in its past.

▶A TOPICAL COLLECTION

Collections of musical instruments—whether made up of gleaming brass horns and burnished woodwinds or of reed instruments and log drums—are usually found only in museums. Large and varied groups of instruments may also be owned by private collectors who take part in this costly hobby. But stamps featuring illustrations of musical instruments make an excellent choice for a topical collection—a collection built around one theme. These stamps are not only unusually striking in appearance. They can also help you learn about the musical heritages of different nations. And you will see that people everywhere share a common feeling—the love of music.

CHARLESS HAHN
Stamp Editor, *Chicago Sun-Times*

MANY HANDS COOKING

from France
CROQUE MONSIEUR (krauk mis-YUH)

Long loaves of bread as only the French can make it, crusty on the outside and soft on the inside, are the beginnings of this melt-in-your-mouth sandwich. A *croque* is a sandwich dipped in an egg mixture and fried. The French call the combination of bread, ham, and cheese in this recipe *Croque Monsieur*. Topped with a fried egg, it's a *Croque Madame*.

Try this recipe. Then invent a *croque* of your own. Note: *Croques* can be made with French bread or regular white bread. *Bon appetit!*

INGREDIENTS
4 slices cooked ham
4 slices Swiss cheese
8 slices bread
2 eggs
¼ cup milk
2 tablespoons butter

EQUIPMENT
paring knife
medium bowl
fork or egg beater
large frying pan
wide spatula

HOW TO MAKE
1. Trim the ham and the cheese with the paring knife to fit the bread.

2. Make a sandwich by placing 1 slice of ham and 1 slice of cheese between 2 slices of bread. Make 3 more sandwiches the same way.

3. Crack the eggs into the mixing bowl, add the milk, and beat them together well.

4. Melt the butter in the frying pan over low heat. Be careful the butter doesn't burn.

5. While the butter is melting, dip each side of each sandwich into the egg-and-milk mixture.

6. When the butter is hot and bubbling, place the sandwiches side by side in the frying pan. Sauté them over medium heat for about 3 minutes until they're golden brown on the bottom. To see if they are brown enough, lift a corner of the sandwich with the spatula and peek at the underside. When they are done, turn them with the spatula and cook the other side.

7. Sauté the other side for 3 minutes or until it browns and the cheese melts.

8. Serve at once.

This recipe serves 4 people.

from Venezuela
BREAKFAST COCOA

Buenas días. It's morning in Venezuela. And the Venezuelans, like many other South Americans, enjoy starting the day with a cup of sweet hot cocoa.

Cocoa and chocolate come from the beans of the cacao tree, a tree native to Central and South America. Groves of these trees grow in countries where there are heavy rains and hot sun. So in South America, Central America, and Mexico, cocoa has been a favorite drink for hundreds of years.

INGREDIENTS
¼ cup water
3 tablespoons cocoa
2 tablespoons sugar
2 cups milk
1 teaspoon vanilla

EQUIPMENT
measuring cup
medium saucepan
measuring spoons
mixing spoon
2 cups

HOW TO MAKE

1. Bring the ¼ cup of water to a boil in the saucepan.

2. Stir in the cocoa and sugar until they are blended. Turn the heat very low.

3. Slowly pour the milk into the saucepan with the cocoa mixture. Stirring steadily to keep it from burning, cook it over low heat for about 2 minutes. Do not let it boil or a skin will form on the top.

4. When the cocoa is hot, remove from the stove and stir in the vanilla.

5. Carefully pour the cocoa into the cups. Serve hot.

This recipe serves 2 people.

WHAT'S DIFFERENT?

Let's play a detective game. Look at the two pictures. See if you can spot all the things that have happened to turn winter into spring. (Answers on page 383.)

Help design and decorate your room—and turn it into your castle!

DESIGNING YOUR OWN ROOM

One of the most exciting things that you can do is to design and decorate your own room. After all, your room is your house, your escape into a private and special place. This room can be turned into your castle.

Imagine, an entire room to call your own. You have a door to open and shut, connecting and separating you from the rest of your family. You have a window to let in air and light, allowing you a view beyond your enclosed four walls. Your floor gives you the physical space to house everything, and your four walls frame your personal territory. Even if you share a room with a brother or sister, it offers you a world of opportunity and challenge, an area for work and for adventure, a place where you can have fun.

And who could know better than you what you really want in your own room? Even if your parents could guess just what you'd like to have in your bedroom—colors, textures, decoration—it wouldn't be nearly as much fun as making your own choices. If you select your own things you can help turn your four walls into a magical special place, and you will be able to take pride in the results.

Your room should take on your personality and almost look like you. If you put what you like in your room, it should become who you are. What you're interested in and care most about will be showing.

As you continue to grow and develop, and your physical size and appearance change, your feelings and needs will continue to change also. Your room should change and "grow up" as you do. This process can keep you active as a designer as you go along.

▶A GROWING-UP ROOM

You spend alot of time in your own room. Your parents probably have separate rooms for sleeping, eating, working, and entertaining. But you have only one room. In this one place you have to find space to house several different activities. You'll need a quiet area in which to work and study. You'll also need a play area, where you can explore alone or with friends. You should have a clear understanding of the differences between these activities.

Your room should have the mood of readiness for a flood of activities. Everything should be within your reach. You should set up an order that you can maintain. Ideally, you should be able to flow from one activity to another with ease and enthusiasm.

Start planning with a dream in mind. Go into your room and pretend it is empty. Try and see your room—bare walls, a floor, a ceiling, a window or two, a closet and a door. Think how you can create the perfect room.

Now let's proceed, step by step, to achieve your goals.

Walls. Keep the walls of your room simple. Remember that the four walls are only a background, a backdrop, for your collections, your art, super graphics, posters, books, and banners. Don't think of decoration; think of providing wall space for your activities.

An excellent choice for your walls and ceiling would be an enamel paint. It's the easiest to keep clean. This type of paint usually comes in four different finishes: high gloss, semigloss, satin finish, and dull.

The shiny high-gloss walls and ceiling sparkle and reflect light. It's probably best to use the high gloss unless your walls are in bad condition; then you should use semigloss or satin finish.

Windows. Your windows connect you with the outside world. Be sure they open and close easily. The glass should be clean. Anything you add to your windows should have a function. Don't have curtains unless they can be closed to provide privacy and darken your room for sleeping.

Thin aluminum blinds are an inexpensive and attractive window idea. These blinds let you control light, and they come in over 100 exciting colors. You can create a stripe effect by using two or three different colors. To learn more about these blinds, inquire at a lumber yard or paint store.

Floors. Your floor is an important part of your room. Of the thousands of floor coverings available today, one of the most practical is still a hardwood floor. A wood floor can stand up to the hard wear you'll give it. Check to be sure there are no rough boards that could give you splinters. Sand where necessary. If you have a wooden floor in your bedroom, consider painting it a color, staining it, stenciling it, or having it scraped to lighten the color. To make your floor super strong, you can apply a clear liquid called polyurethane. This will give a hard, shiny surface (like a gym floor), and it is easy to maintain. All you need is soap and water.

Expensive carpeting that covers the entire floor isn't very practical. You need freedom in your room so you can re-arrange your furniture on a whim. But you may want a small area rug, even if it is just a mat in front of your bed.

Lighting. You should have several different light fixtures in your room. On a dark winter day, a ceiling fixture is good to flood the room with light. But you should have a small lamp near your bed. There's nothing worse than having to get out of bed to turn off the overhead light. If your room is big enough and you need lots of light, you could consider track lighting.

Daylight is really best. Study your room at different times of the day so you can best use the light that comes in from your window. You might want to have your desk near the window so you can read and study in natural light.

A desk lamp should take up as little space as possible on your desk. And you should be able to move it around to focus on the project you are working on. The lamps that architects use are ideal. You can clamp one onto your desk, which will keep your entire desk top clear. The neck of the lamp moves from a hinge, so you can avoid glare by adjusting the light. These lamps come in several different sizes, and colors include chrome, black, and white.

There are also clip-on lamps for bed or wall that are appropriate for reading in bed. Because they are attached to your wall or bed, they are safer than a lamp on a table, which could get knocked over.

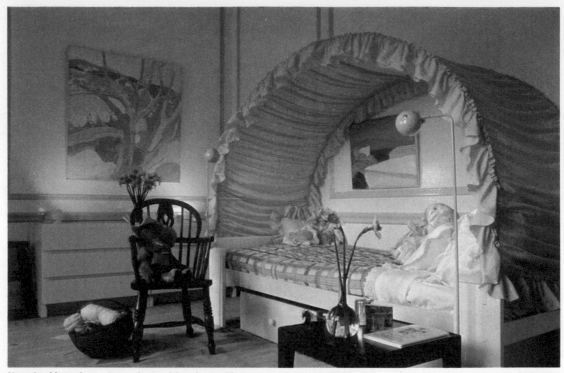

Your bed is an important piece of furniture. Make sure it's comfortable.

If you are a plant lover, fluorescent lighting may be perfect for your needs. You can easily install a fluorescent light *under* a shelf. Or if you need extra light for plants near a window, you can put a fluorescent strip across the top of the window, with a flat board in front of it to hide the fixture. Some people have two fixtures, on separate switches, behind the board: one is a plant light and one is a regular fluorescent fixture.

Your Furniture. Because you may often want to re-organize and re-arrange your room, your furniture should be easy to move around. No matter how positive you are about your room plan today, you may want to change things in a month. The key to your room's success is flexibility. Don't have anything built-in if you can help it.

Your needs should be fairly simple: a bed, a desk, a desk chair, a place for relaxing and enjoying hobbies, and storage space.

By now you have grown enough physically so that you can have furniture that will be just as appropriate ten years from now as it is today. Think about your furniture.

• The most important piece of furniture is your bed. Place it in front of the window so you can see the stars as you go off to sleep.

Is your bed comfortable? You should have a hard mattress.

• Do your have your own desk? It doesn't matter what the desk is like as long as it's your own. Even if you share your bedroom with a sister or brother, you need to have your own place to study.

Check the height of your desk. If it is too tall, can you have the legs cut down? If it is too short, can you add on to the legs?

If you don't have a desk you can easily create one. The least expensive desk would be made from square toy boxes, 14 inches (35 centimeters) on a side. Stack two on each side with a piece of wood cut to fit across the top. Or you could have file cabinets on either side and a wood or formica top. A pair of saw horses purchased from a lumber yard can also be a base for your desk. Paint them a lively red or blue or yellow. Do you want your desk surface to be white or wood or a color?

Put your desk somewhere away from the other furniture so you feel you have a pri-

134

It doesn't matter what your desk is like, as long as it's your own.

vate place to work. Position your desk in such a way that your chair is where you want to sit. Do you want to face the wall or into the room?

• For very little money you can buy a wood swivel desk chair that adjusts from high to low as you grow up. They come in bright primary colors, which add fun to your desk arrangement.

• If your clothes closet is big enough, you can put a chest of drawers inside it. Then you'll have more living space in your room. You can even put your clothes on open shelves. Your clothes rod should be adjustable, on wooden brackets. Then, as you grow taller, you can raise the rod.

You can slide some open storage boxes under your bed. Put them on casters for easy handling.

Or buy several colored plastic storage cubes. If you share a room, each of you should have a different color or set of colors. You could have red, white, and brown—and your sister could have blue, green, and yellow. You can put these bins on casters, too.

• Wall shelves are ideal for books and supplies. The hardware store sells brackets and metal strips that can be screwed or nailed to the wall. You can buy shelves in different lengths and in different finishes, and they can be adjusted to different heights. The brackets come in different depths so your shelves can also vary in width.

One of the most frustrating things about having a hobby you love is to have to stop working. Time is up. You have to go to school or have dinner or play ball. You need a separate shelf or ledge where you can leave the project and then come back and work on it when you have time.

Study your room and see where you could build a ledge. Usually there is some wasted space under your windows or on a wall where there is a radiator. You might decide to have the ledge go the entire length of the wall. Make it deep enough to work on comfortably when you pull up your desk chair or a stool. If you have a record player, measure carefully to make sure it fits securely on the shelf.

Collections. We are all born collectors. If you find you have begun a collection or two of delicate things, you may want to display them on the wall, where they are safe. Miniature porcelain animals or soldiers or rocks or shells—these things need their own place so they won't end up in the vacuum cleaner! You can buy or easily build open display cases. Remember, if you put your treasures behind glass, you can't pick them up and touch them, which is half the fun.

Bulletin Board. No bedroom is complete without a place to pin up notes, cards, invitations, and posters. Get a big bulletin board and put it over your desk. You can buy one at the stationery store, paint the cork one color, and contrast the color of the frame. Use multi-colored push pins to tack on your mementos.

Fabrics. All your fabrics should be washable and soft to the touch. Your bed can be covered in patterned sheets, with a colorful blanket or a matching quilted comforter. Or throw an old quilt on your bed. You can also buy a piece of batik the right size for a single bed cover. If you find an inexpensive cotton fabric you like, you can make a flounce to cover the box spring, make sheets, and make some pillow covers.

Don't think of fabrics only for the bed or on a window. Use a piece of fabric stretched on a wall. You can buy wood stretchers to frame the fabric. Or hang a rug or quilt on one wall. Because you have a plain white background, the patterns will contrast and show up well.

To make pillows, you can buy some pieces of foam rubber and cover them with leftover fabrics of different colors, textures, and patterns. You can create a cozy reading and sitting area in a corner of your room simply by grouping these pillows together.

Color. The colors you select for your room will bring the room to life. As you grow, so will your list of favorite colors. There are no rules to follow. Maybe you want each door in your room to be a different color—one door sun yellow, one door bold blue, and one orange.

Have you ever been lying on your back and wished there were a giant yellow ball on the ceiling. If so, paint a circle.

Bright, colorful fabrics will bring your room to life.

Filled with your own special treasures, your room will become your best friend.

You can buy super stick-on graphics in paint stores. There are also stencil kits you can buy so you can stencil designs on your bed, chair, lamp shade, or chest of drawers. Because your walls are white, be free to paint a mural or a design right on your wall. If you tire of it, cover it over with white and start again.

Use color to accent your room. A slat of your chair, red. A beam, peach. Experiment. Paint is the quickest and easiest way to change the feeling of your room.

Your own things. You should have in your special room only things that mean something to you. Keep your room simple. You will outgrow toys, dolls, trucks, and blocks—things you once cared a great deal for. Don't keep adding more things each year until you have no space to breathe! Even if you can't redo your entire room right now, at least you can weed out the junk. Only you can do this. Your parents don't know what are your treasures and what should go to the thrift store.

Maintenance. If you're old enough to design and decorate your own room, you are also old enough to maintain it. Almost everything in your room is washable—walls, windows, floor, fabrics, and furniture can be cleaned. You should be able to help keep it clean. Pick up your things and keep your room in order.

If you don't keep your room in order, you may lose something, and it could be the last piece of your puzzle or a part of your model airplane or your favorite book. When you put things away, you'll know where they are when you want them. Remember, this is your room.

This should be an exciting project for you. Once you begin to be responsible for the way your room looks and works and feels, you'll be happier. You will find the hours you spend in your room will fly by. Your room and you will become best friends. You'll want to be together.

ALEXANDRA STODDARD
Author, *A Child's Place*

137

NO MORE COWBOYS

Once upon a time, a cowboy was a cowboy and a stewardess was a stewardess. But now times have changed. Today a cowboy is a cowpuncher and a stewardess is a flight attendant.

Not too many years ago, people were expected to play certain roles in our society. Only men were thought to be able to herd cattle. Only young women were considered to be able to wait on airplane passengers. But today we accept everyone's right to choose whatever career she or he wants. Both women and men may become business executives or doctors or flight attendants or cowpunchers.

Some 20,000 different types of jobs currently exist. Until recently, the names of some of them implied that they were meant only for men or for women. The title alone may have discouraged a girl from becoming a repairman. And certainly a boy wouldn't want to be called a maid. But there are girls who want to have jobs where they repair clocks or telephones or cars. And there are boys who would like to work in and care for other people's homes.

To give everyone the same options in choosing a career, the titles of jobs such as repairman and maid—and cowboy and stewardess—have been changed. They have been changed to titles that do not stereotype the job.

Here is a career game for you to play. The numbered column (on the left) lists the old job titles. The lettered column (on the right) lists, in jumbled order, the new job titles. See if you can match each old job title with its new name.

Old Job Title
1. batboy
2. bellboy
3. brakeman
4. cameraman
5. cleaning woman
6. cowboy
7. deliveryman
8. doorman
9. draftsman
10. fireman
11. fisherman
12. flagman
13. housewife
14. maid
15. mailman
16. meterman
17. workman
18. repairman
19. sales girl
20. serviceman
21. stewardess
22. watchman
23. policeman

New Job Title
a. letter carrier
b. sales clerk
c. flight attendant
d. servant
e. cowpuncher
f. firefighter
g. drafter
h. bathandler
i. doorkeeper
j. cleaner
k. bellhop
l. braker
m. guard
n. flagger
o. camera operator
p. deliverer
q. police officer
r. servicer
s. homemaker
t. fisher
u. repairer
v. laborer
w. meter reader

ANSWERS: 1.h;2.k;3.l;4.o;5.j;6.e;7.p;8.i;9.g;10.f;11.t;12.n;13.s;14.d; 15.a;16.w;17.v;18.u;19.b;20.r;21.c;22.m;23.q.

138

The new job titles you have just learned are hidden in this search-a-word puzzle. Try to find them. To find the names, read forward, backward, up, down, and diagonally. If you wish, cover the puzzle with a sheet of tracing paper. Then you can circle each title as you find it. One job title has been circled for you.

F	L	I	G	H	T	A	T	T	E	N	D	A	N	T
F	I	S	H	E	R	M	C	A	R	R	O	T	S	B
R	U	R	N	R	E	F	J	R	H	O	O	L	A	R
R	E	R	E	V	I	L	E	D	O	T	R	E	L	A
E	E	D	E	F	S	A	N	R	M	A	K	T	E	K
L	R	P	A	N	I	G	N	A	E	R	E	T	S	E
D	S	E	A	E	A	G	Y	U	M	E	E	E	C	R
N	E	E	H	I	R	E	H	G	A	P	P	R	L	R
A	R	A	R	C	R	R	L	T	K	O	E	C	E	E
H	V	I	E	V	N	E	E	C	E	A	R	A	R	T
T	I	D	C	E	A	U	R	T	R	R	N	R	K	F
A	C	Y	A	K	B	N	P	Z	E	E	B	R	N	A
B	E	L	L	H	O	P	T	W	S	M	K	I	Y	R
I	R	L	A	B	O	R	E	R	O	A	A	E	L	D
P	O	L	I	C	E	O	F	F	I	C	E	R	U	L

139

HANGING HEARTS

Here is a mobile that will add a touch of color to your favorite room. Hang it anyplace where it will move freely. It also makes a nice present for Valentine's Day or Mother's Day:

What to Use:

red self-hardening clay
heart-shaped cookie cutter
rolling pin
transparent thread

small cardboard box
red felt
ribbon or heavy string
scissors, needle, tape, glue, waxed paper

What to Do:

1. Put the clay between two pieces of waxed paper and roll it flat, just as you would cookie dough.

2. Remove the top sheet of waxed paper. Use the cookie cutter to cut out hearts from the clay. Near the center top of each heart, punch a hole with a pencil. Let the hearts dry and harden. (It may take several days for the hearts to harden completely.)

3. Hang each heart from a double strand of thread.

4. Cut a piece of felt large enough to cover the box, and glue it to the bottom and around the sides.

5. Thread a needle with the line from one of the hearts. Run the needle through the red felt and the bottom of the box. The bottom of the box should be facing downward, toward the hearts, when you do this. Tape the thread to the inside of the box. Repeat with the remaining hearts, but hang the hearts at different lengths. If you need to adjust the height of some of the hearts, carefully remove the tape holding that heart's thread. Adjust and retape.

6. With the point of a scissors, poke a hole in two opposite sides of the box. Push the ribbon through the two holes and securely knot each end inside the box.

7. You can now hang your heart mobile from a hook in the ceiling.

Variations:

You can make many different mobiles in this manner. Use cookie cutters of different shapes. Use different colors of clay. Paint designs or glue colored glitter on the clay after it hardens. Make a circular shape instead of a square from which to hang the hearts.

DISCOVERING CRAFTS

The world of crafts is as big as the world we live in, for it includes anything that can be made by hand. At the same time, it is a very small and personal world, for crafts are whatever you yourself make of them.

People have always used crafts to provide for their physical needs. Spinning and weaving cloth are crafts, as is making tools and utensils for growing and preparing food, building homes, and other basic activities.

Today, because of manufacturing processes, most people do not have to use their hands to make the things they need. But we all still have a desire to create things, and crafts continue to play a role in helping us live more enjoyable lives. While in earlier times people did most crafts because they had to in order to survive, today people do crafts as a hobby, for enjoyment.

With the many materials now available, we can pick and choose from a wide variety of techniques to find the craft that best suits us. Some people like to dabble in many different types of projects, while others prefer to develop skill in just one craft. Some hobbyists like easy techniques that give fast results; others want to spend many hours mastering a challenging craft. In the world of crafts, there is something for everyone—something that will suit each person's interests, skills, and personal tastes.

As in many things, there are trends and fashions in crafts. For several years the most popular have been decorative painting, making miniatures, and the fiber crafts (weaving, basketry, and macramé). However, there are many other crafts that offer opportunities for individual expression. In

You can make many kinds of folk dolls from materials found around the house. This interesting applehead doll is made by carving features on an apple and then letting the apple dry.

142

attempting to find the right craft for you, you should consider as many different types of materials and techniques as you possibly can. Visit your local craft shop and find out about some of the projects you can make from the materials and supplies that are sold. Here are some of the crafts that hobbyists enjoyed in 1978.

▶DOLLS

Dolls have been made throughout human history. They can be found in every culture, from the most primitive to the most advanced. Although they are usually thought of as playthings, they have other purposes as well. Dolls are used to show the dress and customs of other cultures and historical periods. They can also be used as a form of decoration.

There are various kinds of dollmaking. Some of the techniques, such as those for making porcelain dolls, are quite difficult and require special equipment. Other techniques are very simple and can result in some charming, unique dolls. Many of the easier methods have been used by people for generations to make "folk" dolls. Applehead dolls, cornhusk dolls, nuthead dolls, and rag dolls are all folk dolls that can be made from readily available materials.

Folk dolls are not only easy to make, but they are fun too. Applehead dolls, for instance, are made by carving features on an apple and then allowing the apple to dry. One reason appleheads are such fun is that each head is a surprise. As the apple shrivels and dries, the carved features change and take on an expression and character all their own. The faces often resemble those of old folks, but each one is different and has its own personality. The heads are then given bodies, usually made of cloth over wire forms, and dressed in a style appropriate to the face. The body can also be

Many hobbyists have found that working with paper can be challenging and fun. Papier-mâché is one kind of paper craft. You can make all sorts of things, like these cats.

made from throwaway materials. For example, a plastic detergent bottle can serve as an excellent body for the doll. Simply cover the bottle with clothing and put the head on top of it.

▶PAPER CRAFTS

One of the least expensive and most readily available craft materials is paper. Although we may think of it as uninteresting, many hobbyists have discovered that paper can be a very challenging and long-lasting medium.

Papier-mâché is just "chewed up paper," and yet papier-mâché items that are centuries old can be seen in museums. You can make your own paper mash from old newspapers or buy it ready-to-mix in craft shops.

Another popular paper craft is quilling, or paper filigree. You take narrow strips of paper and roll them to form various shapes. They can be glued onto a background as part of a picture (*left*) or glued onto a three-dimensional item, like this little cardboard sleigh (*below*).

Papier tole is a craft in which you can create a three-dimensional "paper elevation."

Either way, it is an excellent modeling material that allows for a free range of your imagination.

Another paper craft that has been popular for several years is quilling, or paper filigree. This is also an old craft, which originated in France in the 17th century. Quilling is simply very narrow strips of colored paper that are rolled to form circles, ovals, and other shapes. These are used in several ways. Often they are glued onto a background to form part of a picture. Sometimes they are glued together to make hanging ornaments. They can even be applied to three-dimensional items such as tiny potted plants or figures. Quillwork has a special charm, and people who enjoy quilling find it fascinating to build pictures from little pieces of paper.

Découpage is a paper craft that has been popular among hobbyists for a number of years. Like quilling, it originated in France, and its name, *découpage,* means "applied cutouts." In découpage, paper cutouts are glued to a surface such as a box, and many coats of varnish are applied over them. When the piece is finished, the cutouts are so deeply embedded in the varnish that the surface is perfectly smooth to the touch. The fun in découpage lies in selecting and arranging the cutouts—the creative possibilities are endless. Découpage is a kind of "painting with paper," and even those who cannot paint at all can achieve striking results.

A variation of découpage is a technique called *papier tole* or dimensional découpage. In this craft, different parts of a print are used to create a three-dimensional "paper elevation." Parts of the print are glued down flat. Other parts are cut out and curled, or contoured, over the original print so that some elements of the picture stand out. This gives a surprisingly lifelike effect.

Whichever craft you decide to explore, you will find that there are many exciting materials and instructions available to make it rewarding for you.

SYBIL C. HARP
Editor, *Creative Crafts* magazine

RIBBONS ROUND HER NECK

Ribbon jewelry is easy to make and fun to wear. It is also a perfect gift for birthdays and other special occasions.

Use your imagination to create unusual designs. Make a neckband to match a dress or to celebrate a holiday. Use nail polish or felt-tip pens to make a polka dot design. Use sequins to spell out "SUPERMOM" or a person's name. You'll quickly think of many other ideas.

What to Use:

Ribbon (velvet and grosgrain ribbons are especially nice)
Decorations (such as lace, rickrack, yarn, felt, pearls, and sequins)
Snaps (1 set for each neckband)
Scissors, thread, needle, chalk, glue

What to Do:

1. Cut the ribbon to the proper length. To do this, you must first use a tape measure to find the distance around the neck of the person who will wear the neckband. Then add about ½ inch (1.5 centimeters). For example, if the neck measurement is 13 inches (33 centimeters) make the neckband 13½ inches (34.5 centimeters) long.

2. Sew the snap onto the ribbon. This is used to close the neckband. The extra ½ inch (1.5 centimeters) of ribbon is for the snaps. Sew one part of the snap onto the end of the ribbon, on the *top* side of the ribbon. Sew the other part of the snap onto the other end, on the *underside* of the ribbon.

3. Decide what design you wish to make. If you want to use buttons, place them on the ribbon in different patterns. Keep rearranging them until you like the way they look. Then lift the buttons off the ribbon, one at a time, and use chalk to mark the position of each button. Put the buttons in a row on the table, in the order they will appear on the neckband.

4. Sew the decoration onto the ribbon. If you are using felt decoration, glue it onto the ribbon.

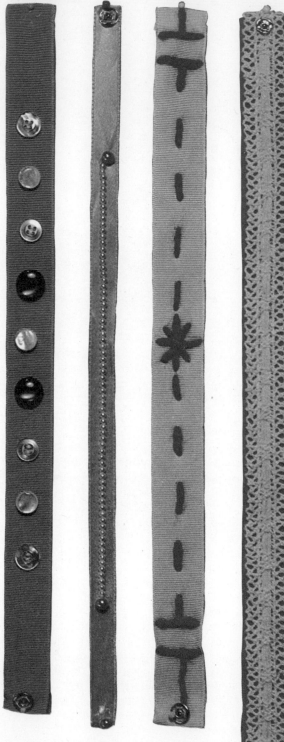

A UFO MAZE

We hear all kinds of stories about people who have spotted UFO's. Well, here's a UFO that has landed on Earth! Some of the alien creatures are leaving their spacecraft through the door. But others have found another way to get off their ship. See if you can find it, too.

Place a sheet of tracing paper over this UFO maze. Begin at the arrow above and try to find your way out of the maze (to the arrow on your right). If you come to a blind alley, try a different-colored pencil and a different route.

The solution is on page 383.

COIN COLLECTING

Throughout much of 1978, gold dominated the world of coin collecting. Investors turned to the yellow metal in growing numbers, many of them buying collector coins. Collector coins often sell for more than the value of their gold because they are prized by hobbyists. They include the U.S. double eagle ($20 gold piece) and growing numbers of modern issues that have been created specifically for collectors.

In 1972 only six nations were issuing gold coins. Since then, about 60 countries have done so. In 1978 the countries that issued gold coins included Afghanistan, Brunei, Cuba, Czechoslovakia, Macao, the Maldives, Mauritania, and Sudan.

In 1978, gold dominated the world of coin collecting. Some of the nations that issued gold coins were Brunei (*above*) and Mauritania (*below*).

▶U.S. COIN NEWS

The ongoing concern of 1978 was over the creation of a new mini-dollar coin, slightly larger than a quarter. After much debate, a likeness of Susan B. Anthony, the pioneer of women's suffrage, was agreed upon for the obverse design. The reverse will feature an adaptation of the "eagle landing on the moon" design from the Eisenhower dollar. The new coins will be released on July 1, 1979.

The new, smaller dollar coin, with a likeness of Susan B. Anthony, will be released in July, 1979.

The new Anthony dollar will replace the Eisenhower dollar in the 1979 proof set offered to collectors. For 1978, the Mint produced 3,200,000 proof sets, which were in great demand because they represented the last year of issue of the Eisenhower dollar.

Collectors themselves made some news in 1978. The American Numismatic Association established a coin-grading service, to start on a trial basis. This was a significant step for the hobby because the quality of a coin—particularly of a scarce or rare issue—is so important in determining its value.

Some interesting rare coins were discovered during the year. First came a number of silver 1977 Eisenhower dollars circulating in the Las Vegas area—a $2,000 "find" for those who were lucky enough to come up with them. The blanks from which these coins were struck had been prepared for collector editions. But they were accidentally mixed in with a batch of clad-metal dollar blanks that were destined for general circulation.

Two new "overdate" coins came to the attention of collectors for the first time in 1978. (In making an overdate, the Mint changes the date on the die from which the coin is made. Sometimes the old date shows through.) The first was a 1943/2 "wartime" nickel, which had gone undocumented for some 35 years. Overnight, lucky collectors who had specimens of this issue found themselves richer by nearly $1,000. The second overdate discovery was a 1958/7 Lincoln cent, the first overdate known in the Lincoln series.

148

This rare 1870 half dime made coin news in 1978.

The year's biggest discovery was the first known example of an 1870 half dime struck at the San Francisco Mint. Carrying a $500,000 price tag, the top-quality specimen is thought to have been part of a set struck for presentation at the dedication of the mint building.

Spectacular discoveries were not limited to the U.S. field, however. Early in the year it was learned that a third specimen of Canada's first dollar coin, dated 1911, had been discovered. Unlike the previously known specimens, which were struck of silver, this one was struck of lead. One of the silver specimens had sold for $110,000 in 1976.

The pattern for Canada's 1911 dollar, struck of lead.

▶A POCKETFUL OF NEW COINS

During 1978, Canada produced its third annual $100 gold coin issue. This limited edition of 200,000 pieces, produced in proof quality, was dedicated to Canadian unity and was eagerly bought by collectors.

Canada's $100 gold piece stressed unity.

The Soviet Union announced its first modern gold coinage, a series of six 100-ruble commemoratives. The first of the series was released in July, in honor of the hosting of the 1980 Olympic Games in Moscow.

A modern Soviet gold coin honored the Olympics.

In Italy, the currency system continued to suffer from inflation. When a new aluminum-bronze 200-lire coin—worth about 23 U.S. cents—was released in December, 1977, it was immediately hoarded. Officials pressed to begin introducing 500,000,000 coins slated for production in 1978.

For the Vatican, 1978 was an extraordinary coinage year. It began with the introduction of the 16th annual set of issues for Pope Paul VI. His death on August 6 caused Vatican City officials to introduce a traditional 500-lire *Sede Vacante* issue, to mark the period between the death of one pope and the election of his successor. The death of Pope John Paul I on September 28 brought forth a second *Sede Vacante* piece, an occurrence unprecedented in modern times.

Ascension Island, a tiny British dependency in the Atlantic Ocean midway between Africa and South America, issued its first coin in 1978. It was a crown commemorating the 25th anniversary of the coronation of Queen Elizabeth II. The coin shows a sea turtle, a reptile for which the island is famed.

Other coronation commemoratives were issued by the British Virgin Islands, the Cayman Islands, the Isle of Man, Jamaica, St. Helena, and Tristan da Cunha. The Tokelau Islands, a New Zealand dependency, also joined the first-ever coin list during the year.

CLIFFORD MISHLER
Publisher, *Numismatics News*

CRAYON MAGIC

It's fun to learn about colors by using crayons. Each crayon will give you a different color, or you can experiment and make new colors, shades, and tints. By working with stencils and textured materials, you can achieve new and exciting effects. And you can draw on many surfaces—paper, fabric, sandpaper.

The tip of your crayon will make straight lines, curved lines, dots, dashes, and letters.

The end of your crayon will make perfect little circles, by pressing down and twisting.

Two crayons taped together will make straight parallel lines and curvy parallel lines.

Remove the paper from a crayon and use the side to make soft lines, as in the picture below.

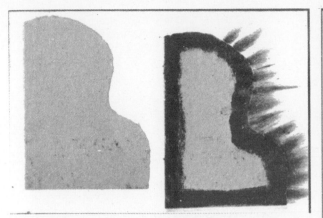

Cut out a shape from construction paper. Both the shape and the hole from which the shape was cut can be used as stencils. Crayon colors along the edges of a stencil can be "pulled out" with a pencil eraser (*above*). Stencils can be arranged under a piece of paper for a crayon rubbing (*right*). Stencil shapes can be repeated, overlapped, or used to create a whole design of many parts (*below*).

Apply a layer of black crayon over a design of many colors. Then, using the tip of a plastic spoon handle, scratch through the top layer of crayon to get interesting effects. You can scratch the design out in different directions (*above left*) or in one direction (*above right*).

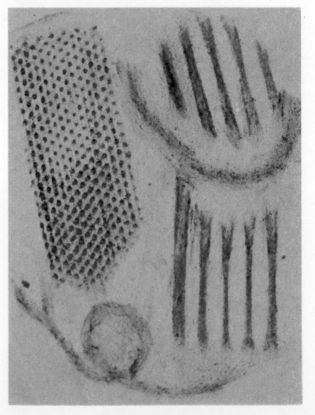

You can place materials that have textured surfaces under a piece of thin drawing paper. Then carefully rub the side of a crayon over the paper. This textured print was achieved by using pieces of window screening, rubber mats, and rope.

Try using your crayons directly on different surfaces. Textured papers, wood, fabric (*above*), and sandpaper (*below*) are some of the surfaces you can experiment with. Make big, bold pictures. Make small, detailed pictures.

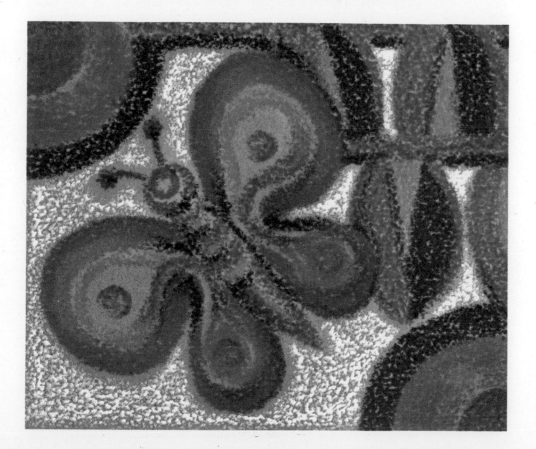

SPOON PEOPLE

This pretty lady was once a plain wooden spoon. Now she hangs on a wall, holding flowers in her pocket. You can make this spoon lady, or any other spoon person you can think of.

What to Use:

a wooden cooking spoon
yarn—about 1 yard (1 meter), of a color to be used for hair
fabric—a 12-inch (30-centimeter) square
felt—small scraps, of colors to be used for lips and eyes
glue, scissors, lace or other decoration

What to Do:

1. Cut a square piece of fabric for the dress. Each side of the square should be as long as the handle of the spoon.

2. Cut a small piece of fabric for the pocket. You can use a contrasting fabric if you wish.

3. Hem the dress on the bottom, and the pocket on all four sides. Sew your decoration onto the dress. Then sew the pocket onto the front of the dress.

4. Assemble all your materials on a clean sheet of newspaper. The "face" of the spoon is the round, convex side.

5. Make a loop with which to hang the spoon: Cut a 6-inch (15-centimeter) piece of yarn. Make a double loop. Glue the loose ends of the loop onto the top back of the spoon. The loop should clear the top of the spoon by about an inch (2.5 centimeters).

6. Cut 10 strands of yarn for the hair. Try arranging the strands in different ways. You may want to cut a few extra short pieces for bangs. When you have a nice arrangement, glue the yarn onto the spoon. The top ends should be glued over the back of the spoon.

7. Cut two eyes and a mouth from the felt. Then glue these onto the face.

8. Glue the dress onto the handle of the spoon. First, glue the center top of the dress onto the front neck of the spoon handle. When this is dry, bring the top edges of the dress around the back of the handle and glue down. Do this at an angle, so that the dress has a nice flared look.

9. The pocket in the spoon person's dress can be used for many things: dried flowers, a box of matches, small emery boards, toothpicks, pencils.

TAPETIME

Here's a quick and easy way to recycle glass bottles and tin cans. In just an hour you can make an attractive vase, candle holder, candy dish, or pencil holder. All you need is a clean can or bottle, a roll of masking tape, a pair of scissors, and some shoe polish wax.

Start by cutting small pieces of masking tape. You can cut the tape straight across. But for variety, you might make rounded edges. This will give a scalloped look to the finished product. Or, for zigzag edges, cut the tape with pinking shears.

Then put the pieces on the container, overlapping each piece, in an attractive design. Press each piece firmly to the glass—you don't want any loose edges. Make a clean edge around the container's opening. If you are covering a glass bottle, be sure to cover the bottom.

When you finish covering the container, apply a coat of shoe polish wax to the tape. Let stand for a few minutes, then rub with a clean cloth until the polish is shiny. Repeat this process several times. When there are four or five coats of shoe polish on the tape, you will have a rich, shiny surface—and a very pretty container.

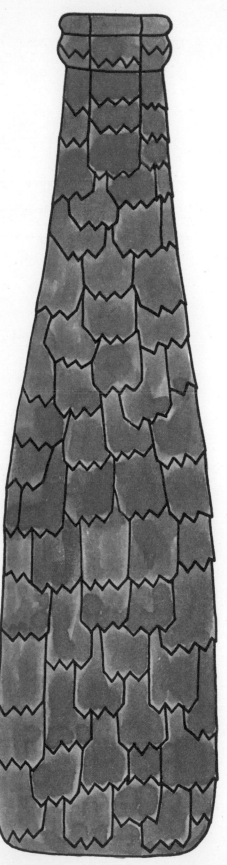

WORLD OF SPORTS

Everybody is running these days—to keep fit and for the joy of it!

Yankee pitcher Ron Guidry was the hero of the World Series, and he won the American League's Cy Young Award.

BASEBALL

The 1978 baseball season was possibly the greatest ever, from the standpoint of public interest. There was record attendance at the 26 major league parks. And about 61,000,000 television viewers watched each of the six games in the World Series—which the New York Yankees won from the Los Angeles Dodgers, 4 games to 2.

It was also a very unusual campaign for the Yankees. It was the 32nd time they played in the World Series and their 22nd triumph. But never before did they have a more difficult journey.

In mid-July, the Yankees were trailing the Boston Red Sox by 14 games in the Ameri-can League's Eastern Division. Also at that time, Bob Lemon became manager of the team, taking over from Billy Martin.

At the end of the regulation 162 games, New York had made a great comeback and was tied with Boston, each with a 99–63 record. The Yankees captured the division title in a one-game playoff, 5–4.

Then New York met the Kansas City Royals, the Western Division winner. It was the third straight year that the two teams ended up battling for the league pennant. And once again the Yankees took the pennant from them, 3 games to 1.

The Yankees seemed to be on a winning

streak as they entered the World Series against the Dodgers, who had defeated the Philadelphia Phillies for the National League pennant. But then New York lost the first two World Series contests to the Dodgers, and many people thought that the Yankees had also lost the Series. The Yankees came back, though, to win the next four games. No other World Series team had ever won four straight after losing the first two. And Bob Lemon became the first American League manager to win a Series after taking on the post in mid-season.

Younger team members, rather than the usual heroes, had carried the Yankees to their third straight pennant and their second straight World Series victory. Ron Guidry, a left-handed pitcher in his second big league season, was the hero throughout the campaign. When he turned back the Red Sox in the playoff for the pennant, it was his 25th victory, with only three defeats. His earned run average, 1.74, was the lowest in the league. And his season's total strikeouts, 248, represented a Yankee team record.

At bat, shortstop Bucky Dent was another top player. His three-run homer was the vital blow in the Boston playoff. And his ten hits for a .417 mark against the Dodgers earned him the Most Valuable Player award in the World Series.

Guidry was the unanimous choice as the winner of the American League's Cy Young Award (for pitchers). But the league's MVP honor went to Red Sox slugger Jim Rice. Rice led the majors in homers (46) and in runs batted in (139), and he was the first batsman in 20 years to accumulate more than 400 total bases (406). Rod Carew of the Minnesota Twins, with a .333 mark, earned his sixth American League batting title in the last seven years.

The major individual honors in the National League went to members of nonwinning clubs. Pittsburgh outfielder Dave Parker was the landslide winner as MVP. His .334 mark gave him the league's second straight batting title. The hurler who gained the Cy Young Award was 40-year-old Gaylord Perry of the San Diego Padres. He had the rare distinction of capturing the trophy in both leagues—he had also won it with Cleveland in 1972.

Pete Rose, of the Cincinnati Reds, won the hearts of baseball fans in 1978. With his 44-game hitting streak, he broke the modern National League record of 38 games and tied the all-time league mark of 44.

1978 WORLD SERIES RESULTS

		R	H	E	Winning/Losing Pitcher
1	Los Angeles	11	15	2	Tommy John
	New York	5	9	1	Ed Figueroa
2	Los Angeles	4	7	0	Burt Hooton
	New York	3	11	0	Jim Hunter
3	New York	5	10	1	Ron Guidry
	Los Angeles	1	8	0	Don Sutton
4	New York	4	9	0	Rich Gossage
	Los Angeles	3	6	1	Bob Welch
5	New York	12	18	0	Jim Beattie
	Los Angeles	2	9	3	Burt Hooton
6	New York	7	11	0	Jim Hunter
	Los Angeles	2	7	1	Don Sutton

FINAL MAJOR LEAGUE BASEBALL STANDINGS

AMERICAN LEAGUE

Eastern Division

	W	L	Pct.	GB
*New York	100	63	.613	—
Boston	99	64	.607	1
Milwaukee	93	69	.574	6½
Baltimore	90	71	.559	9
Detroit	86	76	.531	13½
Cleveland	69	90	.434	29
Toronto	59	102	.366	40

Western Division

	W	L	Pct.	GB
Kansas City	92	70	.568	—
California	87	75	.537	5
Texas	87	75	.537	5
Minnesota	73	89	.451	19
Chicago	71	90	.441	20½
Oakland	69	93	.426	23
Seattle	56	104	.350	35

NATIONAL LEAGUE

Eastern Division

	W	L	Pct.	GB
Philadelphia	90	72	.556	—
Pittsburgh	88	73	.547	1½
Chicago	79	83	.488	11
Montreal	76	86	.469	14
St. Louis	69	93	.426	21
New York	66	96	.407	24

Western Division

	W	L	Pct.	GB
*Los Angeles	95	67	.586	—
Cincinnati	92	69	.571	2½
San Francisco	89	73	.549	6
San Diego	84	78	.519	12
Houston	74	88	.457	21
Atlanta	69	93	.426	26

*pennant winners

MAJOR LEAGUE LEADERS

AMERICAN LEAGUE

Batting
(top 10 qualifiers)

	AB	R	H	Pct.
Carew, Minnesota	546	85	188	.333
Oliver, Texas	525	65	170	.324
Rice, Boston	677	121	213	.315
Piniella, New York	472	67	148	.314
Oglivie, Milwaukee	469	71	142	.303
Roberts, Seattle	472	78	142	.301
Otis, Kansas City	486	74	145	.298
Lynn, Boston	541	75	161	.298
LeFlore, Detroit	666	126	198	.297
Munson, New York	617	73	183	.297

Pitching
(top 5 qualifiers, based on ERA)

	W	L	ERA
Guidry, New York	25	3	1.74
Matlack, Texas	15	13	2.30
Caldwell, Milwaukee	22	9	2.37
Palmer, Baltimore	21	12	2.46
Goltz, Minnesota	15	10	2.50

Home Runs

	HR
Rice, Boston	46
Wynegar, Minnesota	45
Bosetti, Toronto	42
Baylor, California	34
Hisle, Milwaukee	34
Thornton, Cleveland	33

NATIONAL LEAGUE

Batting
(top 10 qualifiers)

	AB	R	H	Pct.
Parker, Pittsburgh	581	102	194	.334
Garvey, Los Angeles	639	89	202	.316
Cruz, Houston	565	79	178	.315
Madlock, San Francisco	447	76	138	.309
Winfield, San Diego	587	88	181	.308
Richards, San Diego	555	90	171	.308
Clark, San Francisco	592	90	181	.306
Rose, Cincinnati	655	103	198	.302
Burroughs, Atlanta	488	72	147	.301
Concepcion, Cincinnati	565	75	170	.301

Pitching
(top 5 qualifiers, based on ERA)

	W	L	ERA
Swan, New York	9	6	2.43
Rogers, Montreal	13	10	2.47
Vuckovich, St. Louis	12	12	2.55
Knepper, San Francisco	17	11	2.63
Hooton, Los Angeles	19	10	2.71

Home Runs

	HR
Foster, Cincinnati	40
Luzinski, Philadelphia	35
Parker, Pittsburgh	30
Smith, Los Angeles	29
Kingham, Chicago	28
Stargell, Pittsburgh	28

LITTLE LEAGUE BASEBALL

The Little League World Series has just about become the private territory of the youngsters from Taiwan. So it was no surprise when a team from Pingtung, Taiwan, captured the 1978 championship with three impressive victories during the four-day tournament at Williamsport, Pennsylvania. It was the seventh triumph since 1969 for the representatives from the island in the Far East. And it was achieved by spectacular pitching and superb defense.

In the climactic title contest, the Taiwanese romped to an 11–1 victory over the Danville, California, team. And that Danville run, scored in the first inning, was the only one allowed by the Pingtung pitchers in their three games. The hurlers, throughout the tourney, were supported by a team that failed to make an error—something that doesn't often happen under the pressure of international competition.

Pan Chao-min, a 12-year-old right-hander, pitched the decisive game. He allowed five hits, struck out 13 Danville batters, and clouted a two-run homer. Pan's performance was awesome considering a shaky first in-

ning, in which he walked three batters and gave up a single that produced the lone run for the losers. Pan Chao-min had also hurled the opening victory for Taiwan, a 12–0 effort against Surrey, British Columbia, during which he rolled up 13 strikeouts.

Taiwan reached the championship game with a 3–0 decision in the semifinal over LaJavilla of the Dominican Republic. Earlier, LaJavilla had beaten Madrid, 13–0, on a no-hitter by the left-handed Jose Pichardo—and the manager had boasted, "We have better pitching than Taiwan." He underestimated the Taiwanese, for the Dominican players were limited to one hit, and 13 of them were struck out. Pan Chao-min played shortstop in that contest, and his double with the bases loaded drove in the three runs for Taiwan. Danville reached the final with a 6–5 victory over Lexington, Kentucky.

By the end of the 1978 championship, Taiwanese teams had won 20 consecutive World Series games in which they participated. They were absent in 1975 when the tournament was restricted to U.S. entries, a ban that was lifted a year later.

Pan Chao-min was the hero in Little League World Series play.

BASKETBALL

Professional basketball seems to be producing a different championship club every year. This continued during the 1977–78 season, as the Washington Bullets emerged from the long, wearisome campaign clutching the title. Twice before, the Bullets had been frustrated finalists. But this time they gained the National Basketball Association (NBA) crown with a 105–99 victory over the Seattle SuperSonics in the seventh game of a spine-tingling series.

The fact that Washington and Seattle played in the NBA championship final was surprising. The Bullets' regular-season record, 44–38, was seventh in the league. And the Sonics, with 47–35, were sixth. The best mark in the 22-team circuit was posted by the defending champion, the Portland Trail Blazers, 58–24. But they were beset by injuries and were eliminated by Seattle, 4

games to 2, in the quarter-final playoff series. The Sonics reached the title round by defeating Denver, also 4 games to 2.

Washington, given little chance to survive the early post-season competition, defeated Atlanta, San Antonio, and Philadelphia to reach the final with Seattle.

At that point, history appeared to be the Bullets' greatest problem. In previous finals, they had lost four straight to Milwaukee in 1971 and had also been swept by the Golden State Warriors in 1975. Adding to this, the Bullets lost a 19-point lead in the opening game with Seattle and went down to defeat, 106–102.

But Bobby Dandridge, Elvin Hayes, and Tom Henderson played brilliantly to break the pattern with a 106–98 victory for Washington in the second game. After five games, the Bullets were trailing 3 games to 2. But

The Washington Bullets beat the Seattle SuperSonics, 105–99, to win the NBA championship.

FINAL NBA STANDINGS

EASTERN CONFERENCE

Atlantic Division

	W	L	Pct.
Philadelphia	55	27	.671
N.Y. Knicks	43	39	.524
Boston	32	50	.390
Buffalo	27	55	.329
N.J. Nets	24	58	.293

Central Division

	W	L	Pct.
San Antonio	52	30	.634
Washington	44	38	.537
Cleveland	43	39	.524
Atlanta	41	41	.500
New Orleans	39	43	.476
Houston	28	54	.341

WESTERN CONFERENCE

Midwest Division

	W	L	Pct.
Denver	48	34	.585
Milwaukee	44	38	.537
Chicago	40	42	.488
Detroit	38	44	.463
Indiana	31	51	.378
Kansas City	31	51	.378

Pacific Division

	W	L	Pct.
Portland	58	24	.707
Phoenix	49	33	.598
Seattle	47	35	.573
Los Angeles	45	37	.549
Golden State	43	39	.524

NBA Championship: Washington Bullets

COLLEGE BASKETBALL

Conference	Winner
Atlantic Coast	Duke
Big Eight	Missouri
Big Ten	Michigan State
Ivy League	Pennsylvania
Mid-American	Miami (Ohio)
Missouri Valley	Creighton
Pacific Eight	UCLA
Southeastern	Kentucky
Southern	Furman
Southwest	Houston
West Coast Athletic	San Francisco
Western Athletic	New Mexico

NCAA: Kentucky

National Invitation Tournament: Texas

Kentucky defeated Duke, 94–88, for the NCAA championship, the Wildcats' first triumph since 1958.

they evened the series with a 117–82 splurge, the greatest margin ever (35 points) in an NBA playoff. One more obstacle remained—the Seattle Coliseum, where the Sonics had won 22 consecutive games. Wes Unseld, the lone survivor of the earliest playoff disaster, came to the rescue with key plays in Washington's triumph.

In collegiate competition, the University of Kentucky recaptured the glory that had frequently been enjoyed by Wildcat teams of the past. Kentucky won the NCAA championship for the fifth time by defeating Duke, 94–88. It was the first triumph for the Wildcats since 1958.

Kentucky and Duke reached the collegiate final with narrow victories over Arkansas and Notre Dame, respectively. The National Invitation Tournament was won by the University of Texas, which defeated North Carolina State in the final, 101–93. The UCLA women's basketball team became the champion of the Association for Intercollegiate Athletics with a 90–74 victory over Maryland.

THE COMMONWEALTH GAMES

The year 1978 marked the 50th anniversary of the Commonwealth Games. The idea of between-Olympics gatherings for athletes from the Commonwealth nations originated during the 1928 Olympics. The first Games, then called the British Empire Games, were held in 1930 in Hamilton, Ontario. Since then, they have been held every four years. The Games are based on the idea of friendly competition among Commonwealth members, rather than nationalistic rivalries.

On their golden anniversary, the Games were again held in Canada, this time in Edmonton, Alberta. The opening ceremonies of the 1978 Games began with a 21-gun salute. About 1,800 athletes from 48 countries prepared to compete in 138 different events. Until 1978, there had been nine categories of Games—swimming, shooting, diving, weight lifting, badminton, cycling, track and field, boxing, and lawn bowling. Canada, as host country for the 1978 Games, was invited to select a tenth category. It chose the increasingly popular sport of gymnastics.

After the ten days of cheers and applause had ended, Canada led the final standings for the first time in the history of the Games. Canadian athletes captured 45 gold medals in many different events. They particularly excelled in swimming. Graham Smith, the superstar of the event, won six gold medals (a Games record)—swimming in his home town in a pool named after his father. Fifteen-year-old Carol Klimpel also set a Games record, in the women's 100-meter freestyle. And the Canadian relay team set yet another, in the 400-meter freestyle.

Another multiple gold-medal winner was cyclist Jocelyn Lovel. He won two individual competitions and captured a third, the

Canadian swimmer Graham Smith won six gold medals, setting a Commonwealth Games record.

tandem sprint, with fellow cyclist Gord Singleton. Carmen Ionesco set a Games record in the discus event, and Diane Jones Konihowski set several more in the course of winning the pentathlon. A young Canadian women's gymnastics team—ranging in age from 13 to 15—won their event, and their counterparts captured the men's gymnastics competition.

Australian swimmer Tracey Wickham set a world record in the women's 800-meter freestyle. Other outstanding performers included Kenyan long-distance runner Henry Rono and England's decathlon winner, Francis Daley Thompson.

The next Commonwealth Games will be held in 1982, in Brisbane, Australia. But many of the athletes who took part in 1978 will undoubtedly be making headlines and setting records before then—at the 1980 Olympic Games.

This long jump helped Diane Konihowski win the pentathlon.

Fifteen-year-old Carol Klimpel swam to a Games record in the women's 100-meter freestyle.

FINAL MEDAL STANDINGS

	Gold	Silver	Bronze
Canada	45	31	33
England	27	28	33
Australia	24	33	27
Kenya	7	6	5
New Zealand	5	7	9
India	5	4	6
Scotland	3	5	5
Jamaica	2	2	3
Wales	2	1	5
Northern Ireland	2	1	1
Hong Kong	2	0	0
Malaysia	1	2	1
Ghana	1	1	1
Guyana	1	1	1
Tanzania	1	1	0
Trinidad	0	2	2
Zambia	0	2	2
Bahamas	0	1	0
Papua New Guinea	0	1	0
Western Samoa	0	0	3
Isle of Man	0	0	1

FOOTBALL

Two teams that have been frequent participants in National Football League (NFL) championship games once again battled it out in the 1979 Super Bowl: the Dallas Cowboys and the Pittsburgh Steelers. Since each had been a winner twice before, one was destined to become the first team

Houston's Dan Pastorini is about to be sacked by Pittsburgh's L. C. Greenwood in the American Conference title game.

to capture the Super Bowl three times. And it was Pittsburgh that got the honor, 35–31.

Both reached the final without too much trouble. Dallas captured the National Conference title with a 28–0 victory over the Los Angeles Rams. In the same afternoon, the Steelers capitalized on nine Houston fumbles and interceptions to gain the American Conference title in a 34–5 romp.

The Steelers-Oilers game was played in heavy rain, and the slippery ball contributed to five Steeler turnovers. But the Steelers' rugged defense blocked the Oiler attack, and their offense cashed in on almost every Houston error. Franco Harris and Rocky Bleier ran for the first two Steeler touchdowns. Terry Bradshaw passed for two more, to Lynn Swann and John Stallworth. And Roy Gerela contributed two field goals. Just before halftime, the Steelers scored 17 points within 48 seconds.

The Dallas–Los Angeles contest, a battle between defensive giants, was also finally decided by miscues. Tony Dorsett broke a scoreless deadlock in the third period with a five-yard run—after Charlie Waters, Cowboys safety man, had intercepted Pat Haden's pass and galloped to the Rams' ten yard line. Another interception by Waters and a Ram fumble set up two fourth period scores, on passes from Roger Staubach to Scott Laidlaw and Billy Joe DuPree. In the closing minutes, Tom Henderson ran 68 yards with an interception for the final frustrating blow to the Rams, who have won six straight division titles without ever reaching the Super Bowl.

In the American Conference, the Oilers qualified for their first playoff appearance since 1969, with a 10–6 record. This earned them a wild-card slot and a meeting with that conference's other wild-card entry, the Miami Dolphins. With Dan Pastorini passing for 306 yards, the Oilers broke a 7–7 deadlock in the final period and went on to a 17–9 victory. A week later, the surprising Houston club advanced to the conference final with a crushing 31–14 triumph over the New England Patriots, who led the Eastern Division with an 11–5 record.

Cowboy Roger Staubach carries the ball for a first down during Dallas' 28–0 rout of Los Angeles in the National Conference title game.

The Denver Broncos, a Super Bowl entry a year earlier, retained their Western Division title with a 10–6 log but ran afoul of the powerful Steelers in the playoff and were trounced, 33–10.

En route to the National Conference championship engagement, Los Angeles beat the Minnesota Vikings, 34–10. And Dallas met surprising resistance from the Atlanta Falcons before winning, 27–20. Dallas and Los Angeles led their respective divisions, East and West, with identical 12–4 records, and Minnesota reached the playoffs with an 8–7–1 mark. Atlanta and Philadelphia were the wild-card entries, and the Falcons survived with a 14–13 squeaker.

Individually, Houston's rookie running back, Earl Campbell, was the NFL's outstanding performer, with 1,450 yards rushed during the regular season. He had been the Heisman winner a year earlier.

The Edmonton Eskimos won the Canadian Football League's Grey Cup, defeating the Montreal Alouettes, 20–13.

COLLEGE PLAY

As often happens, the national championship among the colleges was unresolved. One of the two recognized polls designated the University of Alabama as No. 1, while the other chose the University of Southern California.

Going into the New Year's Day bowl games, Penn State was the undisputed leader, with the only perfect record (11–0) among major college teams. But Penn State fell before Alabama's stars in the New Orleans Sugar Bowl, 14–7. Southern California's bid resulted from a 17–10 triumph over Michigan in the Pasadena Rose Bowl. In Miami's Orange Bowl, Oklahoma reversed an early-season setback by defeating Nebraska, 31–24. And in Dallas' Cotton Bowl, Notre Dame scored 22 points in the final period to nip Houston, 35–34.

The 1978 Heisman Trophy, going to the outstanding collegiate player, was won by Billy Sims, Oklahoma's fleet running back. He led the country in rushing, 1,762 yards, and in scoring, 20 touchdowns.

Oklahoma's Billy Sims was the winner of the 1978 Heisman Trophy, as the best collegiate player.

FINAL NFL STANDINGS

AMERICAN CONFERENCE

Eastern Division

	W	L	T	Pct.	PF	PA
New England	11	5	0	.688	358	286
Miami	11	5	0	.688	372	254
N.Y. Jets	8	8	0	.500	359	364
Buffalo	5	11	0	.313	302	354
Baltimore	5	11	0	.313	239	421

Central Division

	W	L	T	Pct.	PF	PA
Pittsburgh	14	2	0	.875	356	195
Houston	10	6	0	.625	283	298
Cleveland	8	8	0	.500	334	356
Cincinnati	4	12	0	.250	252	284

Western Division

	W	L	T	Pct.	PF	PA
Denver	10	6	0	.625	282	198
Oakland	9	7	0	.563	311	283
San Diego	9	7	0	.563	355	309
Seattle	9	7	0	.563	345	358
Kansas City	4	12	0	.250	243	327

Conference Champion: Pittsburgh

NATIONAL CONFERENCE

Eastern Division

	W	L	T	Pct.	PF	PA
Dallas	12	4	0	.750	384	208
Philadelphia	9	7	0	.563	270	250
Washington	8	8	0	.500	273	283
St. Louis	6	10	0	.375	248	296
N.Y. Giants	6	10	0	.375	264	298

Central Division

	W	L	T	Pct.	PF	PA
Minnesota	8	7	1	.531	294	306
Green Bay	8	7	1	.531	249	269
Detroit	7	9	0	.438	290	300
Chicago	7	9	0	.438	253	274
Tampa Bay	5	11	0	.313	241	259

Western Division

	W	L	T	Pct.	PF	PA
Los Angeles	12	4	0	.750	316	245
Atlanta	9	7	0	.563	240	290
New Orleans	7	9	0	.438	281	298
San Francisco	2	14	0	.125	219	350

Conference Champion: Dallas

1979 Super Bowl Winner: Pittsburgh Steelers

COLLEGE FOOTBALL

Conference	Winner
Atlantic Coast	Clemson
Big Eight	Oklahoma; Nebraska (tied)
Big Ten	Michigan; Michigan State (tied)
Ivy League	Dartmouth
Mid-American	Ball State
Pacific Ten	Southern California
Southeastern	Alabama
Southern	Furman; Tennessee–Chattanooga (tied)
Southwest	Houston
Western Athletic	Brigham Young

Cotton Bowl: Notre Dame 35, Houston 34
Gator Bowl: Clemson 17, Ohio State 15
Orange Bowl: Oklahoma 31, Nebraska 24
Rose Bowl: Southern California 17, Michigan 10
Sugar Bowl: Alabama 14, Penn State 7

Heisman Trophy: Billy Sims, Oklahoma

Nancy Lopez made a tremendous impact on the 1978 golf scene. In her first full season on the LPGA tour, she became the first to win both the LPGA Rookie of the Year and Player of the Year honors.

GOLF

PROFESSIONAL		AMATEUR	
	Individual		**Individual**
Masters	Gary Player	**U.S. Amateur**	John Cook
U.S. Open	Andy North	**U.S. Women's Amateur**	Cathy Sherk
Canadian Open	Bruce Lietzke	**British Amateur**	Peter McEvoy
British Open	Jack Nicklaus	**British Women's Amateur**	Edwina Kennedy
PGA	John Mahaffey	**Canadian Amateur**	Rod Spittle
World Series of Golf	Gil Morgan	**Canadian Ladies Amateur**	Cathy Sherk
U.S. Women's Open	Hollis Stacy		
Ladies PGA	Nancy Lopez		
	Team		**Team**
World Cup	United States	**Curtis Cup**	United States

Montreal's Jacques Lemaire falls head over heels as he collides with Boston's Brad Park. The Canadiens took the Stanley Cup series, 4 games to 2.

HOCKEY

The Montreal Canadiens skate along as the perennial champions of the National Hockey League and there are no signs that the coming years will dim their luster. In 1978 the Canadiens once again captured the Stanley Cup, for the third consecutive season and their 21st Cup triumph. The opposition was able to console itself with the fact that the victory required a little more time than usual.

In the final best-of-seven series for the Cup, the Canadiens were confronted by the Boston Bruins, who had been beaten in four straight games the previous year. This time, the Bruins delayed the ultimate triumph until the sixth contest. After two Montreal victories, 4–1 and 3–2, the Bruins appeared to be on the verge of another swift end. But they fought back to even the series with scores of 4–0 and 4–3 (in overtime). That extra period was the Bruins' last gasp—they were soundly beaten in the final two skirmishes, with identical scores of 4–1.

The keys to Montreal's success were the spectacular veteran goalie, Ken Dryden; the defensive trio of George Savard, Guy Lapointe, and Larry Robinson (winner of the Conn Smythe Trophy as the most valuable performer in the playoffs); and Guy Lafleur (the league's top scorer).

If the league's other teams thought that age would eventually rust the Canadiens' talents, that hope probably disappeared in the closing game. After the Bruins had taken a 1–0 lead, Steve Shutt tied the count for the Canadiens. Then two goals by Mario Tremblay made it 3–1 before Rejean Houle ended the scoring for the winners. Tremblay was a 21-year-old rookie, and the two goals were set up by 22-year-old Pierre Mondou.

On the way to their Stanley Cup triumph, the Canadiens eliminated the Detroit Red Wings in the opening playoff series, 4 games to 1, and swept the Toronto Maple Leafs, 4–0. Montreal had lost one playoff game in 1976 and was beaten twice in 1977 and three times in 1978—for a total of six defeats in 42 post-season engagements. During the regular 1977–78 campaign, the team lost only eleven of its 80 games.

In the six-year history of the World Hockey Association, only the Winnipeg Jets have succeeded in capturing the Avco Cup twice. Beaten by the Quebec Nordiques in a seven-game series in 1977, the Jets won the title in 1978 with a four-game sweep over the New England Whalers. Led by the spectacular Bobby Hull and two Swedish imports, Anders Hedberg and Ulf Nilsson, the Jets swarmed over the Whalers with scores of 4–1, 5–2, 10–2, and 5–3. Winnipeg's previous Cup victory had been achieved in 1976.

The Soviet Union won the world hockey championship tournament, nosing out Czechoslovakia on a difference of goals scored for and against. In hand-to-hand combat, they divided honors, the Czechs winning 6–4, and the Soviets, 3–1. During the three-week tournament, the Czechs scored 54 goals and yielded 21 for a difference of 33. The Soviets scored 61 and allowed 26 for a difference of 35, a winning margin of 2.

In Avco Cup play, the Winnipeg Jets beat the New England Whalers in a four-game sweep.

Jets Ulf Nilsson and Anders Hedberg skate around the arena carrying the Avco Cup.

FINAL NHL STANDINGS

CAMPBELL CONFERENCE

Patrick Division

	W	L	T	Pts.
N.Y. Islanders	48	17	15	111
Philadelphia	45	20	15	105
Atlanta	34	27	19	87
N.Y. Rangers	30	37	13	73

Smythe Division

	W	L	T	Pts.
Chicago	32	29	19	83
Colorado	19	40	21	59
Vancouver	20	43	17	57
St. Louis	20	47	13	53
Minnesota	18	53	9	45

WALES CONFERENCE

Norris Division

	W	L	T	Pts.
Montreal	59	10	11	129
Detroit	32	34	14	78
Los Angeles	31	34	15	77
Pittsburgh	25	37	18	68
Washington	17	49	14	48

Adams Division

	W	L	T	Pts.
Boston	51	18	11	113
Buffalo	44	19	17	105
Toronto	41	29	10	92
Cleveland	22	45	13	57

Stanley Cup: Montreal Canadiens

FINAL WHA STANDINGS

	W	L	T	Pts.
Winnipeg	50	28	2	102
New England	44	31	5	93
Houston	42	34	4	88
Quebec	40	37	3	83
Edmonton	38	39	3	79
Birmingham	36	41	3	75
Cincinnati	35	42	3	73
Indianapolis	24	51	5	53

Avco Cup: Winnipeg Jets

OUTSTANDING PLAYERS

Scorer	Marc Tardif, Quebec
Rookie	Kent Nilsson, Winnipeg
Goalie	Al Smith, New England
Most Valuable Player	Marc Tardif, Quebec
Sportsmanship	Dave Keon, New England
Defenseman	Lars-Erik Sjoberg, Winnipeg
Avco Cup play	Bob Guindon, Winnipeg

OUTSTANDING PLAYERS

Calder Trophy (rookie)	Mike Bossy, N.Y. Islanders
Conn Smythe Trophy (Stanley Cup play)	Larry Robinson, Montreal
Hart Trophy (most valuable player)	Guy Lafleur, Montreal
Lady Byng Trophy (sportsmanship)	Butch Goring, Los Angeles
Norris Trophy (defenseman)	Denis Potvin, N.Y. Islanders
Ross Trophy (scorer)	Guy Lafleur, Montreal
Vezina Trophy (goalies)	Ken Dryden and Michel Larocque, Montreal

NHL champs: Top rookie Mike Bossy of the New York Islanders and . . .

. . . Montreal's Larry Robinson, MVP in Stanley Cup play.

173

ICE SKATING

FIGURE SKATING

World Championships

Men	Charles Tickner, U.S.
Women	Anett Poetzsch, East Germany
Pairs	Irina Rodnina/
	Alexander Zaitsev, U.S.S.R.
Dance	Natalja Linichuk/
	Gennadij Karponsov, U.S.S.R.

United States Championships

Men	Charles Tickner
Women	Linda Fratianne
Pairs	Tai Babilonia/Randy Gardner
Dance	Stacey Smith/John Summers

SPEED SKATING

World Championships

Men	Eric Heiden, U.S.
Women	Tatiana Averina, U.S.S.R.

Irina Rodnina and Alexander Zaitsev of the Soviet Union won their sixth world pairs title.

Hanni Wenzel of Liechtenstein took the women's World Cup skiing championship.

SKIING

WORLD CUP CHAMPIONSHIPS

Men	Ingemar Stenmark, Sweden
Women	Hanni Wenzel, Liechtenstein

U.S. ALPINE CHAMPIONSHIPS

	Men	Women
Downhill	Karl Anderson	Cindy Nelson
Slalom	Phil Mahre	Becky Dorsey
Giant Slalom	Phil Mahre	Becky Dorsey
Combined	Billy Taylor	Cindy Nelson

CANADIAN ALPINE CHAMPIONSHIPS

	Men	Women
Downhill	Ken Read	Kathy Timmins
Slalom	Pete Monod	Vanita Haining
Giant Slalom	John Hilland	Kathy Dreiner
Combined	Ken Read	Laurie Graham

Australia's Tracey Wickham (*above*) broke three world records in the women's freestyle. And America's Penny Dean (*right*) swam the English Channel in 7 hours and 42 minutes, breaking the world records for men and women.

SWIMMING

WORLD SWIMMING RECORDS SET IN 1978		
EVENT	**HOLDER**	**TIME**
	Men	
200-meter individual medley	Graham Smith, Canada	2:03.65
400-meter individual medley	Jesse Vassallo, U.S.	4:20.05
	Women	
100-meter freestyle	Barbara Krause, E. Germany	55.41
200-meter freestyle	Cynthia Woodhead, U.S.	1:58.53
400-meter freestyle	Tracey Wickham, Australia	4:06.28
800-meter freestyle	Tracey Wickham, Australia	8:24.62
1,500-meter freestyle	Tracey Wickham, Australia	16:14.93
200-meter backstroke	Linda Jezek, U.S.	2:11.93
100-meter breaststroke	Julia Bogdanova, U.S.S.R.	1:10.31
200-meter breaststroke	Lina Kachushite, U.S.S.R.	2:31.42
100-meter butterfly	Andrea Pollack, E. Germany	59.46
200-meter butterfly	Andrea Pollack, E. Germany	2:09.87
200-meter individual medley	Tracy Caulkins, U.S.	2:14.07
400-meter individual medley	Tracy Caulkins, U.S.	4:40.83

Sixteen-year-old Pam Shriver was the youngest finalist ever in the women's division of the U.S. Open.

TENNIS

In 1978, the U.S. Open tournament moved from the traditional site in Forest Hills to a new $10,000,000 stadium in Flushing Meadow, New York. With the move came a record attendance of 275,300 people during the two weeks of competition. While the names of the singles champions were familiar—Jimmy Connors and Chris Evert—the huge crowds were more intrigued by a newcomer: Pam Shriver, a high school junior from Lutherville, Maryland. Shriver, 16 years old and 6 feet (183 centimeters) tall, was the youngest finalist ever in the women's division of the U.S. Open.

Although Shriver bowed to the more experienced Evert in the final, 7–5, 6–4, she did it with stubborn resistance. On the way to that climactic match, the youngster had eliminated Martina Navratilova in the semifinal. For the 23-year-old Evert, the triumph was her fourth straight U.S. title, matching the record achieved by Helen Jacobs in the mid-1930's.

Connors gained the U.S. men's title by defeating Björn Borg in straight sets, 6–4, 6–2, 6–2. The 22-year-old Swede, at a disadvantage because of an infected thumb, went down to defeat after a spectacular string of victories that included the Italian and French Open championships, and a historic third consecutive crown on the famed center court at Wimbledon.

Borg crushed Connors, 6–2, 6–2, 6–3, in the Wimbledon final. In winning for the third straight year, Borg equaled the performance of Fred Perry (1934, 1935, 1936). Connors won the first two games of the opening set, then had the upper hand in only five games during the remainder of the match. And Perry, who witnessed the Swede's firepower, commented, "I don't believe any player in history could have lived on that court with Borg today."

In the women's final at Wimbledon, Navratilova defeated Evert, 2–6, 6–4, 7–5. Evert, a winner at Wimbledon in 1974 and 1976, was leading in the third and deciding set, 4–2, before Martina rallied. The defending champion, Britain's Virginia Wade, had been beaten by Evert in the semifinal.

TOURNAMENT TENNIS

	Australian Open	French Open	Wimbledon	U.S. Open
Men's Singles	Vitas Gerulaitis, U.S.	Björn Borg, Sweden	Björn Borg, Sweden	Jimmy Connors, U.S.
Women's Singles	Evonne Goolagong Cawley, Australia	Virginia Ruzici, Rumania	Martina Navratilova, U.S.	Chris Evert, U.S.
Men's Doubles	Ray Ruffels/Allen Stone, Australia	Hank Pfister/Gene Mayer, U.S.	Frew McMillan/Bob Hewitt, South Africa	Stan Smith/Bob Lutz, U.S.
Women's Doubles	not played	Mimi Jausovec, Yugoslavia/ Virginia Ruzici, Rumania	Kerry Reid/Wendy Turnbull, Australia	Billie Jean King/ Martina Navratilova, U.S.

Davis Cup Winner: United States

Henry Rono of Kenya broke four world records in track-and-field competitions during the year.

TRACK AND FIELD

WORLD TRACK AND FIELD RECORDS SET IN 1978

EVENT	HOLDER	TIME OR DISTANCE
	Men	
3,000-meter run	Henry Rono, Kenya	7:32.1
5,000-meter run	Henry Rono, Kenya	13:08.4
10,000-meter run	Henry Rono, Kenya	27:22.5
3,000-meter steeplechase	Henry Rono, Kenya	8:05.4
High jump	Vladimir Yashchenko, U.S.S.R.	7'8"
Pole vault	Mike Tully, U.S.	18'8¾"
Shot put	Udo Beyer, E. Germany	72'8"
Discus throw	Wolfgang Schmidt, E. Germany	233'5"
Hammer throw	Karl-Hans Riehm, W. Germany	263'6"
	Women	
200-meter run	Marita Koch, E. Germany	22.1
400-meter run	Marita Koch, E. Germany	48.9
1,000-meter run	Ulriche Bruns, E. Germany	2:32.7
5,000-meter run	Lea Olafsson, Denmark	15:08.8
10,000-meter run	Lea Olafsson, Denmark	31:45.4
100-meter hurdles	Grazyna Rabeztyn, Poland	12.5
400-meter hurdles	Tatyana Zelencova, U.S.S.R.	54.9
High jump	Sara Simeoni, Italy	6'7¼"
Long jump	Vilma Bardnuskena, U.S.S.R.	23'3¼"
Javelin throw	Evelin Jahl	232'

THE 1978 WORLD SOCCER CUP

The tournament for the World Soccer Cup is held once every four years. In 1978, Argentina, the host country, captured the Cup, which is symbolic of world soccer supremacy. In the final match, the Argentine national team defeated the Netherlands, 3–1, in 30 minutes of overtime. Over 77,000 spectators in the Buenos Aires stadium and a worldwide television audience watched that exciting game.

The triumph brought both tears and joy, for it represented the end of 48 years of frustration. Argentina hadn't reached the World Cup final since 1930, when it was beaten by neighboring Uruguay. For the Netherlands, it was the second consecutive setback in the final. The Dutch had lost to West Germany, 2–1, in the title contest in West Germany in 1974.

The hero of the tournament was 23-year-old Mario Kempes, who, with a total of six goals, led all scorers in the month-long competition. He was also the hero of the final game—he scored the first goal during the

regulation time, and then delivered the decisive goal in overtime. Kempes was set up for his first tally by Osvaldo Ardiles, who dribbled past his foes, fell, but managed to push the ball to Leopoldo Luque. Luque then passed to Kempes, who turned suddenly and sent a low kick past the Dutch goalie, Jan Jongbloed, for a 1–0 halftime lead.

The Dutch sent in fresh players, including Dirk Nanninga, for the second half. This move paid off—temporarily. Nanninga came through with the tying goal in the 81st minute of the 90-minute game, when he leaped over a group of players and tipped his head to bounce the ball past the Argentine goalie, Ubaldo Fillol.

The rules dictated two 15-minute extra periods in the event of a tie. If still deadlocked, the teams would then have played again two days later. But the Argentines gathered their forces to maintain a tradition—that no European entry ever has won a World Cup in South America. In the

Holland's Arie Haan is unable to stop Mario Kempes from making his first goal. Argentina went on to win the World Cup, 3–1.

104th minute, Kempes shot through a confused tangle of players in front of the Dutch penalty area to break the tie, and the stadium exploded with blaring horns and whirring ratchets. Daniel Bertoni scored the remaining goal on a pass from Kempes and made the victory secure.

In the battle for third place in the tournament, Brazil defeated Italy, 2–1. Brazil, winner of the World Cup three times, was undefeated in its six games of the round robin but was edged out of the final by Argentina, on the basis of goal average.

Argentina and the Netherlands reached their climactic clash with impressive victories in their semifinal matches. Argentina routed Peru, 6–0, while the Dutch defeated Italy, 2–1.

It was necessary for Argentina to defeat Peru by at least four goals in order to reach the final, for Brazil was still in contention. The Argentinians achieved their purpose with two to spare as Kempes and Luque each scored twice.

The Italians were also in the running for a slot in the final prior to their semifinal engagement with the Netherlands. That contest had a strange moment when Holland's fullback, Ery Brandts, scored a "wrong way" goal for Italy, giving the Italians a 1–0 lead. Brandts also collided with the Dutch goalkeeper, Piet Schrijvers, who was carried off on a stretcher and replaced by Jongbloed. But the Dutch stormed back in the second half, as Brandts made up for his earlier error with a thundering goal in the right net from 25 yards out. With 15 minutes of play remaining, Arie Haan won the game for Holland on a tremendous drive from 40 yards out.

The 16 teams that competed in the five Argentine stadiums were the survivors of two years of qualifying play, during which 104 countries participated in 251 games. The finalists battled back from early failures. Holland had lost to Scotland, 3–2, while Argentina had been beaten by Italy, 1–0. The West Germans, the defending champions, were among six teams that were still in contention when they were upset by Austria, 3–2.

Since the tournament was first held in 1930, Brazil has won the most championships (three). Brazil also had the world's most famous player, Pelé, who led his team to victory in 1970. But the 1978 Jules Rimet Cup, as the World Cup is officially called, will spend the next four years in the hands of 25,000,000 Argentinians, for whom soccer is a national passion. And the victory gives Argentina automatic entry in the next tournament, in Spain in 1982.

Headquarters of World Championship Soccer, reads the poster.

SPORTS BRIEFS

The sun was rising over the British Isles on the morning of August 17, 1978. A British coastguardsman gazed upward and spotted "a silver ball in the sky, like an upside-down pear." What he saw was a huge balloon—the first balloon to sail across the Atlantic Ocean. In a gondola hanging beneath the balloon (the *Double Eagle II*) were three men from New Mexico: Ben Abruzzo, Max Anderson, and Larry Newman. Their six-day voyage had not been an easy one. The men had been hounded by freezing cold, a perilous drop of many thousands of feet, and the knowledge that five other balloonists had died in previous attempts to cross the Atlantic. But after their balloon had made the voyage from a clover field in Maine to a wheat field in France, they had become authentic heroes.

As 1978 ended, the big story in boxing was the same as always—Muhammad Ali was still heavyweight champ. But for seven months of the year, a young ex-Marine named Leon Spinks had held the title, having won it from Ali in February. (Spinks had boxed his way to a gold medal in the 1976 Olympics.) The loss of the championship seemed like the end of the line for Ali. But he grunted and groaned his 36-year-old body into shape. In September, he climbed through the ropes and took his title back from Spinks in a decisive rematch. Muhammad Ali thus became the first boxer ever to hold the heavyweight championship at three different times.

Eighteen-year-old jockey Steve Cauthen and the magnificent horse Affirmed (*right*) teamed up in 1978 to win the Triple Crown of horse racing: the Kentucky Derby, the Preakness, and the Belmont Stakes.

The first U.S. National Sports Festival was held in Colorado in 1978. Lasting four days, it was a "national Olympics," complete with a torch-lighting ceremony. It was like the ones already held in the Soviet Union, Japan, and other countries. More than 2,100 amateur athletes competed in 26 different sports. The athletes came from all parts of the U.S.—the youngest in his early teens, the oldest a 64-year-old archer. Some had been Olympic competitors, but many were unknown athletes on their way up. The festival's sponsor, the U.S. Olympic Committee, hopes that a yearly sports festival will help develop U.S. athletes of Olympic caliber.

In May, 1978, Al Unser won the Indianapolis 500, America's most famous auto race. He became the fifth driver to win the Indy three times: 1970, 1971, and 1978.

Baguio, in the Philippines, was the site of the longest championship chess match in history—32 games. The players were world champion Anatoly Karpov of the Soviet Union and challenger Viktor Korchnoi, who had defected from the Soviet Union and lives in Switzerland. For three months in 1978, the men swapped pawns and clashed queens. When it was over, Karpov still reigned, having won six games to Korchnoi's five. The 21 draws they had played did not count.

GIRLS IN SPORTS

The pitch comes in. The batter swings. Crack! A sharp grounder spurts past the pitcher toward second base. The shortstop darts behind the bag, neatly gloves the ball, and in a smooth motion whips it to first base. Out!

"Nice play, fella!" someone calls to the shortstop from the stands.

"That's no 'fella' " someone else says quietly. "The shortstop is a girl."

If the shortstop's only problem is that she is sometimes mistaken for a boy, then perhaps she is lucky. Little by little, girls have begun to play on previously all-boy teams, and many of them have met with problems more serious than mistaken identity.

The main problem that girls have faced is nonacceptance by boys. "Girls aren't good enough to play on our teams," is what some boys say. The fact is, however, that as more girls get involved in sports, many of them become as good as, or even better than, a lot of boy athletes. But this leads to another problem: some boys are afraid of being outplayed and "shown up" by girls. So the problem of not being accepted by boys cuts two ways: to some boys, girl athletes are "not good enough"; to other boys, some girl athletes are "too good."

▶ **THE PHYSICAL QUESTION**

"Girls aren't as strong or as physically fit as boys" is another argument against coed competition. But, especially at the pre-teen level, this just isn't so. Until the age of 11 or 12, girls are, on the average, bigger and heavier than boys. And physical fitness doesn't depend on one's sex at all. If you have the proper exercise, you will be in good physical condition, whether you're female or male.

There is no question that as boys and girls get older, the boys will, on the average, get taller, stronger, and heavier. If some pre-teen and early teen girls play coed football, what will happen to them as they get older? Will they still be able to play well against stronger boy opponents? Perhaps not. So in contact sports such as football and hockey, coed teams may also be rare.

But in other sports, the physical differences between males and females do not always favor the males. Women and girls are more flexible than men and boys. That is, they are more loose-jointed. This would give females an edge in gymnastics, for example. And some scientists claim that girls and women are less likely to be injured than are boys and men. Because of the structure of a female's body, some of her vital organs are better protected than those of a man. Being less injury-prone is a definite "plus" in any sport.

Women may, on the average, even have more endurance than men. This is hard to prove, but the evidence suggests that it is so. There are women marathon swimmers, such as Diana Nyad, who are among the best long-distance swimmers in the world, male or female. And women running in races of 50 miles (80 kilometers) or more have often done better than men runners.

▶THE SUCCESSES

Even with all the problems, many girls have done well on previously all-boy teams. Consider Tammy Lee Mercer. She played tackle for the Amherst Regional High School football team in Massachusetts. Tammy Lee was an excellent football player and an exceptional athlete who kept herself in fine condition.

Anne Babson, of Ipswich, Massachusetts, was the only girl on her junior high's football team. Barbara Potter was the number one tennis player on her school's tennis team in Watertown, Connecticut.

In Houston, Texas, 18-year-old Linda Williams played right field for her high school baseball team. She was no superstar, but she played well, and had a lot of support from her male teammates. But Linda left the baseball team in order to concentrate on girls' basketball and volleyball.

As more and more girls play on what were once all-boy teams, the obvious question comes up: how far will it go?

▶THE FUTURE

Some coaches are afraid that if the best girl athletes play on boys' teams, it will be difficult to develop strong girls' teams. Other coaches believe that the best girl athletes should play in the same leagues with the best boys. And the not-so-good athletes, male and female, should play in their own leagues. Talent, rather than sex, would determine who plays against whom.

Perhaps that is what the future holds for coed sports. For preteens and young teens, the number of coed sports teams will probably increase. As the athletes get older, though, the teams may become all one sex, especially in the rough contact sports.

But who knows? Girls and women have only begun to discover what their athletic abilities are. Female athletes have been improving greatly in all sports. In fact, they are improving at a much faster rate than male athletes. So it may only be a matter of time before that girl shortstop gliding smoothly across the infield becomes the first woman to break into a major league lineup.

READY, SET—RUN!

You see them everywhere, it seems: on city streets, country roads, and suburban lanes; along the shoulders of asphalt highways and on narrow dirt paths in parks. Who are they? They're the runners and joggers—men and women, boys and girls, of all ages, sizes, and shapes. They run indoors, too. Take a look in any gymnasium, in any "Y." If you ask, "Where is everybody running to?" you've missed the point. Most runners and joggers only get back to where they started from. A much more important question than "where" is "why." Why is everybody running so much?

People have always felt the urge to run. It is a strong urge, probably dating back to the earliest humans, for whom running was a necessary technique of survival. But besides running to escape from enemies and wild animals, those early people probably also ran just for the joy of it. Your blood surges within you, your muscles stretch and strain, the wind hits your chest, and your lungs open to receive the air. Put simply, it feels good to exercise your body, and running is one of the best forms of exercise there is. But that is only part of the reason why so many people are running.

▶RUN FOR YOUR LIFE

Until about ten years ago, long-distance runners and joggers were not often seen in North America. Occasionally, you would see one or two loping through a park or along a roadway. People would hoot at them as they went by: "What are you, crazy?" or "Hey, Daddy Longlegs!" Almost all the runners were young men and boys, and most were members of school track teams. But there were also others, mostly older men.

They ran and jogged "to keep fit." They already understood what other people were just beginning to learn: the relationship between running, fitness, and health.

In the 1950's and 1960's, many Canadian and American doctors became concerned about the increase in heart disease. A well-known cardiologist (heart doctor), Dr. Paul Dudley White, began telling people that strenuous exercise was good for the heart. By "strenuous" exercise, Dr. White did not mean a Sunday afternoon game of softball or a round of golf. He meant exercise during which the heart beats fast for a long time, twenty minutes or more. The heart is a muscle, and to become strong a muscle needs strenuous exercise.

What sports offer strenuous exercise? The answer is, those sports that require constant motion and hard breathing. Basketball is good, as are handball, tennis, and soccer. But even better are cycling, swimming, cross-country skiing, and running. For cycling, though, you need a bicycle. For swimming, a pool. For cross-country skiing, snow and equipment. But for running, all you need is a very good pair of running shoes.

By the early 1970's, many people had become aware of the importance of strenuous exercise. They began to run. Some started with a mile (1.6 kilometers) a day but soon found that they could run even five miles (8 kilometers) daily. And the more they ran, the more certain things began to happen:

• They felt better, both healthier and happier. Running seemed to lift their spirits as well as make them stronger.

• Their hearts worked more efficiently. Their pulses, at rest, were slower and stronger. Those with high blood pressure often found that it dropped to healthier levels.

• They lost weight. Their bodies were trimmer. How fast they ran did not seem to matter. What mattered was that they ran, or jogged, regularly (at least three times a week) and that each run lasted for twenty minutes or more.

As time has passed, doctors have noticed a wonderful thing—heart disease seems to be decreasing in North America, especially among people who exercise regularly. Certainly, the decrease in heart disease is not

For most marathon runners, the joy is not so much in winning but in finishing the race.

only due to running. But the general concern for physical fitness seems to have a lot to do with it. And so, just as the earliest humans ran for their lives in order to escape from enemies, many people today have begun to run for their lives—in order to escape, or at least lessen, the chance of heart disease.

Thousands of young people, from the earliest grades on up, have taken up jogging and running. But why should young people have to think about heart disease? It is because good health habits must start early. So, many schools in North America have started jogging programs in their gym classes. And the young people love it.

▶**RUNNERS AND JOGGERS**

What's the difference between running and jogging? Speed. But there is no clear line between the two. When most people first start, they just plod along as far as they can. After a few weeks, plodders become joggers. They go faster. They go farther. And then, at a certain point, some joggers become runners. But it is difficult to say just what that point is.

A good rule of thumb is this: while you're jogging, you can comfortably carry on a conversation. But if you have to gasp for air between words, then you're running.

The difference is not important. Both running and jogging are excellent ways to keep fit. A person who runs, though, may not only be keeping fit. He or she may be running in order to compete. The runner may want to race against other runners. Or the runner may wish to compete against herself or himself and try to beat her or his own best times over certain distances.

There are millions of joggers and runners in North America. Many have increased the distance they run to the point that they feel ready to take on the marathon—the most exciting long-distance race of all.

▶**THE FINISH LINE**

After the Battle of Marathon in 490 B.C., a young Greek soldier named Pheidippides ran a great distance to his city to tell of the victory. "Rejoice, we conquer," he gasped, and then he died. It is in his honor that the "marathon" race is named.

The marathon is 26 miles, 385 yards (42 kilometers, 352 meters) long. The course over which it is run may be hilly or flat, depending upon where the race is held. Actually the marathon is a "race" for only a very few of the competitors. Of the hundreds who may run in a marathon, only a few are actually good enough to win. For all the rest, merely finishing the marathon is considered a victory.

The best male marathoners in the world usually finish the race in about two hours, ten minutes. The best women marathoners, in about two hours, forty-five minutes. And for even the greatest runners, the marathon is grueling and painful. Even they cannot be sure they will complete the race until they have crossed the finish line.

People in their seventies have completed marathons, as have people under the age of ten. But in spite of how different they may seem to be, all marathoners have one thing in common: the desire to challenge their bodies to run despite the pain and to experience the joy of finishing.

▶**PAIN AND JOY**

Pain? Of course. Joy? Yes, joy too. To push your body to its limits—that creates pain. The joy comes from feeling your body get stronger and from going farther or faster than you have ever gone before. And sometimes there is a magic moment, when your breathing becomes easy, and when all pain disappears. You feel free. Your legs seem to move themselves, and easily and fluidly you glide on and on and on. At that moment, running is pure joy.

If you want to start running or jogging, follow these rules.

1. Get a medical examination first. Running is strenuous. Make sure you're in good health.
2. Get a good pair of running shoes. Running can be hard on the feet, legs, and back. Good shoes will provide cushioning and support.
3. Do warm-up exercises before each run.
4. Until you build up your endurance and strength, don't go too far or too fast.
5. Stick to it. Run at least three times a week.

A good running program is important in training for any sport. Running skills will improve your performance in sports like tennis, soccer, and basketball, and also in bowling and golf, where leg strength is the key to solid body support. A good running program develops upper body strength, too. Running and jogging help your lungs to process more oxygen, and your heart to pump more blood through your body. And there is another advantage to being in shape and feeling fit. When you wake up in the morning and feel in shape, and know that your training has paid off, you will look forward to competing—and to doing well.

Different sports, of course, require different types of running programs. A training program for basketball or tennis should be based on wind sprints, which cover shorter distances. Soccer or field hockey, on the other hand, require both wind sprints and longer, jogging-type distances.

Regardless of what type of running program you as an athlete decide on, you must go about it consistently. Sporadic training—where you run two or three times a week for a few weeks and then drop off to once a week and then go back to four times a week—just doesn't do the job. You must develop a program and then stick to it.

Personally, I like to run in the morning. I enjoy it the most then. Some people like to run after work or school because it helps them to get rid of the tension of the day. But it doesn't matter when you train, as long as you are consistent and diligent. After a while, you will find that you hate to give it up and, in fact, get more and more out of it. You will realize that you have put in a lot of work and feel very good for it. You won't want to see it all slide by.

I participated in track and field for twelve years before the 1976 Olympics. In 1970, I decided to concentrate solely on the decathlon. So for the six years from 1970 until Montreal, I worked every day of every month training for that event. For the last three years before the Olympics, I worked six to eight hours a day. I developed an athletic program that was strenuous without being boring.

I began each day at nine o'clock with twenty minutes of stretching. Then I ran for

an hour and followed that with light calisthenics. After lunch I did technique work for a few hours, some hard running, and finished up with weightlifting. I had to train that much if I wanted to win the decathlon. And in 1976 at the Olympic Stadium, all my work paid off. But, even if I hadn't won, it was all worth it. Because the Olympic experience was the high point of my life—and there could be no substitute for it.

BRUCE JENNER

189

LIVING HISTORY

Early mapmakers believed in the existence of an undiscovered southern continent, as shown on this map drawn in the late 1500's. Captain James Cook was one of a great many explorers who searched for *Terra Australis Nondum Cognita* ("southern land not yet known"). Cook's voyages in the 1700's proved that the southern continent as shown on this map did not exist.

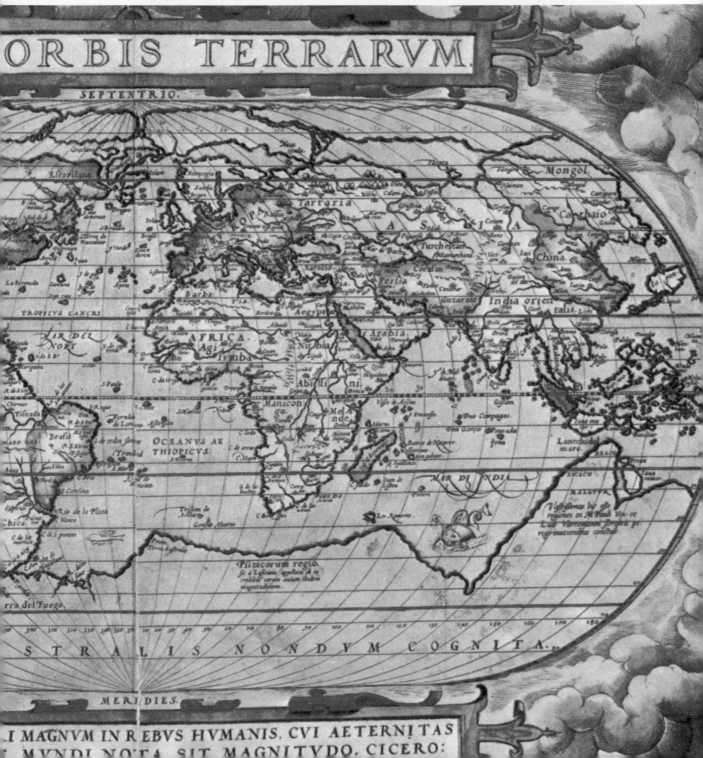

ENTRY TO THE TRAITORS GATE

THE TOWER OF LONDON

The Tower of London has been a fort, a palace, a prison. It once housed the Royal Observatory. For more than 500 years it was home to leopards, bears, and other animals of the Royal Menagerie. Today it is one of England's most important monuments and tourist attractions. People come from all over the world to see it and the treasures it contains. In 1978 the historic Tower celebrated its 900th anniversary.

Visiting the Tower of London is like walking through the history of England, for so many important events took place here. Perhaps best known is the story of two princes—Edward, Prince of Wales, and his brother, the Duke of York. The year was 1483. Edward was 12 years old; his brother was 9. Their father, the king, had died unexpectedly, and plans were being made for Edward's coronation as King Edward V. In the meantime the two boys were living in the Tower, under the protection of their uncle Richard. But Richard decided that he wanted to be king, and he arrested those

who opposed this move. The two young princes remained in the Tower after their uncle was crowned Richard III. Eventually the boys disappeared. To this day no one knows what happened to them, but many people think that they were murdered by their uncle. The Tower is no longer used as a prison. What is it like today? What treasures does it hold? Let's find out.

▶TURRETS, WALLS, AND MOATS

The Tower of London was begun nine centuries ago, in 1078, by William the Conqueror, who wanted to protect and control London. The first structure to be built was a stone tower, today known as the White Tower. It is the tallest building in the complex, with a basement, two floors, a gallery, and a turret at each of the four corners.

As the centuries passed, other rulers added to the fortress. A great stone wall with thirteen towers was built around the White Tower and its grounds. A moat was dug and filled with water. Later, another outer wall was built. The moat, now between the two walls, was filled in and a new moat was dug outside the fortress.

As you can imagine, the Tower became a well-protected place. Kings often lived there, especially during times of unrest. In fact, it was said that whoever held the Tower held the keys to the kingdom.

There were only two entrances to the Tower. One was from land, across a drawbridge. The other was from the Thames River. This was not an entrance that most people wanted to use. One guide at the Tower calls it "London's original one-way street." It was through here that prisoners entered the Tower—prisoners who often were on their way to the scaffold, where they were beheaded. (Beheading was a death reserved for royalty and the upper class. Poor people were hanged.) This entrance from the river is known as Traitors' Gate. Among the famous people who passed through the gate on the way to their deaths were Sir Thomas More and two wives of King Henry VIII: Queen Anne Boleyn and Queen Catherine Howard.

Above Traitors' Gate is a tower. Origi-nally it was called the Garden Tower, but now it is known as the Bloody Tower. This is where the young princes are thought to have been murdered. It is also where Sir Walter Raleigh lived during most of the twelve years that he was imprisoned in the Tower of London. Although a prisoner, Raleigh had a decent apartment and two servants to wait on him. He also had a little laboratory in a shed in the garden, where he did chemistry experiments. Raleigh's wife and son lived with him for a while, and he had frequent visitors, including Queen Anne and her son.

Raleigh had many chances to see the "beasts and birds" that were kept at the Tower. By the early 1800's—some 200 years after Raleigh's death—the menagerie had grown quite large. But in 1835 one of the lions bit a soldier. The Duke of Wellington, who was Constable of the Tower, ordered that all the animals be removed and sent to the new London Zoo.

▶THE CROWN JEWELS

The best-known treasures kept in the Tower today are the Crown Jewels. These

The most famous treasures kept in the Tower of London are the Crown Jewels.

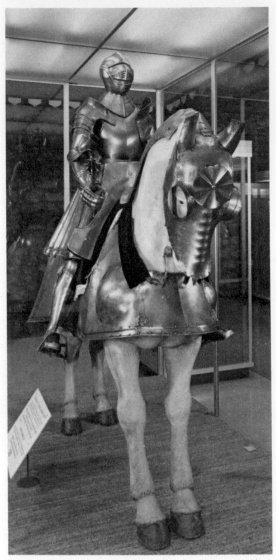

The royal collection of armor contains the armor that was worn by Henry VIII and his horse.

Royal Sceptre, which contains a 530-carat diamond, the largest cut diamond in the world. There are the coronation rings, consisting of diamonds, rubies, and sapphires. There are gold and silver dishes used at the coronation banquet. And there are spectacular crowns, set with many beautiful jewels.

The Crown Jewels have been kept at the Tower since the 1300's. But they have not always been kept safely. Occasionally, a king would be in debt and would pawn some of the jewels. During the 1650's, England was ruled not by a king but by Oliver Cromwell. Cromwell sold or destroyed many of the Crown Jewels. Some of the jewels that survived were used in later crowns. The Imperial Crown of State, worn after the coronation and on other special occasions, contains some of these jewels. Altogether, this crown contains more than 3,000 jewels, mostly diamonds and pearls.

Another important crown is St. Edward's Crown, made for the coronation of Charles II in 1661. It is the heaviest crown in the collection, weighing nearly five pounds (2.5 kilograms). It has been used for every coronation since 1661. It is placed on the sovereign's head for only a short time, but it signifies that he or she is now ruler of England.

In 1671, Charles II was broke. He looked for ways to make some money. He decided to let "strangers" see the Crown Jewels. So you see, tourism is a very old business at the Tower of London.

▶THE ARMOR COLLECTION

Another tourist sight at the Tower that dates back hundreds of years is the royal collection of armor and weapons. Housed in the White Tower, the collection was begun by Henry VIII. Henry, it is said, had enough weapons at the Tower to equip 100,000 soldiers.

The exhibits show the changes that were made as years passed. There is body armor made of interlinking iron rings, which was worn in the early Middle Ages. It was gradually replaced by plate armor, which covered the body from head to toe—with matching armor for the warrior's horse! Weapons changed, too: clubs and crossbows eventually gave way to pistols and muskets.

are the jewels of the Crown—the person who is the sovereign, or king or queen, of Britain. Most of the jewels are connected with the coronation, the ceremony during which the prince or princess is made king or queen. They were last used in 1953 for the coronation of Queen Elizabeth II, Britain's current sovereign.

The Crown Jewels are very beautiful and extremely valuable. There are the Swords of Justice, which are carried in front of the sovereign during the coronation. There is the

The Ceremony of the Keys is enacted every night when the main gates of the Tower are locked.

▶TOURISTS AND RESIDENTS

Today, 3,000,000 tourists visit the Tower of London every year. Guiding them and safeguarding the Tower are the Yeoman Warders, more popularly known as the "Beefeaters." These men are members of the British Armed Forces and are easily recognized by their red and black uniforms.

At the end of each day the tourists leave and the gates are locked. This is done in a special Ceremony of the Keys. Carrying the keys and a lantern, a Yeoman Warder locks the outer gates. As he moves toward the center of the fortress, he passes the Bloody Tower. A guard challenges him:

"Halt! Who comes there?"
"The Keys."
"Whose keys?"
"Queen Elizabeth's Keys."
"Pass, Queen Elizabeth's Keys, all's well."

After being allowed to pass, the Yeoman Warder leaves the keys in the Governor's residence for the night.

The Yeoman Warders and their families live in the Tower of London. So do the Governor, the Curator of the Jewels, and others. Altogether, about 200 people call the Tower home. If they plan to visit other parts of London in the evening, they can return to the Tower after the gates are locked. But if they return after midnight, they have to know the secret password, which changes every day.

"It's very pleasant living here," the Chief Yeoman Warder told one visitor. "There're no peddlers or fear of theft. But it does get a bit noisy on days when we have 30,000 people coming through."

JENNY TESAR
Sponsoring Editor, *Gateways to Science*

OLD FORT WILLIAM

A birchbark canoe eases up to the landing near the main gate of a fort surrounded by a wall of pointed logs. A half dozen French-Canadian *voyageurs,* dressed in colorful shirts, baggy pants, and moccasins, hop out of the canoe. Moments later, they hoist heavy loads of beaver skins over their shoulders and walk briskly through the gate, followed by their Ojibway Indian guides.

Inside the fort, the *voyageurs* shout a cheery *bonjour,* the French "hello," to a group of men in cutaway frock coats and high hats. The men return the greeting and inquire about the new arrivals' long river journey. The smell of freshly baked bread wafts from one of the many log cabins enclosing the great square in the middle of the fort. A blacksmith's hammer rings loudly. Nearby, a kilted bagpiper plays a lively Scottish reel.

Everywhere people are going about their daily activities just as they would have more than 150 years ago. For we have arrived at Old Fort William, on the banks of the Kaministikwia River, in the city of Thunder Bay in Canada's province of Ontario.

Old Fort William is a faithful and accurate re-creation of an actual fur-trading post that flourished in the early 1800's. Here, only a short distance from the site of the original Fort William, history springs back to life. You leave the 20th century and enter the world of hardy adventurers and fur traders of another era.

The government of Ontario spent about $12,000,000 to create this replica of Fort William, which was the inland headquarters of the North West Company from 1803 to 1821. During those years, the fort was the center of the Company's vast fur-trading empire.

Nearly deserted throughout most of the year, the fort bubbled with life each July when the Great Rendezvous took place. It was then that the Company's *voyageurs* would arrive by canoe from the northern and western posts to exchange furs for trade goods brought by Company agents from Montreal and beyond.

The *voyageurs* were a hardy breed of tough little men. By Company rule they had to be short and lightweight so they wouldn't overload the canoes used to transport goods. At the Great Rendezvous, the *voyageurs* and Indians set up encampments just outside the fort. For the next two weeks they let loose in a nonstop celebration that included feasting, drinking, and other forms of merrymaking.

Today you can relive those exciting and colorful days by visiting Old Fort William, which is open to the public from late May to early October. You will be plunged back into an earlier age. All the people who work at the fort—the tradespeople, *voyageurs,* and Company officials—are dressed in the costumes of that period.

You can wander over to the canoe yard to see the huge *voyageur* canoes being built out of the same materials the Indians used. They are made of birch bark, and the seams are carefully sewn with spruce roots. Then they are covered with pitch to make them waterproof.

At the infirmary, a kindly doctor peers over his steel-rimmed glasses and offers an old 19th-century remedy for whatever ails you. He shows off his assortment of surgical tools—all from the 1800's—and explains what each was used for.

Voyageurs and an Ojibway guide arrive at Old Fort William, in a re-creation of fur-trading days.

You can see Ojibway tribe members do leatherwork (*right*), and visit the canoe yard to watch the construction of the huge canoes (*below*).

A few houses away, you can eavesdrop on a meeting of the North West Company's partners. They are discussing the problems they are having with the Company's arch rival—the Hudson's Bay Company.

There is also the Indian encampment, where members of the Ojibway tribe practice their native crafts. If you are hungry, you can wander over to the Cantine Salope (the fort's restaurant) for thick stews, tasty puddings, and bread baked in the same sort of brick ovens used 150 years ago.

There's enough to keep you pleasantly busy for a whole day. And when you leave Old Fort William and return to the 20th century, you will carry with you a better understanding of the fur trade that formed an important part of Canada's early history.

HENRY I. KURTZ
Author, *Captain John Smith*

197

THE LIGHTHOUSE

Imagine that you are at sea. The sky is dark. The sea churns and waves pound against your ship. You know that there are dangerous rocks in the area—rocks that could smash your ship to bits. But you don't know how near the rocks are because your ship doesn't have radar. Suddenly the sailor on watch sees flashing lights. You are safe. A lighthouse beacon has told you where the dangerous rocks are located. Now your captain will be able to navigate around them.

A modern lighthouse is more likely to be a steel platform than a romantic stone tower that juts up from the sea. And computers have probably replaced the keepers who once kept the lights burning at remote stations. But many of the old towers still stand, and their keepers live on in legend.

▶ **EARLY LIGHTHOUSES**

Early navigators had only very crude navigational charts and maps. They didn't have radar or radios. They sailed by trial and er-

ror. Ships would be dashed to pieces on rocks or would be unable to find the mouth of a harbor. As the years passed, people began to use lights as homing beacons to guide ships to port. Usually the homing beacon was an open wood or coal fire, built on a high point of land or on a high platform. These fires didn't work too well because they couldn't be seen from very far away. Rain and wind put them out. And if the weather was foggy, the light couldn't penetrate the fog.

In the 17th century, sea trade expanded, and people ventured farther from home. But the hazards of sea travel were still great. Navigational equipment and sea maps were poor. Ships were small and made of wood, and they were easily broken up when they came upon hidden rocks or reefs. Soon people began to use warning lights to point out hazards at sea as well as to mark harbors. These beacons at sea needed to be strong enough to stand up against the

Montauk Light, at the eastern tip of Long Island, New York, was one of the first lighthouses to be built after U.S. independence. Today it is threatened by erosion.

Cape Florida Light is part of Cape Florida State Park on Key Biscayne. In 1836 a rebel band of Seminole Indians set fire to this lighthouse, and its keeper was rescued by a passing ship.

pounding of ocean storms. Lighthouses—towers of stone or wood topped with guiding beacons—were built to stand guard at dangerous zones.

Perhaps the most famous of the early lighthouses was the Eddystone Light, 14 miles (22.5 kilometers) off the coast of Plymouth, England. It was built at the end of the 17th century to warn ships that they were approaching the fearsome Eddystone rocks, which were often called a sailors' graveyard because of the great number of ships that were dashed to pieces there. Its beacon was a series of huge candles. This structure was washed away in a storm. A second version of the Eddystone Light was destroyed by a fire in 1755.

A third structure, built of stone, proved more long-lasting and became a model for other lighthouses.

The first lighthouse in North America was the Boston Light, built in 1716. It was destroyed in the Revolutionary War, and another light now stands in its place. In the 19th century, when clipper ships and steam-ships plied the seas in stiff competition for booming trade, lighthouses sprouted all along North America's Atlantic coast. By 1900, a chain of beacons guided sailors from Newfoundland to the Florida Keys. And a wealth of stories—some fact, some fantasy—grew up around the lighthouses and their keepers.

▶A LONELY LIFE

The life of a 19th-century lighthouse keeper was a lonely one. Sometimes the keeper, and perhaps an assistant, lived alone in cramped apartments in the light tower, surrounded by crashing waves. Or the keeper might live with his family in a house next to the tower, perhaps on some lonely point of land or island. Usually supplies were brought in by boat. The work was hard and the hours were long. The keeper's most important job was tending the light—filling the oil lamps, trimming the wicks, polishing lenses, and cleaning windows. The keeper also repaired storm damage and sometimes rescued people from capsized boats.

A lighthouse keeper's life was dangerous, too. The story of Abbie Burgess illustrates just how dangerous it could be. Abbie's father was the keeper of Matinicus Rock light, off the coast of Maine. Her family lived in a house next to the light tower. Her mother was an invalid, and she had three younger sisters.

In 1857, soon after Abbie's 14th birthday, her father left the island to get supplies. He planned to be gone for just one day. But that night a terrible storm blew up. It churned up the sea and pounded the rocks. Huge waves crashed against Matinicus Rock. The Burgess house was in danger of being swept away. Quickly, Abbie moved her mother and her sisters up into the light tower. The waves wrecked the house and rose up to the base of the tower. The storm raged for four weeks, and Mr. Burgess was not able to return to Matinicus. But the light shone brightly each night because Abbie and her young sisters tended it. They never let it go out once!

▶ MODERN LIGHTHOUSES

Today most lighthouses are automated and require no keepers. Computers are used to turn the lights on and off and adjust their signals. Technicians travel from site to site, inspecting the lighthouses to make sure that all systems are in good working order.

Beacons have changed, too. Early lighthouses were not much more effective than land fires because their lights could not be seen from far away. By the end of the 18th century, oil lamps had largely replaced candles, and reflectors made of mirror or highly polished tin were being placed around the lamps to increase their light.

Then, in the 19th century, lighthouses were revolutionized by the development of

Sandy Hook Light, built in 1764 on the New Jersey shore, is now the oldest lighthouse in the United States. Some historians believe that the top level of the lighthouse was lopped off by soldiers during the Revolutionary War.

Cape Henry Light, at the entrance to Chesapeake Bay, was built in 1881. An earlier tower, built in 1792, still stands nearby and has been preserved as a historical monument.

the Fresnel lens, invented by French physicist Augustin Jean Fresnel. The Fresnel lens consists of highly polished prisms combined into a large lens. Light rays bounce off the prisms, creating a very strong light.

Today powerful electric lights are used, and the lenses are huge. And a modern lighthouse may have a radio beacon, which sends out radio waves that can be picked up by ships.

New lighthouses are often metal frames that are built on shore and then towed out to dangerous spots, where they are bolted into place. Quite a few of the old towers are still in use, however. Others have fallen into disrepair. But some are preserved as museums and historic sites. If you visit one of these lighthouses, you can learn firsthand about the life of a lighthouse keeper.

HOW TO "READ" A LIGHTHOUSE

Every person has fingerprints that are different from everyone else's fingerprints. Each lighthouse, too, is different from all other lighthouses because each has certain light characteristics and color. This information is usually found on navigational charts.

Here are the three basic kinds of lights:

1. Fixed light—the light burns steadily.

2. Flashing lights—the light flashes at regular intervals. The period of light is less than the period of dark.

3. Occulting lights—the light flashes at regular intervals. The period of light is longer than the period of darkness.

CAPTAIN JAMES COOK: A GREAT EXPLORER

The sun had not yet come up on the morning of January 18, 1778, when the lookout on the British ship *Resolution* shouted "Land Ho!" He had spotted an island looming ahead, barely visible in the pale dawn light.

Captain James Cook, the *Resolution's* commander, raised a telescope to his eye for a closer look. Later that day, he wrote in his journal: "An island was discovered and soon after we saw more land bearing north and entirely detached from the first; both had the appearance of being high land."

The two islands Cook and his men saw that day were Oahu and Kauai—part of the island chain we now know as Hawaii. And Captain Cook and his British seamen were the first Europeans known to have set foot on Hawaii.

Cook claimed the islands he had "discovered" for King George III of England. Actually, Polynesian islanders had discovered them centuries before. But they were unknown to Europeans until Cook visited them 200 years ago.

In 1978, Hawaiians celebrated the Cook landing. A pageant commemorating the event was held on Kauai, and the state of Hawaii issued a bronze medal in honor of the Cook bicentennial. A special exhibit at the Bishop Museum in Honolulu featured native carvings and other items that Cook had brought back to England after his voyages to the Pacific.

In addition, several new biographies of Captain Cook were published, for 1978 was also the 250th anniversary of the birth of this brilliant naval officer. He won fame and honor in his day for his explorations and for his work as a navigator who used the latest scientific methods. Many consider him the greatest of all British explorers.

Cook was born in Yorkshire, England, in 1728. His family was poor, and young James had to limit his education and go to work when he was only 12 years old. After serving as an apprentice for a shipping company, he joined the Royal Navy as an ordinary seaman. A smart and ambitious young man, Cook was promoted quickly. By 1759, he was the master of his own ship.

Cook studied mathematics, astronomy, and geography in his spare time. Because of his scientific knowledge, Cook was chosen to lead an expedition to the Pacific. His mission was to observe the planet Venus passing between Earth and the sun, a rare occurrence. But Cook also carried secret orders to look for new lands in the South Pacific that could be settled as British colonies.

Leaving England in the summer of 1768, Cook's ship, H.M.S. *Endeavour,* sailed around Cape Horn and reached the tropical island of Tahiti a year later. As ordered, Cook and the scientists who accompanied him observed the passage of Venus. From Tahiti, Cook continued on to New Zealand, whose coasts he explored and mapped.

Early in 1770, Cook reached the previously uncharted east coast of Australia. The British seafarer claimed the territory for England and named it New South Wales. When Cook returned to Britain, he was promoted to captain.

Besides finding new lands, Cook accomplished something else on this voyage. He helped to improve the lot of the average British seaman, whose living quarters were often dirty and rat-infested. Cook required his men to bathe regularly and to keep the ship clean and free of vermin. And he had the sailors eat fresh vegetables and fruit containing vitamin C in order to prevent scurvy—a serious gum disease.

In 1772, Cook once again put out to sea. His two ships, the *Resolution* and the *Adventure,* headed for the southern oceans where some scientists predicted an undiscovered continent would be found. There was no southern continent, but his voyage did result in the discovery of New Caledonia and Norfolk Island, and his ships were the first to cross the Antarctic Circle.

Cook sailed off on his third and final voyage in 1776. It was during this voyage that he came upon the Hawaiian Islands, which he named the Sandwich Islands in honor of his patron, the Earl of Sandwich. Cook found the islanders to be "an open, candid, active people and the most expert swimmers we had met with."

From Hawaii, Cook moved up the west coast of North America, which he explored as far as the Bering Strait and the Arctic Ocean. Only when his way was blocked by solid ice did he turn back. Late in 1778, Cook returned to Hawaii. There, on February 14, 1779, he was killed during an argument with some islanders who he believed had stolen one of his small boats. It was a tragic ending to the life of one of the greatest seagoing explorers of all time.

HENRY I. KURTZ
Author, *John and Sebastian Cabot*

Captain James Cook discovered the Hawaiian Islands in 1778, on his third great voyage.

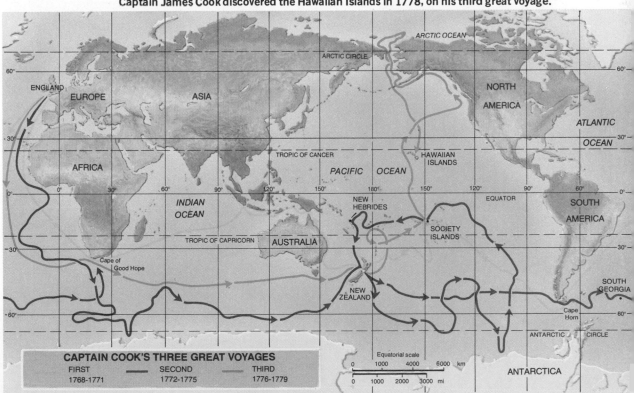

CAPTAIN COOK'S THREE GREAT VOYAGES

FIRST	SECOND	THIRD
1768-1771	1772-1775	1776-1779

The Iron Age volunteers built their community in England's countryside, far from civilization.

THE IRON AGE COMMUNITY

On March 31, 1978, a group of people in England "returned" to the 20th century. For one whole year, they had been living in the Iron Age of 2,200 years ago. They had lived without automobiles, pollution, frozen dinners, television, and almost everything else that commonly belongs to the modern world. They had gathered their own food, made their own clothes, and dwelt in a hut deep in the woods. Why? They were making an experiment in living the way the ancient Celts had lived, 200 years before the time of Christ.

The Celts (pronounced *selts* or *kelts*) were tribes that lived in western Europe beginning more than 3,000 years ago. They learned how to take iron from rocks and make it into weapons and tools. Therefore, the Celtic era is known as the Iron Age.

Many of today's Britons are descended from the Celts. That is why western England was a logical setting for the "Iron Age Experiment."

▶MADE FOR TV

The experiment was sponsored by the British Broadcasting Corporation (the BBC). In 1976, BBC television producer John Percival decided to make a series of TV films about how the Iron Age Celts had lived. He could have made films that showed only where the Celts had lived and what kinds of tools they had used. But Percival thought the films would be more interesting if they showed people who were actually living as the Celts had lived. He did not want actors pretending to be Celts. Instead, he wanted to film people who were living with all the problems, pleasures, and attitudes of the ancient Celts.

Percival put ads in British newspapers asking people to volunteer for the Iron Age Experiment. Over 1,000 people responded. From these volunteers, Percival chose six couples. One couple brought their three children. Among those chosen were students, teachers, a doctor, a nurse, and a builder.

To prepare themselves for the experiment, the volunteers first had to learn some Iron Age skills, such as weaving, blacksmithing, agriculture, livestock raising, carpentry, and pottery making. By April, 1977, the 15 volunteers were ready to go back in time 2,200 years. They settled together in Wiltshire, southwest of London. Far away from civilization, they lived in an Iron Age community.

Except for the TV camera team who came to film them every week, the volunteers were completely shut off from the outside world. Their exact location was kept a secret, to keep away curious 20th-century visitors.

▶THE CELTIC WAY

The volunteers worked hard at doing things the Celtic way. They used ancient tools to build the large hut that housed them all. The hut was made out of wattle (interwoven sticks and branches) and daub (a primitive plaster made of mud and animal hair), and had a cone-shaped roof. For clothing, they sewed animal hides and wove wool from their sheep. For food, they gathered wild roots and vegetables and grew their own peas, beans, and wheat. They made cheese out of goats' milk, and they raised hogs, cattle, and chickens for meat. They caught and ate squirrels, rabbits, and rats. They ground flour and baked bread.

Cooking had to be done over an open fire. It took a whole day to bake a loaf of bread.

Doing things the Celtic way wasn't easy. But the Iron Agers learned to adapt to their primitive way of life. Without soap, they washed themselves with clay. Without toothbrushes and toothpaste, they cleaned their teeth with twigs. Many British people are tea drinkers, and one woman especially missed her afternoon tea. So she learned to use substitute drinks made from dandelions or mint leaves. The doctor in the group learned to treat flu, headaches, and asthma with various roots, herbs, and barks. And he treated cuts and bruises with soothing honey from the group's beehives.

The volunteers weren't always sure they were doing things the way the ancient Celts had actually done them. They often talked and argued about what was "proper" for the Iron Age. When one man made a chair, he had to destroy it because Iron Age people almost certainly didn't have chairs. But just as real Iron Agers had done, they made their own dyes from barks and mosses. They entertained themselves by telling stories and by playing Celtic musical instruments such as the lyre (a stringed instrument), pipe, and drums.

The volunteers also tried to follow the religious beliefs and traditions of the ancient Celts. Instead of Christmas, they celebrated the Winter Solstice, which marks the first

The volunteers raised goats and made cheese from the milk, just as the ancient Celts had done.

day of winter. But they couldn't follow all the Celtic religious traditions exactly. For one thing, they didn't always know the correct Celtic prayers or chants. For another, the ancient Celts used to sacrifice one of their people as a way of asking the gods for a good harvest. None of the volunteers was ready to follow that particular tradition!

▶ THE 20TH CENTURY—GONE BUT NOT FORGOTTEN

In spite of the volunteers' attempts to make everything authentic, the 20th century sometimes tried to poke its way into their lives. British building inspectors didn't approve of the hut as a living place, but they agreed to let it stand. British school authorities wanted the children to keep up with their lessons, so some 20th-century books and papers had to be allowed into the Iron Age. And animal protection societies insisted that the hogs could be killed only by "humane" 20th-century methods.

At times, the Iron Agers found that certain modern items were very necessary. The volunteers were allowed to use some 20th-century health devices, and an "outside" doctor came to the camp a few times during emergencies. Producer John Percival took the group for a short summer "vacation" at the seashore. While the vacation wasn't really necessary, it was probably a very welcome rest for the volunteers.

▶ DID THE EXPERIMENT WORK?

How well did this group of modern people succeed as Iron Agers? Pretty well, it seems. They were able to provide all their own food and clothing.

Living together in a group had its problems, but the Iron Agers seemed to get along fairly well. Each couple had its own private area in the hut, but nearly everything was done in a group. You may wonder if any one person became the group leader. Apparently not. When the group was building the hut, the men gave directions and acted as leaders. But once the hut was built, day-to-day life centered around food preparation and household chores. Since the women were more experienced at these tasks, they acted more often as group leaders.

In time, the volunteers found that they were changing personally. They were walk-

Two volunteers prepare a meal over the fire, which was kept burning inside the large hut.

The group learned that working together requires co-operation and consideration of others.

ing and talking more slowly than they had in the 20th century. They learned that living in a group requires lots of self-control and consideration for others. And they also learned that Iron Age life was by no means easy. Most of each day was used for gathering and preparing food. Still, the volunteers had time to refine their skills in such Iron Age crafts as pottery making and weaving.

For the most part, the Iron Age volunteers enjoyed the experiment, but not always. In August, 1977, one of the men decided to hitchhike to a beach resort. Within two days, however, he changed his mind and returned.

In December the family of five left the community for good. One of the children was sick, and his parents insisted on taking him to a modern doctor. Five couples remained.

Some of the volunteers reported that arguments often arose within the group. One woman said that the arguments came up because without TV, books, and newspapers, the group had very little mental recreation. So they exercised their brains by arguing with each other.

▶RETURNING TO "NOW"

On March 31, 1978, the ten remaining volunteer Celts walked out of the Iron Age and returned to the 20th century. All were happy to come home. One of the women had especially missed her family and friends, chocolate, and her Bob Dylan records. One of the men had missed beer and cigars. The woman who had had to drink dandelion and mint tea could have her regular tea again. There were some 20th-century things that they hadn't missed at all—noise, pollution, and inflation. One of the women said that after a year in the woods, she didn't think she would ever want to live in a city again.

But for better or for worse, they were back. Producer John Percival had enough film for twelve TV shows for the BBC. And the volunteers had memories of a very unusual experience—plus $2,000 each, their "pay" for spending one year in an Iron Age community.

DANIEL J. DOMOFF
Consulting Editor
Educational Developmental Laboratories

CELEBRATION FOR JOHN BUNYAN

John Bunyan was an English writer and preacher who lived during the 17th century. He is the author of one of the all-time great classics of English literature—*The Pilgrim's Progress*.

In 1978, there was a double celebration for John Bunyan—that year was the 350th anniversary of his birth and the 300th anniversary of the publication of *The Pilgrim's Progress*. How this poorly educated man came to write one of the world's most widely read books is a story of great faith and determination.

▶PREACHER AND WRITER

John Bunyan was born near Bedford, England, on November 30, 1628. He was the son of a tinker (a maker and mender of pots and pans) and attended school for a very short time before taking up his father's trade. When he was 16, he became a soldier in the parliamentary army, a very dis-ciplined Puritan group. Parliament disbanded his regiment in 1646, but the experience had introduced him to Puritan thought and to a wide variety of people. A few years later, he married a woman whose religious views also greatly influenced him, and he began to read and think about religion.

Spurred on by his deeply religious beliefs, Bunyan became a member of a nonconformist church in Bedford. In 17th-century England, certain religious groups were called nonconformists because they refused to recognize the Church of England as the only true church.

Bunyan began preaching to small groups of nonconformists throughout the countryside. But the government tried to force everyone to belong to one religion, and Bunyan was arrested. He was kept in prison for almost all of the next twelve years. During this period, he began to write. Finally freed in 1672, Bunyan was granted a license to

John Bunyan was the author of the great classic *The Pilgrim's Progress*. This statue of him, with a scene from the book, stands in Bedford, England.

preach. He spent the rest of his life as pastor of his Bedford congregation.

But earning the preacher's license did not earn Bunyan a peaceful life. He was imprisoned again, for a short time in 1675. During this second prison term, he finished *The Pilgrim's Progress*. For more than 200 years, this book was more widely read and owned than any other book except the Bible. In fact, it was one of the first books printed in America after the Pilgrims had settled.

The Pilgrim's Progress is the kind of story known as an allegory. This means that Bunyan used people and places to represent spiritual and human qualities, such as faith and hope and doubt. As the story begins, Christian (the pilgrim) flees the City of Destruction to look for the Celestial City. During the journey he meets many temptations and pitfalls. He finds himself in such places as the Slough of Despond, By-path Meadow, Doubting Castle of the Giant Despair, and Vanity Fair. Along the way, Christian meets many companions. Some try to help him, and others try to keep him from reaching his goal. Such characters as Faithful, Mr. Worldly Wiseman, Hopeful, Lady Feigning, Obstinate, and Ignorance reveal Bunyan's keen understanding of human nature. This has been one reason for the book's long-lasting popularity.

The Pilgrim's Progress teaches that people are responsible for the salvation of their own souls. From this point of view, the book is an important piece of religious writing. For many years the book was read and reread regularly in many Christian homes. Today, people are as likely to read and enjoy *The Pilgrim's Progress* for its story as for its religious instruction. There is a single, straightforward plot—the travels of a hero and his companions. The scenes are vividly described and the dialogue is realistic and natural. Bunyan had a good imagination and a knack for making written words come to life.

▶CELEBRATIONS AND FESTIVITIES

In 1978, John Bunyan's hometown of Bedford celebrated the double anniversary throughout the year. Visitors flocked there to take part in the festivities. There were dramatizations of *The Pilgrim's Progress*,

In this drawing from *The Pilgrim's Progress*, the hero (Christian) is chased by Obstinate and Pliable.

country dancing, and demonstrations of 17th-century games. With the help of a special map, modern "pilgrims" could even follow in Christian's footsteps and reach some actual landmarks mentioned in *The Pilgrim's Progress*.

History buffs were able to visit a Bunyan museum and see some of his personal possessions, as well as rare copies of his book. And at nearby Elstow, the village where Bunyan was born, buildings and furniture from the 17th century had been preserved, giving visitors a true taste of Bunyan's world.

The determined tinker would no doubt be pleased to know that his writings and his memory have survived for more than three centuries.

DON JAY SMITH
Educational writer
American Telephone and Telegraph

209

TRAVELING TRUNKS

One morning, you arrive at school and see a large, old trunk in your social studies classroom. The trunk has a curved top and a big iron lock. You can tell that it has had hard use because it is scarred and worn. Would the trunk make you think of old letters? Of packing for camp? Or would you think of pirate treasure—of heaps of beautiful gold coins buried long ago? If you lifted the top of this special trunk you *would* find treasure. Not gold and silver, but the treasures of an American family. You would be looking into a West Virginia Heritage Trunk.

▶A UNIQUE PROJECT

The West Virginia Heritage Trunk project was designed to teach eighth-graders about their heritage, or their roots. The Children's Museum and Planetarium of Sunrise, Incorporated, developed the project for the West Virginia Department of Education. It helps students learn about life in West Virginia—as it was lived from 1863 to 1873.

Trunks filled with specially chosen items have been put together, and they travel from school to school throughout West Virginia. The traveling trunks are like traveling social studies textbooks. In each one, students find things that were used by the West Virginians of 100 years ago—things like clothes, toys, books, and family records. They are not the belongings of presidents, generals, or other famous people we usually read about in history books. They are the belongings of ordinary people.

This particular historic period was a special time because West Virginia had just become a state. It was also the time of the Civil War, when the country was divided and many people suffered great hardships. During this decade the war ended, and people worked hard to bring the states together again.

How would you go about learning how your family lived 100 years ago? Well, you could start with your parents. They will be too young to have been around, but they may remember stories that their grandparents told. If you are lucky enough to have grandparents or other elderly relatives, they will remember stories, too. You can also look through old photograph albums. Perhaps your family has other old records—birth certificates, diplomas, marriage licenses, letters, and death certificates. These, too, will help you learn about your family's heritage.

Talking and investigating is just what the Heritage Trunk people did. A team of interviewers traveled around West Virginia and talked with many older citizens. One woman, Fanny Cobb Carter, was interviewed just before her 100th birthday. Mrs. Carter had a very good memory. She even remembered Booker T. Washington, the famous black educator. He had visited her grandmother when Mrs. Carter was a little girl. Rebecca Morgan also shared stories told by her grandmother, a woman who managed the family farm and took care of her children while the Civil War raged around her. Her husband, an officer in the Confederate army, was killed in a duel.

When all the interviewing was finished, the team wrote the life stories, or biographies, of six families There were 36 people in these families. But the people never really existed. They were invented from all the information that the interviewers had gathered in their research. Their "lives" represent the lives of the ordinary people who lived more than 100 years ago.

▶WHAT WAS PUT INTO EACH TRUNK?

In addition to interviewing, some researchers looked for old trunks and for objects that could be put into the trunks. They searched through attics and basements and they shopped in secondhand stores. The trunks they picked had actually been used by early families as they moved from one place to another.

Here are some of the items that were selected to go into each trunk.

• A mountain dulcimer (DUL-suh-mer)—a musical instrument once common in West Virginia. A mountain dulcimer looks something like a violin without a neck. It is played by plucking and strumming the strings. Even today the strange sounds of the mountain dulcimer are heard as an accompaniment to blue grass and other folk music.

• A quilting kit. A quilt is a colorful blanket made from bits of fabric. Nineteenth-century women learned to make quilts when they were children. They used scraps left over from sewing projects and from worn out clothing. These people had very little money, so nothing was ever wasted. A quilt, in addition to being colorful, was thrifty. Students can actually make a quilt using the materials found in each trunk.

• Materials to make a sampler. A sampler is an embroidered picture. A hundred years ago, every young girl was taught needlework. A sampler was used to practice the various embroidery stitches. A traditional sampler began with a picture at the top. The picture was usually of the girl's home or her family. Below the picture was a verse, often taken from the Bible. The girl's name and the date were also worked into the sampler. First the picture and verse were drawn onto a piece of cloth. Then they were embroidered with colored threads. Some of the samplers were beautiful, with tiny, perfect stitches. Each trunk contains a printed sampler that can be stitched by the students.

• A mountain woman's wardrobe—two dresses (a simple calico for everyday wear and a silk dress with a lace collar that was worn on special occasions), a sunbonnet, a fan, and a pair of pantaloons. Women wore pantaloons under a dress to hide their legs from view. Nineteenth-century women were very modest, and it was not considered proper for legs or ankles to be seen. The clothes included in each trunk are for trying

A reproduction of an ivory fan.

A cornhusk doll.

A family of puppets.

on. But they are not authentic. They are reproductions. Girls and women from earlier times were much smaller than modern girls and women. Today's eighth-graders just wouldn't fit into the clothes that were worn 100 years ago.

• A working man's wardrobe—a pair of pants, a coonskin cap, and a wamus. A wamus is a fringed jacket made from the skin of an animal. If you compared the men's and the women's clothes, you would notice one thing for sure—women's fashions have changed a lot more than men's fashions. You would also notice that all the clothes were made from natural fibers like cotton and wool and silk. Our early relatives didn't have synthetic fabrics like nylon or Dacron. And the clothes weren't permanent press, either.

• Toys. The children of that period didn't have as much time to play as today's children do. They were expected to work—tending animals, gardening, cooking, and taking care of the younger children. Their toys were simple. Dolls were made from cloth and stuffed with rags. Corn husks, too, were used to make dolls. Each trunk contains a selection of toys, including a family of puppets.

• Documents. Every family had records that were kept at home. Often, statistics were entered in the family Bible—births, marriages, deaths. Each trunk includes copies of family documents, as well as of business records—a land grant, a doctor's leave of absence from a Civil War hospital, a shipping bill.

• A copy of the *McGuffey Reader* and a copy of *Noah Webster's Spelling Book*. These books were used 100 years ago to teach reading and spelling. You wouldn't find them much fun—there are few pictures and no color. School was serious business and, for most children, lasted only a few years.

▶HOW STUDENTS USE THE TRUNK

The trunk that arrives at a West Virginia school contains all the items just described. It also contains 36 cards. Each card describes a member of one of the six families. Look at the three sample cards on the following page.

These biography cards are used for role playing. In role playing, each student takes on the personality of another person. By "getting into someone's head" and by acting the way you think that person would act, you can learn a lot about that person. In this project each student becomes one of the 36 West Virginians and takes part in activities that these early settlers could have participated in. When you perform some of the jobs that the settlers needed to do just to survive, you will learn just how hard life was 100 years ago. When you attend some of their parties, you will realize that they also had fun.

Perhaps a student "family" might invite neighbors in for a spelling bee. The Webster's speller in the trunk could provide the words. There might be a simple prize for the winner. Not very exciting by modern standards, but it was probably a nice way for weary people to relax at the end of a hard day's work—during a time when there were no movies, no TV, and not even any electric lights.

All the families in a community might have a square dance. A hundred years ago, square dances were held in farmers' barns. The women wore their prettiest dresses. There was cider to drink and food prepared by the women. Nearly everyone attended, even small children. There was a fiddler to provide music and a caller to lead the dancing. Modern students might hold a similar square dance in their school gym.

Soapmaking is a long, hard job. It is dangerous, too. The soapmaker mixes melted fat and lye, a chemical that can burn the skin. The 19th-century family would save fat, perhaps for months. When enough fat had been collected, a day would be set aside for soapmaking. Enough soap to last the family for several months would be made at one time. A modern science class might try soapmaking.

It is possible to learn many things about the past by studying people's belongings and by role playing. This is just what the people who developed the West Virginia Heritage Trunk project thought. Thousands of West Virginia students think so, too. And maybe one day an antique traveling trunk will reach your school.

WHO ARE YOU?

You are **Carrie Brown** (September 10, 1862-1960) You are the daughter of a slave now free and working in the household. You are being carefully brought up and taught by the women of the McNeill household. They teach you to read, teach you your catechism, see that you have proper clothing. You help with little chores such as dusting and sweeping. You are very much at ease in the household as a little girl, because the McNeills are interested in you. You are more fortunate than many other Negroes. You are to go to Storer College and become a teacher.*

* Parts of this fictitious profile are suggested by the life of Mrs. Fanny Cobb Carter as told in an interview.

WHO ARE YOU?

You are **Richard Abshire** (January 19, 1857-1939) You are a farm boy who loves to know how things work. When your father got the beater, you were really excited. You are very interested in the water wheel at the grist mill. You made a water wheel in a smaller size. One of your jobs is to take the corn to the mill to be ground. Sometimes you take a little longer than necessary to do this so you can look around at the mill and at the blacksmith's shop too. The railroads are beginning to interest you.

There is no science taught in your one-room school, but your schoolmaster encourages you in learning how things work.

You love to eat—especially apple cobbler made from the apple trees on the farm. You live long enough to see great developments in machines and technology.

WHO ARE YOU?

You are **Rebecca Brown McNeill** (December 15, 1839-1905) Your family came from England to the United States before the American Revolution. You are a determined woman capable of doing many things. While Dr. McNeill was away during the Civil War, you defended your house when a very much disliked southern general wanted to take it over. When you refused to turn it over to him and his troops, he said that he would return the next day and take it by force. He returned, but you stood firmly in the doorway with your children beside you. When the general gave the command to shoot at the house, his men refused to do so.* You also hid a slave in the corn stacked for harvest when the doctor felt he must sell her. When the steamboat arrived to take her, she was nowhere to be found.*

* These situations were suggested by the true stories told by Mrs. John Morgan about the life of her grandmother, Mrs. Littlepage.

THE RENAISSANCE PLEASURE FAIRE

Every summer, in an oak forest north of San Francisco, a 16th-century English village comes into being. There are half-timbered cottages and colorful stalls. Gracious noblemen and their ladies, dressed in rich velvets and laces, walk along the streets. There are minstrels and jesters, too, and tradespeople selling wonderful toys, food, and clothing.

Suddenly, there's a loud cry: "Make way! Make way! The Queen is coming!"

People move to the sides. Some cheer, others bow, as Queen Elizabeth I and her entourage pass by.

Moments later, the crowd's attention is focused on a fire-eater. Nearby, a young maid plays a sad ballad on her harp.

These are just a few of the many activities that are part of the Renaissance Pleasure Faire, a yearly event that gives 20th-century people a chance to take part in the life of 16th-century England. The fair is much like

ones that took place in rural England in the late 1500's. At the end of the summer, the farmers and other country people would take a break from the hard work that made up their everyday lives. They would gather at the fair to see friends and celebrate a good harvest.

The present-day fair is produced by the Living History Centre. In addition, the Centre holds free workshops during the year at which people of all ages can learn Elizabethan dancing, Elizabethan language, and how to make clothes like those worn in England during the latter half of the 16th century.

Several thousand people work on the Renaissance Pleasure Faire. Some of these people set up the village. They assemble the town, put up tents, and carry in some 6,000 bales of hay, which are used as seats at the fair's theaters and rest areas. Some of the workers are entertainers. Professional actors, musicians, singers, dancers, mimes, acrobats, fire-eaters, and jesters provide continuous entertainment in the theaters and on the village streets. All these people are dressed in 16th-century costumes. Many visitors to the fair also wear costumes. They come as merchants and milkmaids, lords and ladies, rich folk and common folk. Other visitors wear modern casual clothes. Look around and you may see a child in T-shirt and shorts chatting with a child wearing a full-sleeved linen shirt, knee breeches, and a velvet cloak. One will be speaking American slang, the other Elizabethan English. One child may be nibbling on a jester cookie—a chocolate chip cookie that is wider than a large dinner plate.

They may wander over to the games area. There they can watch the sword fighting and the archery. Perhaps they'll make some candles at the dipping wheel or join in a dance. There are so many things to do. For when you travel 400 years into the past, "All the Faire's a Stage, and all those who gather in festive Spirit are its Players."

Listen to a musician . . .

. . . and attend a play at the Renaissance Pleasure Faire.

215

THE REINDEER LAPPS

Most of us think of reindeer once a year, at Christmastime. But in Lapland, reindeer have long been an important part of people's daily lives.

Lapland is an area in northern Europe. It covers about 150,000 square miles (390,000 square kilometers) in northern Norway, Sweden, and Finland, and on the Kola Peninsula in the northwestern corner of the Soviet Union. Over half of this area lies north of the Arctic Circle. It is a rugged land. There are tall mountains, many lakes and swamps, and huge evergreen forests. Winters are long; for months, there is no sun. Summers are short, and for a time there is no night. This is the land of the midnight sun. After long, cold, snow-filled winters, there is a burst of color from wildflowers, a burst of song from visiting birds—and a plague of bites from millions of mosquitoes.

The people who live in this region call themselves Sameh. Outsiders call them Laplanders or Lapps. In all, they number only between 35,000 and 45,000. They have their own language, Lappish, although most of them also speak the language of the country in which they live and of which they are citizens.

The Lapps have lived in their northern homeland for more than 2,000 years. They first came to hunt the reindeer, wild animals that migrated great distances with the seasons. The Lapps followed the reindeer herds on their migrations. Slowly, the people were able to domesticate the reindeer, much as people in other parts of the world domesticated, or tamed, wild cattle and horses. The Lapps thus became reindeer herders.

The Lapp herders get many necessities

Over the years, the Lapps tamed the wild reindeer and became reindeer herders.

Traditionally, the Lapps migrated with their reindeer. When the animals grazed, the Lapps put up tents (*above*) and warmed themselves around a fire (*right*).

from their reindeer. They drink the animals' milk and use it to make cheese. They eat reindeer meat. They use the skin to make clothing, blankets, and tents. Thread can be made from the sinews. The fat can be burned to give heat and light. And the herders also sell the animals to make a living.

▶THE REINDEER

Reindeer are a type of caribou, which is a species of deer. Reindeer are unique in that both males and females have antlers. The antlers are long and curved, with several branches, and a new set is grown every year. The antlers grow from knobs on the reindeer's forehead. They get bigger and bigger until autumn, when the animals mate. Thereafter, the antlers begin to harden. In late winter they fall off, and soon afterward a new set begins to form.

Male reindeer have larger antlers than the females. The males are also bigger animals. They may weigh as much as 300 pounds (135 kilograms). Females weigh between 150 and 250 pounds (65 and 115 kilograms).

Reindeer are well adapted to their Arctic home. They have very large, broad hooves. These enable the animals to travel over snow or soft, marshy ground. They can also swim. Reindeer coats are a combination of short, dense fur and long hairs. This keeps the animals warm when winter temperatures drop to −30°F (−34°C) or lower.

Reindeer are migrating animals. That is, they travel back and forth between two regions. In spring many herds move north to low mountain pastures, where they spend the summer. Their main food is a lichen known as reindeer moss. They also eat grasses, mushrooms, blueberries, and other small plants.

Soon after the reindeer reach their summer home, the females give birth. The young are called calves. The young reindeer can walk when they are only two hours old.

As summer ends, the reindeer move south to the forests, where they spend the winter. Here they live almost entirely on lichens. The animals dig through the snow, pushing their noses down to reach the food.

▶ON THE MOVE

Traditionally, the Lapps made the same journey with the reindeer. A family, or a group of families called a *sida,* followed its herd north in spring and south again in autumn. When the animals stopped to graze, the Lapps put up tents and rested for a while, warming themselves around a fire in the center of the tent. But when the reindeer moved, so did the Lapps.

The people's belongings were carried on sleds. Usually there was a string of sleds, each with a particular purpose. One carried the children and the puppies. Another carried the tent, a third carried clothing, and so on. The sleds were pulled by reindeer. Other reindeer carried heavy loads on their backs.

There were many dangers on the journey. Sudden storms brought icy winds and deep snow. Flooded rivers had to be crossed. Wolves attacked and killed reindeer that strayed.

Some Lapp herders now use snowmobiles to follow their reindeer.

The Lapps helped the reindeer through deep snowdrifts and across rivers. They and their dogs guarded the reindeer against wolves. They skied after straying animals and brought them back to the herd. (The Lapps, by the way, invented skis.)

When the people and their herd reached the summer grounds, the people set up camp. Everyone had a job to do. Some people set up tents. Some cut branches. These were put on the floor of the tent and then covered with reindeer skins to make a bed.

The camp was always in the same place, perhaps near a lake or among a small cluster of birch trees. Some buildings in the camp were permanent and were used from year to year. Storage houses, for example, held meat from animals slaughtered the previous year. The cold weather kept the meat frozen. This meat was a treat after the long trip north, during which the Lapps had to make do with tough, dried meat.

The Lapps' main interest then became the calving ground, where the female reindeer gave birth. The greater the number of calves, the richer the people would be. The Lapps kept the male reindeer away from the females during this time, and did everything possible to make sure the calving ground was a quiet place. They also guarded against bears, whose favorite food was newborn reindeer.

▶A CHANGING LIFE

Until 100 years ago, almost every Lapp followed the reindeer herds. But today only a few thousand Lapps live the way you just read about. The others have given up the traditional way of life—a way of life that is in danger of ending forever.

The outside world has entered Lapland. The Lapps have found themselves faced with different lifestyles, new opportunities, and modern appliances.

People from southern Scandinavia and the Soviet Union began moving into Lapland several hundred years ago. At first, only a few farmers came. But in this century the number of southerners has increased. They have come to exploit the mineral resources and other natural wealth of the land. They have built mines and lumber camps, railways and roads, towns and cities.

This means less grazing land for the reindeer. The herds are smaller now, and it is harder for the Lapps to make a living following them. But new conveniences make life a little easier. For example, some herders now use snowmobiles to follow the reindeer. The families spend the winters in modern homes instead of log huts. In fact, the wives and children may stay in the home the year round while the men go off with the migrating reindeer.

The Lapps who have given up the nomadic life live in the Arctic towns and cities or have moved south out of Lapland. They have become doctors, lawyers, factory workers, and farmers.

Will the old way of life die out? Will the children forget Lappish, their native language? Will they forget the arts and crafts and music of their ancestors? These questions worry the Laplanders and the Scandinavian governments because there are no easy answers.

▶TRAVELING IN LAPLAND

You can go to Lapland on special tours called reindeer safaris. If you go, you will travel across snowy fields and frozen lakes on a sled drawn by a reindeer. It's a bumpy trip—tourists often find themselves face down in the snow after their sleds tip over.

At night you will stay in a hut called a *lapinkota*. It is circular and has thick log walls that slant inward toward a smokehole at the top. There's a fireplace in the center of the floor and your Lapp guides will build a fire. They will melt snow, then boil the water to make coffee. And they will cook dinner—a meal that probably will include reindeer meat.

You'll sleep on the floor, perhaps on pine branches covered by reindeer skins. As you doze off, you may hear the tinkling of bells. Those are the bells worn by the reindeer that wait outside the hut. Tomorrow they and your Lapp guides will take you through more of the land that is their home.

If you visit Lapland, why not go on a reindeer safari? You will travel across fields of snow on a sled drawn by a reindeer.

FAIREST OF THE FAIRS

If you take a trip to Montreal, Canada, you can take a trip around the world at the same time. How can this be? Well, while staying in Montreal you can visit Man and His World—a fair held each summer on two beautiful islands in the St. Lawrence River. At Man and His World, displays from many faraway countries are housed in elegant buildings called pavilions. The exhibits are so real and so well presented that you truly feel you are in each distant country. And besides the country exhibits, there are "theme pavilions," each devoted to one fascinating subject or idea.

Man and His World grew out of a world's fair called Expo 67. That fair opened in Montreal in 1967 and was praised as the most handsome and impressive world's fair ever held. Because of its success it was "held over" and called Man and His World, although the exhibitions are not exactly the same as those that appeared at the original fair in 1967.

Each year, the fair is centered around a special theme. For 1978 the theme was "I'm in love with the world." In keeping with that thought, four countries entered the Man and His World community for the first time: Cuba, Venezuela, Portugal, and Italy. UNESCO (the United Nations Educational, Scientific, and Cultural Organization) also got its own pavilion for the first time in 1978. And the fair honored UNESCO with its own special day, July 2, dedicated to the whole world.

▶SOME COUNTRY PAVILIONS

Every country at Man and His World has vivid exhibits of its arts, folk handicrafts, and industrial products. Often a country will show how it has been making progress in the modern world. Iran, for instance, stresses progress in education by showing arts, crafts, and even movies made by Iranian children. And the People's Republic of China demonstrates its treatment of minority peoples by showing a model of a minority village with scenes from daily life. China also shows a model of a factory village.

Some of the displays are startling. In Haiti's pavilion, there is a Voodoo Corner devoted to this mixture of African magic and Christianity. The corner boasts a typical voodoo altar. Venezuela's pavilion has a kind of mirrored tunnel where visitors feel they are right in the middle of the Amazonian jungle.

Some other country exhibits that are clever or unusual are Cuba's display of sands from its beaches, Italy's display of costumes from movies made by director Luchino Visconti, and Portugal's diorama of the history of the Cistercian order of monks.

▶SOME THEME PAVILIONS

Of all the theme pavilions, the strangest is the one called Strange, Strange World. It features exhibits about UFO's (Unidentified Flying Objects) and about odd forms of power, or "energy," that are said to cause bizarre events. One display shows "energy currents" swirling about the human body.

The Endangered Species Pavilion will interest anyone who likes animals and wants to protect them. And the Village of Yesteryear shows in exact detail what life in Canada was like during the years from 1900 to 1910.

Quebec Village is another popular stop at the fair. This replica of a village in interior Quebec has eleven different craft shops where you can buy things such as wood carvings you would rarely find anywhere else.

▶LA RONDE

Quebec Village is located in the fair's amusement park, called La Ronde. Here you can find unusual rides, restaurants, discotheques, and, in the 1978 season, a festival of folk singing. At the entrance to La Ronde, in a colorful candy shop, is a merry new addition to Man and His World—a huge lollipop. It seems to say to the passersby, "Be happy, everybody!"

One especially interesting display at Man and His World is the Voodoo Corner in Haiti's pavilion.

WORLD OF YOUTH

Young people have the starring roles in *A Circle Is the Sun*, performed by the Children's Theatre Company.

YOUNG PHOTOGRAPHERS

Today's young photographers are learning early that photography is not just a hobby but a real art form. They know that their work can be as striking and as haunting as the greatest painting or the finest poem. So they work hard to produce remarkable photographs like the ones shown on these pages.

All these photographs were winners in the 1978 Scholastic/Kodak Photo Awards program. And the young photographers who took them gained as much satisfaction from producing excellent photographs as they did from winning awards.

Old North Church,
by Randy Le Duc, 14, Burbank, California

Hang Glider, by Chris Lombardo, 17, Reseda, California

Man's Best Friend, by Bob Fries, 14, Bellevue, Washington

Fantasy Sunrise, by Scott Headley, 16, Rochester, New York

Untitled, by Kenneth Glenn, 17, Burbank, California

On a Rainy Afternoon, by Theresa Papp, 17, Cicero, New York

Fishing Escapade, by Joseph Tomassini, 17, Waukegan, Illinois

A Colorful Creature, by Vernon Nobles, 14, St. Clair Shores, Michigan

TOYING AROUND WITH AN IDEA

How would you like to go to a toy shop where there are more than 28,000 different kinds of toys? There is such a "shop"—the U.S. Patent Office, in Arlington, Virginia. There, among more than 4,000,000 patents for all sorts of inventions, you will find descriptions and drawings of every imaginable toy.

There are spaceships, rocket launchers, and robots that look like something out of *Star Wars*. There are dancing bears, power-operated soap-bubble makers, toy theaters, and inflatable swords that won't hurt you when you duel. And there are dolls that hug, kiss, smile, dance, talk, walk, sing, pick themselves up, feed themselves, and burp. There is even a doll that you can "cure" of a variety of illnesses, including cough, fever, and fractured bones.

Researching the patent applications that are classified as "Amusement Devices and Toys" keeps three patent examiners busy. It is their job to decide whether or not a patent should be issued. Patents are documents granted by the government that give inventors the exclusive right to make, use, and sell their inventions for a fixed number of years. Each week the Patent Office publishes descriptions and drawings of almost 1,500 newly patented inventions, among them perhaps four or five toys. Some of these toys find their way to the shelves of toy shops. But others are never produced.

A talking and singing doll patented in 1890 by Thomas A. Edison was manufactured and sold for a number of years. The doll had a small phonograph inside. Edison, who invented the phonograph and the electric lamp, had a total of 1,093 patents to his name.

A flying doll was patented by Orville Wright in 1925, some 22 years after he and his brother Wilbur had successfully flown the first powered airplane. The doll was shot into the air by a spring-operated catapult, flew for a considerable distance, turned a somersault, and hooked onto a swinging bar with its curved arms.

Many of the patented toys are quite elaborate. A toy circus patented in 1922, for example, was complete with elephants, clowns, acrobats, jugglers, trapeze artists, and other acts.

More recent patents include one for an electrically lighted hula hoop. The built-in lights flash on and off as you spin the hoop around your body—very dramatic when you hula in a darkened room.

Robert Patch was granted a patent for this toy truck when he was only 5 years old. He built it out of empty shoe boxes, bottle caps, nails, and tape. The truck could be taken apart and put back together in different ways.

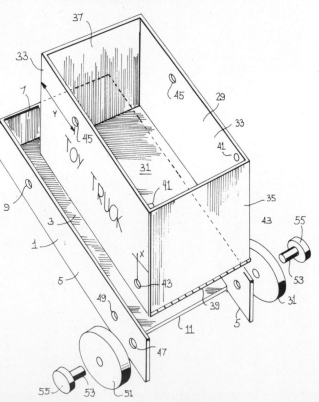

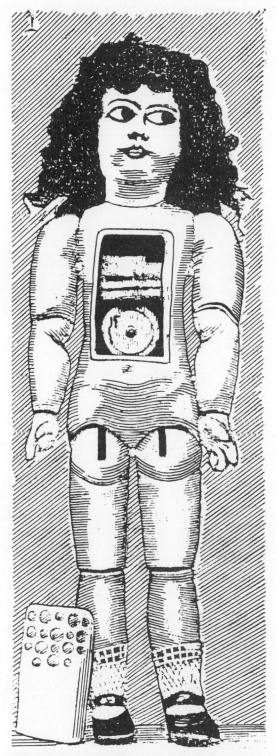

This talking and singing doll, with a phonograph inside its body, was patented by Thomas Edison.

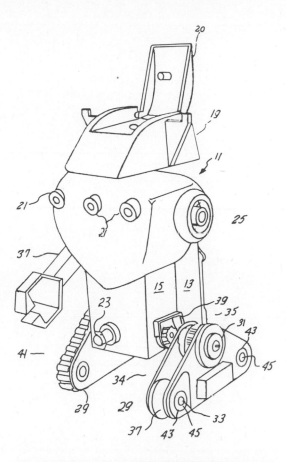

This patented toy robot has interchangeable parts and is driven by an electric motor inside the body.

There are a great many patents for toy robots that operate in most unusual ways. One delivers a karate chop. Another has interchangeable body parts. A third kind of robot is remote-controlled and can be moved into all kinds of positions and shapes.

Robert W. Patch is believed to be the youngest inventor to be granted a patent. He was only five when he filed a patent application for a toy truck that he had assembled out of empty shoe boxes, bottle caps, nails, and transparent tape. The truck could be taken apart and put back together in several different ways. Robert's father filled out the application for him, and Robert signed with an X.

Perhaps, one day, you will be the inventor of a patented toy.

HARRY GOLDSMITH
Former Patent Counsel

BOY SCOUTS

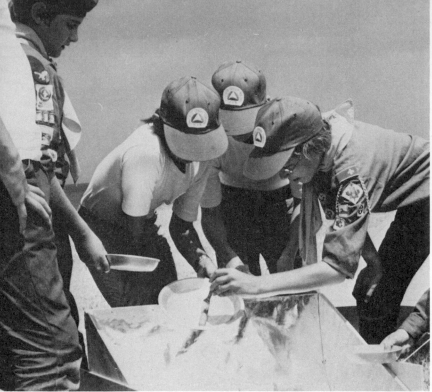

By cooking hot dogs in a solar oven, these Canadian Boy Scouts are learning about a source of energy that is becoming more popular today—the sun.

In 1978, Eagle Scout Mark Leinmiller of Georgia (*center*) was chosen to go to the Antarctic as a member of a National Science Foundation scientific expedition. Here, Leinmiller is in New Mexico, teaching Scouts how to orient a map.

The Boy Scouts of America continues its effort to reach inner-city youngsters. Here, a group of New Jersey Explorers who are specializing in aviation learn more about the operation of small aircraft.

Many opportunities are offered for Scouts around the world to travel and share experiences with fellow Scouts from other nations. These two Swedish Scouts were among a group that visited the United States in the summer.

Scouting continues to emphasize "outing," as this unit from North Carolina demonstrates. But the activities are kept relevant: while Scouts learn how to treat snake bites, they must also know how to handle a rat bite—a realistic problem for many city kids.

This trio from Pennsylvania is Number One! They won the 1978 Cub Scout Physical Fitness Contest and were chosen the fittest of the 2,000,000 Cub Scouts in the United States.

One of the highlights on the Exploring calendar was the 1978 National Explorer Olympics, held at Fort Collins, Colorado. It attracted some 2,000 top Explorer athletes in the United States.

Nancy Winecoff of North Carolina was elected the 1978 National Explorer president. She is the second woman to be elected head of this 400,000-member senior program of the Boy Scouts of America. Exploring, geared to the 15 to 20 age group, is co-educational.

YOUTH IN THE THEATER

Who knows what magic is? Is it magic when something grows grand and wonderful, or is it magic when something make-believe becomes real and true? Is it magic when joy and understanding flow from a young person's spirit? If all of these are magic, then there is in Minneapolis, Minnesota, a very magical place, because all these wonderful things have happened there. And perhaps the most wondrous thing is that this place is not a sorcerer's castle or an elf's wood or a fairy garden. This magical place is a theater—and what's more, a school—the Children's Theatre Company and School of Minneapolis, Minnesota.

▶SOMETHING VERY LITTLE

In 1961, a little group of adults borrowed a little money and set up a little theater. They called themselves the Moppet Players, and they began presenting plays for children in the back room of a Minneapolis restaurant. They put on eight plays that year, and word started to get around that the Moppet Players put on very good children's theater.

In 1962 they moved to larger quarters, an abandoned police station. That same year a young man named John Clark Donahue joined the Moppets. He directed, painted, designed, and taught (which he still does today). Guided by the idea that children's theater should be every bit as good as adult theater, the Moppet Players started to grow. They put on such plays as *Winnie the Pooh, The Reluctant Dragon,* and *The Princess and the Swineherd.* More than 10,000 people—children and adults—came to their performances each year.

During those early years, the Moppets also started giving classes in dramatics, dance, and play production. No one knew it at the time, but magic was happening: something little was growing into something grand and wonderful.

Students at the Children's Theatre Company and School perform in such plays as *Aladdin* . . .

▶SOMETHING MAKE-BELIEVE

By 1965, the Moppets had gotten too big for the police station. So Donahue, now artistic director, took the Moppet Players to the Minneapolis Institute of Arts. Besides a new home, they now had a new name: the Children's Theatre Company (CTC).

The people of the CTC believe that good children's theater is educational. They know that a play tells a wonderful story to its audience. They also feel that it must try to reach inside each person in the audience and give him or her some understanding of what it means to be human. This is what education should be about. Donahue says, "If I can make a child laugh or cry through the work on the stage, I'm teaching so much more than the ABC's." And this is how the magic make-believe of the stage becomes real and true—when the play touches the human feelings of each of the people in the audience.

Following the conviction that plays must be educational, the CTC expanded the theater classes it taught to young people from the Minneapolis–St. Paul area. In 1969 the CTC became the Children's Theatre Company and School, and since then, the theater and the school have grown together.

▶JOY AND UNDERSTANDING

In 1974 the CTC moved again, this time to a $4,500,000 theater and classroom building designed especially for them. The school now has about 100 students, most aged between 11 and 18. Each afternoon, after attending their regular schools in the morning, these young people come to learn the magic of the theater. Taught by Donahue and other artists, they study dance, music, acting, theater literature, theater history, pantomime, gymnastics, improvisation, directing, writing, puppetry—and more. They also learn what goes on backstage. They study theater lighting, sound, makeup and costuming, set construction, and stage management. And they study hard—four hours a day, five days a week.

The CTC now performs for more than 150,000 people each year. Some of the students take part in the plays, such as in *The Snow Queen* (from the story by Hans Christian Andersen) or *The Dream Fisher* (by

. . . and *Treasure Island*.

John Clark Donahue). There aren't always many roles for the students, since adult roles are filled by adult actors. Nor are students required to act in the CTC's productions. But when they do, the skills they have learned have deepened, and they have returned to their classes with a greater understanding of the dramatic arts.

Most striking about the CTC is its belief that human growth is the most important aspect of education and of theater. The school has been compared to a "garden" where people, both children and adults, flourish. Students and teachers nourish each other. Like the best of schools, it not only teaches skills, but it helps people learn to be whole human beings. And that is perhaps the greatest magic of all.

DANIEL J. DOMOFF
Consulting Editor
Educational Developmental Laboratories

235

GIRL SCOUTS AND GIRL GUIDES

Girl Scouts and Girl Guides are members of a worldwide organization—the World Association of Girl Guides and Girl Scouts (WAGGS). In some countries, including the United States, members are known as Girl Scouts. In other countries, including Canada, they are known as Girl Guides. Each nation's organization operates independently, shaping programs to fit the needs of its people. But all Guides and Scouts are linked together in international friendship.

This is the new Girl Scout emblem, which was chosen in 1978. The three-profile silhouette is designed to point up the organization's female focus. It also keeps the basic shape of the three-leaf clover, the traditional Girl Scout symbol that signifies the three parts of the Girl Scout Promise.

In 1978, many television viewers watched "Girl Scouting and the Wild Kingdom" and saw what American Girl Scouts are doing to aid in the conservation of wildlife. Girl Scouts were shown at California's North County Wildlife Rescue Treatment Center, caring for wild animals that were injured or orphaned.

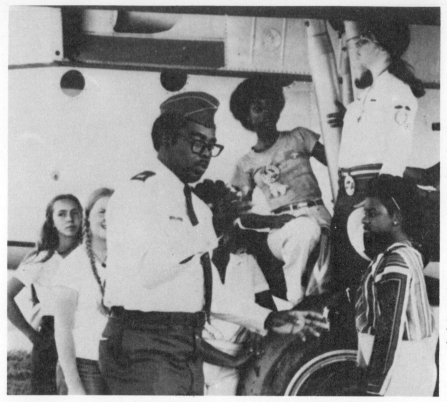

During the summer, Girl Scouts from the United States and Girl Guides from Britain and Sweden took part in the "Arkansas Wing Ding." During the ten-day event, the girls explored women's careers in commercial, private, and military aviation. They visited Little Rock Air Force Base, where they "piloted" a C–130 simulator, learned to read a radar screen, and toured a control tower.

In Europe, Girl Guiding is an important part of society. Girl Guides often work with Boy Scouts and other organizations to help fill the needs of Europe's young people. In Germany, Guides are involved with handicapped children. Girl Guides and Boy Scouts operate a camp for handicapped and nonhandicapped youth, where all can enjoy the outdoors.

There are more than 133,000,000 children in Latin America. Girl Guiding helps them see their own worth as individuals and gives them a sense of community responsibility. These Peruvian Girl Guides have provided activities for hundreds of children in rural areas through a traveling recreation program. There are similar programs in other Latin American countries.

Many Girl Guide/Girl Scout Associations in Africa are engaged in self-help projects, such as planting trees in Rwanda to help conserve soil and tending groundnut and rabbit farms as part of the "Feed Yourself" campaign in Ghana. Here, Tanzanian Girl Guides teach sewing at the Cottage Industry Center, where girls are trained to become independent wage earners.

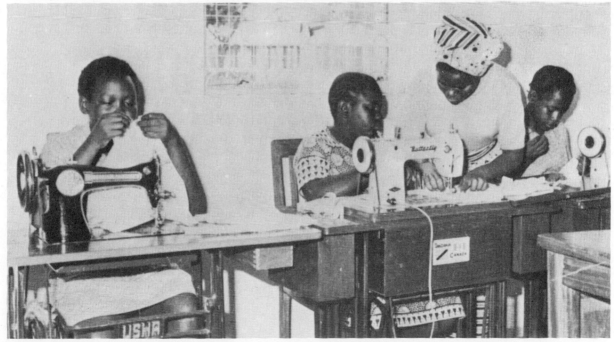

TOMORROW'S LEADERS . . . TODAY

It was 9 A.M. and selling began on the floor of the New York Stock Exchange. Upstairs, 123 teenagers sat in the Board of Directors room. They had come from every state in the United States plus eleven foreign countries. Some had never been away from home before, never flown in an airplane, never stayed in a hotel. But that didn't mean that the teenagers weren't on top of things. They were questioning the chairman and other members of the Stock Exchange about government regulations, foreign investors, and socialistic trends.

This meeting was one of seventeen seminars in which the students took part. They quizzed corporation presidents on how they run their businesses, asked sports superstars to justify their huge salaries, and challenged television and newspaper reporters. It was all part of the 1978 Hugh O'Brian Youth Foundation International Leadership Seminar on America's Incentive System.

O'Brian is the actor who portrayed the legendary lawman Wyatt Earp on television. He has organized and held these seminars for twenty years. Says O'Brian, "The purpose of this program is to give students with leadership potential the opportunity to develop their talents. By letting them speak with recognized leaders in business, government, and education, they are given the chance to better understand and appreciate America's economic system."

▶WHOM DID THE STUDENTS MEET?

The young students, their counselors, and O'Brian formed an easy-to-recognize group as they walked around the Stock Exchange or toured a company. They all wore bright red windbreakers decorated with the American flag and the foundation emblem. The students also wore name tags, showing the states or countries they represented.

The 1978 seminars included authorities from many walks of life:

New York City leaders spoke about the problems of running a city.

Top executives of W. R. Grace and Company discussed manufacturing and retailing.

Scientists from Columbia University described world resources.

IBM executives explained why computers are so important in our economy.

NBC anchorman John Chancellor and other journalists discussed the role of television and newspapers in a free society.

Officers of Texaco and Gulf Oil spoke about the energy crisis.

Muhammad Ali dominated the seminar "The Business of Sports."

Executives from Coca-Cola, American Telephone and Telegraph, Allstate Insurance, and other firms explained the role of money in the American economy.

But the most exciting for many of the teenagers was the seminar "The Business of Sports." The presidents of Texaco and IBM were unknown names to most of the students before they attended the seminars. But Muhammad Ali and Rod Gilbert were heroes. These two sports greats were bombarded with questions. Ali dominated the evening. He talked about his career and his religion. He told the students how important attitude is in determining whether you are a success or a failure. He even recited the poem he had written about his scheduled rematch with Leon Spinks.

▶ HOW IT ALL CAME ABOUT

The inspiration for the seminars came during Hugh O'Brian's trip to Africa in 1958. During that trip, O'Brian spent a week with Dr. Albert Schweitzer, the medical missionary who won the 1952 Nobel peace prize for his work among the sick and poor. Dr. Schweitzer's observations were very stimulating. But one remark particularly struck home with O'Brian. "The most important thing in education is to make young people think for themselves," Schweitzer had said.

As soon as O'Brian returned home, he began to put Dr. Schweitzer's words into action. He set up the foundation to bring together 10th-grade students and distinguished national leaders, so that the two groups could interact.

From 1958 to 1967, the Leadership Seminars took place in Los Angeles, for students from that area. Since 1968, the program has grown to include national and international participants.

All high school sophomores are eligible to compete for the honor of attending the week-long, all-expenses-paid program. At least two students from each state are chosen. O'Brian asks only one thing of the students who attend the seminars: that they write to him each year on their birthdays, until they reach the age of 30. He asks them to write about their accomplishments and successes, as well as about their defeats and frustrations in reaching their goals. In turn, he writes to them each year on his birthday.

"The young people's letters show that they are putting to practical use their leadership potential," says O'Brian. "The majority of them have become active in student government in high school or college. And 70 percent of the students are pointed to careers in business and industry, law, and the health sciences. They really are tomorrow's leaders."

Ann Berk, station manager of NBC, was one of the many executives who spoke to the students.

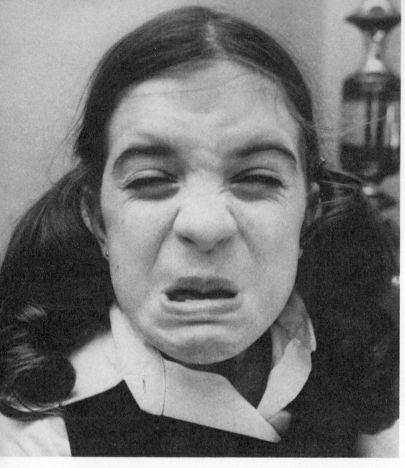

YOUNG HEADLINERS

Good things often come in small packages. In 1978, when she was only 10 years old, Quinn Cummings was nominated for an Academy Award as best supporting actress for her role in the popular movie *The Goodbye Girl.* Here, Quinn is going through her routine of facial expressions.

In April, 200 young musicians demonstrated their skills in the Suzuki International Children's Concert held at Carnegie Hall in New York City. Half of them were Japanese and half were Americans, and they ranged in age from 5 years to the mid-teens. In the applauding audience was Shinichi Suzuki. He founded the world-famous Suzuki method of teaching music to children.

"How do you spell 'deification'?" The correct answer to that question made Peg McCarthy of Topeka, Kansas, the winner of the 51st National Spelling Bee. In the background, the runner-up shows her great disappointment.

This young artist is 13-year-old Wlodek (VWO-deck) Koss. His paintings hang in many art galleries. And in 1978 he had his own one-man show at a major New York gallery. Wlodek went to America from Poland when he was 6 years old and soon began to paint. To Wlodek, painting is "always new. There are always new colors, new shapes—and my imagination."

ANDY GIBB: A SINGER IN HIS OWN RIGHT

Nearly everyone has heard of Robin, Maurice, and Barry Gibb. They're the famous Gibb brothers, better known to millions of popular music fans as the Bee Gees. But while the Bee Gees were busy climbing to the top of the music charts with the songs they wrote for the film *Saturday Night Fever,* another Gibb brother was making a name for himself. Andy Gibb, the youngest member of the Gibb family, moved from the shadow of his famous brothers to become a singer and songwriter in his own right.

Andy was just 20 years old when "I Just Want to Be Your Everything" became his first gold record. He followed that single with another hit, "Love Is Thicker Than Water."

His first album, *Flowing Rivers,* sold well over half a million copies. "Shadow Dancing," written by Andy and his brothers, became his third consecutive single and the title song of a best-selling album.

Andy Gibb grew up surrounded by music—and by his brothers' fame. He was born on March 5, 1958, in Manchester, England. His mother had been a singer, and his father was the drummer and leader of a big band. When Andy was six months old, his family moved to Australia, where his brothers started their music careers. Nine years later, the Gibbs returned to England. His first taste of fame came during this period—his brothers' popularity was so high that hundreds of Bee Gees fans gathered around the Gibb house every day.

But it was quite a while before the same kind of adulation was directed at Andy. He made his singing debut when the Gibbs moved to Ibiza, a small island off the coast of Spain. When he was 13, Andy was performing at local clubs on the island, receiving free cokes and food as his pay. And when Andy's family moved again (this time to the Isle of Man, an island off the coast of Britain in the Irish Sea), Andy formed a band that played regularly at local clubs.

Following the advice of his brothers, Andy returned to Australia to get his act together when he was 16 years old. He had planned to spend five years studying and perfecting his craft. But Andy's popularity with Australian audiences caught the attention of Robert Stigwood, the Bee Gees' manager. He invited Andy to the United States to make some demonstration tapes. And the rest is show business history.

Though greatly influenced by his brothers, Andy Gibb has a style that is definitely his own. "I like ballads," Andy has said, "but energetic as well as romantic, not dreary tearjerkers. They have to be up-tempo things, positive energy." He calls his own compositions "beagle"—a cross between the Bee Gees and the Eagles, another popular singing group. Whatever his music is called, Andy Gibb offers a positive note to the late 1970's music scene.

TRACY CAULKINS: IN THE SWIM OF THINGS

Tracy Caulkins, of Nashville, Tennessee, has probably made the biggest splash in swimming news since Mark Spitz won seven gold medals at the 1972 Olympic Games.

By the end of 1978, 15-year-old Tracy had succeeded in capturing three world swimming records and ten U.S. records. She was the first woman to swim the 200-meter individual medley in less than two minutes. And perhaps her most astounding accomplishment was a time of 4:40.83 in the 400-meter individual medley—a time that beat the former women's mark by nearly two seconds. In all, she has been awarded more than 500 medals in swimming competitions on four continents.

Tracy's swimming career began when she was eight years old. At that age, she concentrated on perfecting her backstroke because she didn't like to get her face wet. But she was winning in Amateur Athletic Union competitions within a year. And at the age of 11, she was setting records for her age group.

Now Tracy does every stroke. But because swimmers may compete in no more than four individual events, she concentrates on the butterfly and the breaststroke, her strongest strokes. She also swims in freestyle and backstroke events.

Becoming a champion is no easy accomplishment. To reach peak performance, Tracy has set rigid rules for herself. She is in the pool six mornings a week at 6:30 A.M. and swims as much as 10 miles (16 kilometers) a day. She rounds out her training by running and by lifting weights three times a week. There isn't much that can keep Tracy out of the water. Even when she broke her right leg in 1977, she swam for six weeks in a specially designed fiberglass cast.

Although she takes five weeks off each school year to attend swimming meets, Tracy manages to do well at her school in Nashville. And the hard work of training produces results. In August, 1978, Tracy was awarded five gold medals and one silver medal at the World Aquatic Championships in Berlin.

Tracy's extraordinary achievement helped her team end the dominant role of East Germany's women swimmers, who had been winning in international competitions for five years. The East German team had won eleven of thirteen gold medals at the 1976 Olympic Games. But the U.S. women's swimming team, with Tracy Caulkins, now has high hopes of capturing a good share of the medals at the Olympic Games that will be held in Moscow in the summer of 1980.

A MUSEUM JUST FOR YOU

Use a windmill to pump water. Play "Chopsticks" on a calliophone. Run a steam engine and mill some grain. Examine a flintlock gun and an insect collection. Relax and listen to folktales.

At the Brooklyn Children's Museum, there are dozens of things to do and see. The museum, in New York City, opened in 1899. It is the oldest children's museum in the world. A few years ago, it moved into a new home that is mostly underground. And it has been designed just for you!

Visitors enter the museum through an antique kiosk that once marked the entrance to a New York City subway station. Then they walk down a ramp, into a long corrugated tunnel. This is the People Tube. In the tube and in nearby open areas are all sorts of displays and equipment. Visitors are encouraged to use machines, play instruments, climb inside a giant diamond, and look through microscopes. You will have many exciting, fun-filled hours at the Brooklyn Children's Museum.

This aerial bridge leads to the roof of the museum, where there is a Sky Theater.

You can operate this steam engine. By attaching various tools to the engine's drive shaft, you can make it do different kinds of work.

This insect collection is just one of the many fascinating exhibits found at the museum.

Children examine a collection of bones. In the background is a model of a diamond crystal — 8,000,000,000 (billion) times larger than the real thing.

The museum holds many workshops. Here, children are designing their own masks after having studied carved wooden masks that come from western Africa.

A stream of water runs through the neon-lit People Tube. You can operate pumps, valves, and other equipment, thereby raising or lowering water levels — or even stopping the flow of water completely.

These children are playing a drum from Ghana. The museum also has a Japanese zither, a Nigerian flute, and a New Guinea drum that is shaped like a crocodile.

YOUNG ARTISTS

These lovely works of art are all from the Eighth International Children's Art Exhibition, which was seen around the world in 1978. Young people aged 5 to 15 from 65 countries sent in their artworks. A panel of Japanese art teachers chose which of the many entries would become part of the year-long exhibition.

The artworks that were selected were imaginative and unusual, rather than just skillfully drawn. They all show how young people from many nations see the world around them. If you look carefully at the pictures, you will see the differences—and similarities—in the ways people live.

To find out how to enter a future exhibition, write to:

International Children's Art Exhibition
2715 Columbia Street
Torrance, California 90503

Raking Autumn Leaves,
by Lisa Schimmens, 8, Canada

Untitled, by Lamio Fissal, 11, Qatar

Mr. Pot, by Albert Lake, Jr., 14, United States

Timbers, by Yoshie Hoyashi, 15, Japan

Untitled,
by Sandra Onosato, 8, Brazil

Our House, by Samanto Broaders, 5, Ireland

The Sleeping Sun,
by Repusseau Hughes, 12, France

Lunch Is Ready, by Tanya Parshintzewa, 11, Soviet Union

THE CREATIVE WORLD

Many of the peasants of China are now painting as well as working in the fields. In 1978 their colorful art, which reflects their way of life, toured the United States for the first time.

Pompeii, as it stands today.

ONE DAY IN POMPEII

It was August 24, in the year A.D. 79. The place was Pompeii—a Roman city located in Italy, south of Naples. About 20,000 people lived there.

As the sun rose in the early morning, it brought the promise of a beautiful day. People awoke and got up. They saw the sun and were happy. Soon the people were busy working. Pompeii had many restaurants, wine shops, bakeries, and stores. There were shops where wool fabrics were woven and factories where pottery and iron tools were made. There were olive groves and vineyards in the city's outskirts.

In the homes, women gave orders to their slaves. Perhaps they went outside into their gardens. And as they picked flowers, perhaps they looked up at nearby Mount Vesuvius. "How beautiful the mountain looks," they may have thought. "How peaceful is the day."

BOOM! Around midday the peace was shattered by a huge noise. It sounded like thunder, and the ground shook. In the homes, all kinds of objects tumbled from shelves.

When people looked up at Vesuvius, they saw the most amazing sight. It had blown its top! Never before in recorded history had Mount Vesuvius done this. Flames and rocks were shooting from the mountain, and liquid rock (lava) poured out. Clouds of ash and poisonous smoke formed.

Soon the day turned as dark as night. Rocks and ash began falling on Pompeii. The fiery red lava ran down the mountainside toward the town. The people were confused and didn't know what to do. Some

Archeologists uncovered this magnificent dining room in a town near Pompeii.

This wall portrait of a man and his wife was found in a home next to a Pompeii bakery.

Many beautiful treasures that were found in Pompeii toured the United States in 1978. Included were this wall painting of a leopard (*above*); this silver hand mirror (*left*); and these emerald-and-gold earrings (*below*).

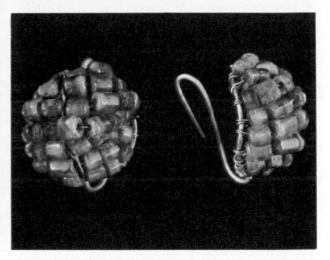

gathered in the town's big exercise ground, near the arena. Others sought safety in their homes. They closed the shutters and doors and waited for the eruption to end. A few of the richer families loaded their belongings onto donkeys and began to leave town. Chances are, they didn't escape. Like those who stayed behind, they were probably trapped by the flowing lava or choked to death by the poisonous gases.

In less than three days, Mount Vesuvius was calm again. The eruption was over. All was very quiet in Pompeii. It was quiet because the city had disappeared—buried beneath 20 feet (6 meters) of lava and ash. And all its inhabitants were dead and buried, too.

As far as we know, no one from Pompeii escaped and lived to write about this terrible event. But we have an account of the eruption written by a young Roman named Pliny. He was staying in a seaside town west of Mount Vesuvius. Wrote Pliny:

"On August 24, in the early afternoon, my mother drew attention to a cloud of unusual size and appearance . . . best expressed as being like an umbrella pine, for it rose to a great height on a sort of trunk and

This marble panel shows theater masks portraying characters in Greek comedy.

then split off into branches ... on Mount Vesuvius broad sheets of fire and leaping flames blazed at several points."

The buildings in the seaside town were shaking and, the next day, Pliny and his mother left the town. Together with many other people, they traveled along a road that led away from the mountain. "Ashes were already falling, not yet very thickly," wrote Pliny. "I looked around: A dense black cloud was coming up behind us, spreading over the earth like a flood.

"[Soon] darkness fell, not the dark of a moonless or cloudy night, but as if the lamp had been put out in a closed room. You could hear the shrieks of the women, the wailing of infants, and the shouting of men."

Time passed and, eventually, "the darkness thinned and dispersed like smoke or cloud ... the sun actually shone out, but yellowish, as it is during an eclipse. We were terrified to see everything changed, buried deep in ashes like snowdrifts."

Several towns were permanently buried by the eruption. But the thick layer of lava and ash preserved the objects it covered. It kept them from rotting or rusting. It saved them from being stolen by robbers.

For almost 1,700 years, Pompeii remained buried—and forgotten. The city was discovered in the 1730's, and in 1748 people began excavating. This work continues even now. There are still parts of the city and its suburbs to be uncovered.

But archeologists (scientists who study the remains of past human activities and civilizations) have uncovered large areas of the city. Today tourists can walk along roads where chariots raced. They can enter temples where the people of Pompeii worshipped. They can sit in theaters where Greek comedies were performed.

The archeologists also found many beautiful objects that were used in the buildings of Pompeii. Some of these are displayed at Pompeii. Others are kept in museums elsewhere, particularly in Naples. And in 1978, and exhibit of 300 of the most interesting treasures began a tour of the United States. The exhibit opened in Boston, went to Chicago and Dallas, and will end in New York in 1979.

The exhibit includes models of Pompeii and of one of the city's houses. There are sculptures, mosaics, and wall paintings. There are toys, tools, and gold jewelry. But perhaps the objects that one remembers longest are two plaster casts. As they uncovered Pompeii, archeologists found impressions of bodies in the ash. They made casts of these. One is of a sleeping dog. The other is of a young woman. She holds her dress up over her face, trying to keep from breathing the poisonous air. But her efforts were in vain. Like the bakers and woolmakers, the wine merchants and chariot riders, she died on that terrible August day 1,900 years ago.

DESIGNS FOR LIVING

Have you ever seen photographs of people who lived about a hundred years ago? Chances are that the women in the pictures had very long hair piled high atop their heads. The men were probably wearing vests. At that time, women often held their hair in place with beautiful combs carved of ivory or tortoise shell. And across the vest of every well-dressed man ran a gold chain connected to a pocket watch. The watch was usually set in a molded gold case that snapped open to show the time.

The woman's comb and the man's pocket watch have something in common. They are both examples of what we call the "decorative arts." This means they are finely designed objects that are both beautiful and useful.

▶ **WHERE ARE THEY NOW?**

Over the years, crafted combs, pocket watches, china bowls, glass vases, and other objects may have been carelessly thrown away. But with a little luck, some of the pieces may have found their way to a new museum of design in New York City—the Cooper-Hewitt Museum. This museum is a part of the famous Smithsonian Institution in Washington, D.C.

The collection of decorative art in the Cooper-Hewitt Museum was actually started back in 1897, by the spirited and wealthy Hewitt sisters—Sarah, Eleanor, and Amelia. They were the granddaughters of Peter Cooper, who founded one of the best-known schools of design in the world, the Cooper Union in New York City.

While still in their teens, the girls began buying fabrics from Europe as examples of fine design. Gradually, they collected other types of decorative art and design. These ranged from furniture and wallpaper to ceramics and glassware. As time went by, the collection grew and grew.

For many years the collection was housed in the Cooper Union building. But in 1963 the school announced that it could no longer keep the Cooper-Hewitt collection. Private citizens then began a search for a new home for the decorative arts. Finally, in 1972, the Andrew Carnegie mansion on Fifth Avenue was left as a gift to house the collection. And in 1976, the Cooper-Hewitt Museum was officially opened to the public.

The Cooper-Hewitt collection contains a wide variety of objects. You can even see a drawing that was used to make *The Yellow Submarine,* the Beatles' movie.

This stunning vase was designed by the French craftsman René Lalique. Can you see the scarab figures outlined in the glass?

Swirling vines and leaves adorn this fabric from 17th-century Italy.

▶ WHY THIS MUSEUM IS SPECIAL

You have probably visited more than one kind of museum. Perhaps you have been to an art museum, a historical museum, or a museum of natural history. Some types of objects from all three of these may be in the Cooper-Hewitt Museum. But the Cooper-Hewitt has a very special purpose that makes it different from the others.

From the very beginning, the collection was put on view to show the history of design and the decorative arts. By studying the designs of things created by people of the past, we may understand how those people saw the world around them. For example, people who lived hundreds of years ago were very close to the world of nature. Their tables and chairs might have been made of sturdy oak or walnut. The designs carved into this furniture were often of leaves, acorns, and flowers. And thousands of years ago, some peoples worshiped certain animals such as the cat. The design of a cat may spring out at you from their jewelry or wall drawings or from boxes and containers of every shape and size. This, then, is the Cooper-Hewitt's most important purpose. It houses objects whose designs are like mirrors to the past—reflections of times gone by.

On any visit to the Cooper-Hewitt, you may see beautifully embroidered materials, gem-studded jewelry from ancient Egypt, cups or spice jars made from gold or marble. You may also see elegant birdcages, which once held canaries and other songbirds that delighted royal courts of the past. You may even see toys and games such as puppets and magic lanterns—the toys of children who lived many years ago. The list is almost endless. Can you think of a more enjoyable way to begin to understand the people of history? Look at their designs. Study their decorative arts. See what they can tell you!

And should you spot an ivory comb or a gold pocket watch catching the light in what seems to be a smile, it's only because it has found a proper home at last.

ON TOUR: THE ARTS OF CHINA

China is the world's most populated nation. Almost one out of every four people in the world lives there. In all, the People's Republic of China (the official name of the mainland country) has more than 850,000,000 citizens.

For many years, the Chinese isolated themselves from the rest of the world. As a result, we knew little about the people and their everyday lives. Nor did we know about their art—their painting, music, dance.

Now things have changed. China has opened its doors. Westerners (people of Europe and the Americas) are visiting the huge country, and the Chinese are visiting us. They are also showing us examples of their rich culture. Two recent tours have been especially popular with people in Europe and North America. One was an exhibit of Chinese peasant art. The other was a touring company of performing artists.

▶THE PAINTERS OF HU-HSIEN

In central China, there is a county named Hu-hsien (Hu County). It is a lovely rural area, consisting largely of farms, small villages, and many streams.

About 20 years ago, many of the people of Hu-hsien began painting in their spare time. They painted during lunch breaks. They painted at night, after working all day on the farms or in offices. And they developed a style of painting that is different from art styles found elsewhere.

Most of the Hu-hsien paintings are landscapes. They show the peasants in their natural surroundings, doing their everyday work. One shows people digging a well. Another shows the gathering of bamboo. A third shows fishermen pulling in a net filled with fish. A fourth shows people running machines in a factory.

The paintings are very colorful and are filled with details. On first view, they look decorative and much like folk art of the Americas. However, unlike Western art, almost every painting has an instructional or political message. In one painting, for example, a straw hat bears the words, "Serve the people." A drilling rig in another paint-

Many of the Hu-hsien paintings show the peasants at work. Children, too, have jobs to do.

Everyone in China works together, and you will often see women working side by side with men.

ing has words that say, "In agriculture learn from Tachai [a model farm community]."

The titles of the paintings also tend to be instructional or political. *Electricity Comes to a Mountain Village, Celebration of Water Conservation Project, Scientific Farming Gets Results, Grasp the Gun Firmly, We Love Chairman Hua,* and *Every Family has Money in the Bank* are some examples.

The paintings always show workers who are happy and healthy—not sad or starving. The workers are always smiling. They smile while dancing and while chopping wood. They smile while pulling heavy carts and while hoeing the ground.

The buildings and land shown in the paintings are always clean and well kept. The people are always cleanly dressed, even while digging a well or planting crops. The machines look new and run correctly. And the fruits and vegetables growing in the fields are huge.

Perhaps these paintings, which show a nearly perfect kind of life, are the result of something said by the late Chinese leader, Mao Tse-tung, in 1942: "Life as reflected in works of literature and art can and ought to be on a higher plane . . . nearer the ideal, and therefore more universal than actual everyday life."

In 1976, the art of the peasant painters of Hu-hsien went on exhibit in Paris. Since then, similar paintings have been exhibited elsewhere in Europe and in North America. Westerners have learned a lot about rural life in China by studying the paintings. Most farm work there is still done by hand, using tools such as those used centuries ago. There are some trucks and tractors, but missing are the gigantic machines found on the large farms of Canada and the United States. Not missing are women: whether digging a well, pulling carts, or gathering crops, the work is shared between men and women. This sharing of work, known as collective labor, is universal in China. Everyone works together to do jobs that need doing. The paintings show people working together for the good of all—not working alone for self-reward.

263

▶**PERFORMING ARTS COMPANY**

Differences between life and thought in China and in the West can also be seen in the performing arts. Americans had a chance to enjoy some of China's best actors, singers, musicians, dancers, and acrobats when a group of them toured the United States in 1978.

Called the Performing Arts Company, the group presented selections from various Chinese art forms. The variety of numbers on the program gave Westerners a hint of the rich culture to be found in China. There were folk dances and ballet. There was music played on traditional Chinese instruments such as the bamboo flute, the erhu (a two-stringed violin), and the pipa (a lutelike instrument). There were selections from the famous Peking Opera.

Again, there were often instructional messages and patriotic themes. For example, one song includes these words: "When you

In *Red Silk Dance,* the dancers gracefully wave long ribbons of bright red silk.

drink tea from our Red base, you will never forget our revolutionary tradition."

One ballet tells of a peasant girl who is being whipped by a wicked landlord. She is found and rescued by members of the Red Army. In *Laundry Song,* Tibetan girls wash clothes for soldiers, while the soldiers fetch water for the girls. In *Militiawomen of the Grassland,* a group of booted women dance behind a red banner, waving swords and guns. Whereas in Western ballets the dancers' hands are usually delicately opened, here they are closed into fists. While in traditional Western ballets the women wear tutus, here they wear work clothes or military outfits. But not everything has a political message. In *Red Silk Dance,* twelve dancers move gracefully across the stage, waving long ribbons of bright red silk.

Perhaps the most popular number on the tour—and one of the most popular in China, too—was a selection from the Peking Opera called *Monkey Makes Havoc in Heaven.* It is a story about the Monkey King and the Jade Emperor of Heaven. The Emperor does not invite the Monkey King to the Celestial Peach Banquet. The Monkey King is very unhappy and decides to get even. He goes to the banquet anyway, eats everything in sight, tosses around peach pits and wine glasses—and makes a big mess!

The Celestial Army comes after the Monkey King, but they are clumsy and he is clever. The battle is a wonderful sight to watch. There are lots of acrobatics and exciting swordplay. Of course, the Monkey King, with some help from the other monkeys, wins. To celebrate the victory, there is baton twirling. There are only three batons but you think there are hundreds—the batons twirl so fast that all you see is a huge blur on the stage.

Monkey Makes Havoc in Heaven is a spectacular number. The actors wear gorgeous costumes of silk and other rich fabrics. Their makeup forms exotic designs of red, blue, black, and white. And there is a great deal of action, much of it funny. The audience doesn't get an inspiring political message. But it is entertained—and impressed by the great artistic talents of the Chinese people.

Monkey Makes Havoc in Heaven is a spectacular selection from the Peking Opera. It tells what the Monkey King (*right*) does when he attends the Celestial Peach Banquet (*below*).

Woody Allen (best director) and Diane Keaton (best actress) in *Annie Hall* (best picture).

1978 ACADEMY AWARDS

CATEGORY	WINNER
Motion Picture	*Annie Hall*
Actor	Richard Dreyfuss (*The Goodbye Girl*)
Actress	Diane Keaton (*Annie Hall*)
Supporting Actor	Jason Robards (*Julia*)
Supporting Actress	Vanessa Redgrave (*Julia*)
Director	Woody Allen (*Annie Hall*)
Foreign Language Film	*Madame Rosa* (France)
Song	"You Light Up My Life" *(You Light Up My Life)*
Documentary Feature	*Who Are the DeBolts? And Where Did They Get Nineteen Kids?*
Documentary Short	*Gravity Is My Enemy*
Cinematography	Vilmos Zsigmond (*Close Encounters of the Third Kind*)

Richard Dreyfuss (best actor), Marsha Mason, and Quinn Cummings in *The Goodbye Girl*.

Vanessa Redgrave (best supporting actress) and Jane Fonda in *Julia*.

Donna Summer—the queen of disco music.

THE MUSIC SCENE

Discotheques became a national craze in 1978. Partly as a result of the huge success of the film *Saturday Night Fever,* discos seemed to appear almost overnight—with spinning mirrored balls, ear-splitting recordings, and strobe lights that flashed to the beat of the music. For years, people had been doing "their own thing." Suddenly, body-contact dances like Time Warp, Detroit Shuffle, the Bump, and the Hustle were back in. Instead of guitars and romantic ballads, the records being played in the discotheques featured groups of singers and musicians that brought back the days of the big band swing era of the 1940's.

Donna Summer, the queen of disco music, took the music scene by storm. Her whispery rendition of "Love to Love You Baby" launched a career that led to a starring role in the film *Thank God It's Friday,* the best-selling album *Live and More,* and two smash singles—"Last Dance" and "MacArthur Park."

Other solo singers and groups also cashed in on the disco phenomenon. "Disco Inferno" exploded into a hit for the Tramps. "Boogie Oogie Oogie" was a number-one best seller for a Taste of Honey. Even the Rolling Stones added to the disco craze. They released their hit "Miss You" in two versions, the longer one for disco audiences.

▶NOSTALGIA: STILL POPULAR

Movies, music, and nostalgia went hand in hand in 1978. John Travolta, the popular star of the television series "Welcome Back Kotter" and the smash film *Saturday Night Fever,* hit new peaks in his career. His popularity reached fever pitch in 1978 when the film version of the long-running Broadway musical *Grease* was released. Olivia Newton-John co-starred with Travolta in this nostalgic film tribute to the 1950's. Together, these superstars recorded two Top Ten singles, "You're the One That I Want" and "Summer Nights," both from the film. Olivia had her own hit with "Hopelessly Devoted to You," another song from the *Grease* soundtrack.

Names from the past continued to crop up in 1978. Frankie Valli, who sang with the Four Seasons in the 1960's and early 1970's, returned to the charts with the title song from *Grease.* The Bee Gees, who have been a part of the popular music scene since 1967, reached superstar status thanks to the huge success of *Saturday Night Fever.* They wrote the score for the film and recorded many of the songs. And their soundtrack album of the film was heading past the 20,000,000 mark at year's end. The Bee Gees' top singles for the year included "Stayin' Alive," "Night Fever," and "How Deep Is Your Love." The Bee Gees also wrote and produced popular hits for their younger brother Andy Gibb ("Love Is Thicker Than Water") and for Samantha Sang ("Emotion").

In addition to *Grease,* there were other 1978 films that mixed nostalgia with music. Two popular ones were about the rock scene of the 1950's and 1960's. *The Buddy Holly Story* was a study of the career of the 1950's singer who died in an airplane crash. And *American Hot Wax* was based on the life of disc jockey Alan Freed (who coined the term "rock 'n' roll"). While not a major box-office success, the film version of the Beatles' celebrated album *Sgt. Pepper's Lonely Hearts Club Band* attracted enthusiastic audiences. The film starred singer Peter Frampton, the Bee Gees, and comedian George Burns.

Echoes of a bygone era could also be heard when folk groups from the civil rights and antiwar movement period re-appeared on the music scene. The Limeliters, the Kingston Trio, and Peter, Paul, and Mary all made their marks in 1978. After a separation that lasted for seven and a half years, Peter, Paul, and Mary re-assembled and played to sellout crowds in an eighteen-city tour. In the past, these fine musicians were able to get their message across with voices and guitars. Now, however, they have joined the electronic age. The trio was backed by electronic keyboards, an electronically amplified drum set, and an electric bass. The trio topped off their reunion by recording a new album, appropriately titled *Reunion.*

Nostalgia took its most curious form in the number of singers who suddenly popped up as imitators of the late Elvis Presley. They not only sang the songs he had made popular, but they also duplicated his style, mannerisms, and dress.

An interest in the past was also seen in two lively Broadway musicals. *Ain't Misbehavin',* named after a hit song written by the legendary Fats Waller, re-created the Harlem entertainment scene of the 1920's and 1930's. The musical score of *Ain't Misbehavin'* was filled with songs that Fats Waller either had written or had been associated with.

The music of ragtime pianist-composer Eubie Blake, now in his mid-90's and still active, was the basis for *Eubie!,* another Broadway blockbuster. *Eubie!* featured the tunes that Blake and Noble Sissle wrote for the all-black musical *Shuffle Along* in 1921.

▶SINGERS SING THEIR SONGS

The most controversial song of the year was "Short People," written by Randy Newman. Newman, a master of ironic humor, meant the song to be a satirical swipe at narrow-mindedness. However, the song was attacked by some groups who mistakenly thought it was a put-down of short people, and it was banned by several radio stations. In contrast to this negative reaction, Newman had his first gold album in *Little Criminals,* from which "Short People" emerged as a number-one song.

Singer-songwriter Billy Joel, who earned a gold album in 1973, returned to the best-seller charts again in 1978 with *The Stranger.* The album yielded four hit singles: "Movin' Out," "Only the Good Die Young," "Just the Way You Are," and "She's Always a Woman." Columbia Records predicted that *The Stranger* would surpass in sales its all-time best

John Travolta and Olivia Newton-John starred in the film *Grease,* a nostalgic look at the 1950's.

seller—Simon and Garfunkel's *Bridge Over Troubled Water.*

Bob Seger, Warren Zevon, Teddy Pendergrass, and Willie Nelson, each a different stylist, were other writer-performers who reached new heights in 1978. Seger dealt with his long pursuit of national recognition in *Stranger in Town,* a Top Ten album that yielded a Top Ten single in "Still the Same." Warren Zevon, a satirist like Randy Newman, achieved a high position on the record charts with his second release, *Excitable Boy. Life Is a Song Worth Singing,* featuring the hit single "Close the Door," won a platinum album for singer Teddy Pendergrass.

Legal battles kept Bruce Springsteen away from the recording studios for three years. However, 1978 saw the end of his difficulties and the debut of his new album, *Darkness on the Edge of Town.* Like his earlier albums, this, too, quickly made its way onto the Top Ten chart. "Bombastic rock," as Springsteen's explosive style was

Meat Loaf became a hit with *Bat Out of Hell.*

termed, found a new participant in Meat Loaf. Twenty-nine-year-old Marvin Lee Aday (Meat Loaf's real name) became a chart-maker with his debut album, *Bat Out of Hell,* and the single "Two Out of Three Ain't Bad."

Canada's gift to the music world is long-time favorite Gordon Lightfoot. Lightfoot's recordings have a habit of landing on the Top Ten charts shortly after their release. His latest album, *Endless Wire,* was no exception. Another Canadian, 21-year-old Dan Hill, made a hit with his third LP, *Longer Fuse.* This album produced a Top Ten single, "Sometimes When We Touch."

Britain's Elvis Costello developed his own style—a mixture of pop, rock, and punk rock. Within a year's time he delivered two albums containing 24 of his original tunes, *My Aim Is True* and *This Year's Model.*

Art Garfunkel, who kept a mysteriously low profile in music circles for several years, produced a new album, *Watermark.* He also made a 40-city tour around the United States, his first since 1970.

Linda Ronstadt maintained her position as the queen of country rock with "It's Easy," from her best-selling album *Simple Dreams.* Roberta Flack continued her string of hits with "The Closer I Get to You," from the album *Blue Lights in the Basement.* Johnny Mathis duetted with Deniece Williams to gives us one of the biggest singles of the year, "Too Much, Too Little, Too Late." And Barry Manilow showed his popularity as a middle-of-the-road performer with "Can't Smile Without You" and "Copacabana," both from his Top Ten album, *Even Now.*

▶BORDERLINE COUNTRY MUSIC

For many years, honky-tonk songwriter-singer Willie Nelson, along with Waylon Jennings, mocked the Nashville establishment. They became known as outlaws of country music. This reputation remained with the release of their album *Waylon and Willie* and their hit single "Mamas, Don't Let Your Babies Grow Up to Be Cowboys." But then Nelson surprised everybody by recording an album of romantic ballads written by Irving Berlin, George and

Gordon Lightfoot's 1978 hit album was *Endless Wire.*

Ira Gershwin, and Duke Ellington. *Stardust* quickly became a number-one album and showed Nelson's versatility as a singer and performer.

Other singers were also stretching country music boundaries. Emmylou Harris, Crystal Gayle, and Dolly Parton were just a few of the country artists who recorded distinctly non-country songs. Dolly Parton landed on the Top Ten charts with "Here You Come Again," while Crystal Gayle contributed "Don't It Make My Brown Eyes Blue" to the best-seller list.

▶A BLENDING OF VOICES

The Rolling Stones, led by Mick Jagger, toured the United States for the first time in three years. This tour was unique in that some of the antics that marked the Rolling Stones as "bad boys" of rock were omitted from their act. The Stones also recorded a highly controversial album, *Some Girls.* This album was viewed by many listeners as sexist, while others thought it was typical pessimistic Stones music.

Earth, Wind & Fire presented a pleasant change to the 1978 music scene. Not one of the nine-member group smokes or drinks. Most of the musicians are vegetarians, and they all meditate before each concert to achieve "oneness of mind." They descend onstage inside huge glass cylinders and they claim to offer music for spiritual uplift, with a blend of gospel, jazz, hard rock, and even disco. Earth, Wind & Fire made four albums that sold over 2,000,000 each. Their 1978 best seller was *All 'n All,* while "Got to Get You Into My Life" became a hit single.

Exile, a soft-rock group, became a new hit combo with "Kiss You All Over" from the album *Mixed Emotions.* Little River Band, Australia's contribution to the group effort, recorded a pop-country-style single, "Reminiscing," from their album *Sleeper Catcher.* Little Feat, one of rock's most popular groups, again hit the charts with their album *Waiting for Columbus.*

Devo, one of the hottest new bands around, took the music scene by storm with

Earth, Wind & Fire descend on stage inside large glass cylinders. Their music blends gospel, jazz, rock, disco.

Country music singers Crystal Gayle and Dolly Parton sang some non-country-style songs in 1978.

their debut album, *Q: Are We Not Men? A: We Are DEVO!* It's a record of infectious primal pop, pounding rhythms, and lyrics that satirize the frustrations of urban life. And Talking Heads, a group known for their anti-showbiz and anti-glitter behavior, recorded their second album, *More Songs About Buildings and Food.*

▶ALL THAT JAZZ

Jazz made big news in 1978 when President Jimmy Carter held a concert at the White House celebrating the 25th anniversary of the famed Newport Jazz Festival. New York City also bestowed a high honor on the world of jazz: By official proclamation, 52nd Street between 5th and 6th avenues was declared a historic landmark. In the 1940's this busy street was jammed with clubs featuring jazz musicians. It drew jazz fans from all over the world. Plans were announced to create a "jazzwalk" on the city block with the names of jazz greats embedded in the pavement.

Jazz also found a new popular entertainer in Chuck Mangione, the man with the smiling face and happy flügelhorn. His "Feels So Good" became a best-selling single and album.

▶THE SHAPE OF THINGS TO COME

With the 1970's drawing to a close, disco appears to be the one new important trend in popular music. But the rock scene is still marked by an ever-growing blending of styles—a mix of pop, jazz, gospel, and rock. The breakup of the much-heralded British Sex Pistols on their first appearance in the United States seemed to signal the end of Punk Rock, the rowdy challenge to studio rock. To many music lovers, the increased presence on best-seller charts of soft, mellow, romantic songs—with a beat—indicated a rise in the popularity of beautiful music.

ARNOLD SHAW
Author, *The Rock Revolution* and
52nd St.: The Street of Jazz

1978 GRAMMY AWARDS

Record of the Year	"Hotel California'"	Eagles, artist
Album of the Year	*Rumours*	Fleetwood Mac, artist
Song of the Year	"Love Theme from A Star Is Born"	Barbra Streisand and Paul Williams, songwriters
New Artist of the Year		Debby Boone, artist
Pop Vocal Performance—female	"Love Theme from A Star Is Born"	Barbra Streisand, artist
Pop Vocal Performance—male	"Handy Man"	James Taylor, artist
Pop Vocal Performance—group	"How Deep Is Your Love"	Bee Gees, artist
Rhythm and Blues Vocal Performance—female	"Don't Leave Me This Way"	Thelma Houston, artist
Rhythm and Blues Vocal Performance—male	*Unmistakably Lou*	Lou Rawls, artist
Country Vocal Performance—female	"Don't It Make My Brown Eyes Blue"	Crystal Gayle, artist
Country Vocal Performance—male	"Lucille"	Kenny Rogers, artist
Original Score for a Motion Picture	*Star Wars*	John Williams, composer
Score from an Original Cast Show	*Annie*	Charles Strouse and Martin Charnin, composers
Classical Album	*Concert of the Century*	Leonard Bernstein, Vladimir Horowitz, Isaac Stern, Mstislav Rostropovich, Dietrich Fisher Dieskau, Yehudi Menuhin, and Lyndon Woodside, artists
Recording for Children	*Aren't You Glad You're You*	Christopher Cerf and Jim Timmens, artists

HAPPY BIRTHDAY, MICKEY MOUSE

He is known as Topolino in Italy, Mikke Mus in Norway, Mikki Hiiri in Finland, Miki in Turkey, Micky Maus in Germany, Raton Mickey throughout South America, Mouse Pigg in Sweden, and just plain Mickey Mouse almost everywhere else.

And in 1978, Mickey Mouse celebrated his 50th birthday!

The famous little guy with the big ears is more than just another cartoon character. He has become a unique part of our cultural heritage. For generations he has held a special place in the hearts of people everywhere—both young and old. His face is possibly more familiar to more people in more countries of the world than any other face.

But despite his long career and his great fame, Mickey Mouse is still a rather modest and unassuming character, trying to laugh at and cope with the world around him.

▶FIFTY YEARS AGO . . .

It all began with Walt Disney, who created his first original animated cartoons in 1920. Soon after, he perfected a new method for combining live action and animation. Then came Mickey, who was born in Disney's imagination in 1928 on a train ride from New York to Los Angeles.

Mickey's talents were first used in a silent cartoon entitled *Plane Crazy*. However, before the cartoon could be released, sound burst upon the motion picture screen. And so Mickey made his screen debut in *Steamboat Willie,* the world's first sound cartoon. It premiered at the Colony Theater in New York on November 18, 1928.

With the success of *Steamboat Willie,* Disney added sound to *Plane Crazy* and to another silent Mickey cartoon, *Gallopin' Gaucho.* (As with all of Mickey's pictures through World War II, Walt Disney himself supplied Mickey's voice. In 1946, when Disney became too busy to continue, Jim Macdonald, a sound and vocal effects man from the Disney studio, took over.)

Mickey's skyrocket to fame didn't take long. His cartoons became so popular that people would ask if a movie house was running a "Mickey" before they would buy a ticket. Soon, theaters were displaying posters that read "Mickey Mouse playing today!" Audiences would often sit through a feature twice to see Mickey again.

In 1929, Mickey's popularity led to the Mickey Mouse Club, which met every Saturday in local theaters for an afternoon of cartoons and games. The several million Mouse

On November 18, 1928, Mickey made his screen debut in *Steamboat Willie* — the world's first cartoon with sound.

275

Soon Mickey was appearing in comic strips, on toys and other merchandise, and on TV.

Clubbers had a secret handshake, a special member greeting, a code of behavior, and even a special club song—"Minnie's Yoo Hoo."

But Mickey's popularity wasn't confined to the silver screen. By 1930 his likeness was appearing on dozens of items, including wooden toys, drums, rubber balls, rattles, cups and plates, soap, candles, glass figurines, bookends, puppets, and clothing. The first Mickey Mouse comic strip appeared January 13, 1930. The strip is still published daily in hundreds of newspapers. And the famous Mickey Mouse wristwatch, first manufactured in 1933, is now a much valued collector's item. Today, more than a thousand companies produce Disney character merchandise worldwide—from T-shirts to toothbrushes, encyclopedias to earmuffs. These items feature not only Mickey, but Donald Duck, Goofy, Snow White, Peter Pan, Winnie the Pooh, and dozens of other Disney-designed personalities.

The peak of Mickey's golden decade oc-

curred in 1940, with his starring role in the feature-length film *Fantasia*. A major artistic innovation, it interpreted music in colors, shapes, movement, and story. The animation techniques, which were years ahead of their time, have never been matched. *Fantasia* also introduced stereophonic sound to theaters, an element not used by other studios until more than 10 years later.

During World War II, the Disney Studio suspended nearly all commercial activity and concentrated on aiding the war effort with training films, goodwill tours, and the designing of posters and armed forces insignia. Mickey played his part by appearing on insignia and on posters that urged national security and the purchase of war bonds. And, incredibly, the password of the Allied forces on D-Day, June 6, 1944, was "Mickey Mouse."

Following the war, Mickey returned to making cartoons. In 1947 he appeared in his second feature, *Fun and Fancy Free,* in which he costarred with Goofy and Donald

Mickey had the starring role in *Fantasia* — which interpreted music in colors, shapes, and movement.

Duck in a new version of Jack and the Beanstalk.

Through the 1940's and 1950's, Mickey made fewer cartoons, giving ground to Donald, Goofy, and Pluto, who were more flexible as characters. Mickey's evolution into a Disney symbol made it increasingly difficult to create story situations for him. If he lost his temper or did anything sneaky, fans would write in insisting "Mickey just wouldn't do that."

In 1955, Disney agreed to create an afternoon television program. That was the start of "The Mickey Mouse Club," which became one of the most successful children's shows ever. In 1977, "The New Mickey Mouse Club," featuring twelve new Mouseketeers, made its debut on television.

▶A MOST SPECTACULAR BIRTHDAY

To help celebrate Mickey's 50th birthday, Walt Disney Productions produced a 90-minute TV special on November 19, 1978, called "Mickey's 50." The program was the biggest birthday celebration in Hollywood history, and it traced the creation and career of Mickey Mouse and included highlights from his many films.

Both Disneyland in California and Walt Disney World in Florida held parades down Main Street in Mickey's honor, featuring floats and more than 50 costumed characters. Articles on Mickey appeared in major newspapers and magazines. Dozens of schools, clubs, even whole communities had special activities to celebrate the event. And an Amtrak train, called The Mickey Mouse Special, traveled from coast to coast carrying Mickey on a whistle-stop tour.

Now that Mickey has reached middle-age, we can look back and understand why the Mickey of the 1930's was so popular. He was a little guy, born out of the Depression years, who satirized people's foibles and taught them to laugh. Most importantly, he was a character who dreamed dreams that were shared around the world.

WALT DISNEY PRODUCTIONS

WHAT DO YOU SEE IN THIS PICTURE?

Look carefully at this picture. You will see a young boy, all alone, playing a fife. Rich reds and golds are silhouetted in black, adding striking qualities to the work. The cadet's left foot casts a shadow, but there are no background objects. The painting seems almost flat. It is a direct painting, with no flourishes or showiness.

The Fifer was painted by Édouard Manet, a French artist who was a pioneer of modern art. Today it is considered a masterpiece. But it was not always so.

In the summer of 1865, Manet, then 34, returned to his home in Paris after having spent two weeks in Madrid. He had been studying the works of Diego Velázquez, a Spanish Renaissance painter. Inspired by the simplicity of Velázquez' canvases, he began to paint *The Fifer*. A friend, Commandant Lejosne, arranged for a young cadet musician to pose for Manet, to help make the painting realistic.

Manet spent more than a year preparing the painting for an exhibit at the famous Salon in Paris. There, wealthy, middle-class people gathered to buy artworks that had been selected by a jury. The jury had turned down Manet's work before. In fact, Manet had written to a friend, "Insults pour down on me like hail." But he still hoped *The Fifer* would win a place at the Salon.

Manet finally received word from the jury. His painting had been turned down. The painting's bold, simple lines and lack of depth had offended the critics. They also downgraded Manet's work because it contained no landscape scenes and told no stories. Those were the kinds of paintings that won popularity in his day.

Oddly enough, Manet belonged to the very upper middle class that rejected his masterpieces. He became a rebel in spite of himself.

Born into a cultured family in Paris in 1832, Manet attended College Rollin. He sailed on a naval training vessel to Rio de Janiero, Brazil. But the world of art beckoned irresistibly, and he began six years of study at L'Ecole des Beaux Arts (The School of Fine Arts) in Paris.

Manet interrupted his work with frequent trips to other European countries, where he studied masters like Titian, Velázquez, Rembrandt, and Frans Hals. Manet and his teacher often had long arguments over how paintings should be done. The artist did not intend to rebel against the usual ways of painting. But his instincts led him to do works that looked different from those of other painters of his day.

Manet believed that art should take people and objects from the real world as its subjects. He wanted to capture the richness of his own times on his canvases. "One must be of one's own day and age," he once said. The realism and directness of *The Fifer* show this.

Manet was a very quiet person, and it is said that he lived, ate, and slept painting. A few years after having finished *The Fifer,* he laid down his paintbrush and took up a gun as a member of the National Guard in the Franco-German War of 1870. The last thirteen years of his life were not easy ones. Money problems worried him at times. And an illness, which was to cause his death in 1883, began to plague him.

Nonetheless, bright spots colored the horizon. In 1880 the Salon awarded him a second prize. He had finally won the privilege of exhibiting there. And his friend Antonin Proust, Minister of Fine Arts, arranged for him to receive the Legion d'Honneur, a prestigious award of the French Government.

Furthermore, a new group of artists, now known as the impressionists, thronged about Manet. Their paintings reflected the immediate sensations that subjects made on them.

Today, Manet stands out as a pioneer. He led the way for the development of modern art, where the interest lies in the elements of painting rather than in a story or landscape. Time has proved the critics wrong, and *The Fifer* has won its rightful place as a masterpiece. Today art lovers all over the world appreciate the rich heritage of the talented Édouard Manet.

LOUISE D. MORRISON
The Harpeth Hall School (Nashville, Tennessee)

JOHN MASEFIELD: IN LOVE WITH THE SEA

> I must go down to the seas again,
> to the lonely sea and the sky,
> And all that I ask is a tall ship
> and a star to steer her by.

These words, from the poem *Sea-Fever*, were written by John Masefield, who is often called "the poet of the sea." He was Britain's fifteenth poet laureate, and he held that honor longer than any other writer except Alfred Tennyson. In 1978, we celebrated the 100th anniversary of Masefield's birth.

Masefield was born in Ledbury, England, in 1878. His parents died while he was still a child, and he was brought up by an uncle. When he was 13 years old, he went to sea as an apprentice on a windjammer. Later, he sailed around Cape Horn.

But after only a few years, Masefield abandoned his seafaring life because of illness. He then spent several years working at various odd jobs in and around New York City—baker, stableboy, and bartender. In one of his books, *In the Mill*, he describes his work spotting flaws in rugs at a Yonkers carpet factory.

In 1897 he returned to London to write, working for a time as a journalist on the *Manchester Guardian*. He married in 1903 and had two children.

Masefield's time at sea had been short, but it inspired many of his writings. His first book of poems, *Salt-Water Ballads*, was published in 1902. It contains some of the most famous of his poems celebrating the beauty of the sea.

The readers of Masefield's day knew him best for long, realistic, narrative poems that told of English life. The first of these, *The Everlasting Mercy*, is about a drunken poacher. It shocked the literary world with its frank, earthy language.

But Masefield was also a novelist, a literary critic, and a playwright. His rousing adventure stories attracted wide audiences. Many of his works were based on his own varied and active life. The book *Gallipoli*, for example, was based on his battle experiences as part of a Red Cross unit during World War I. And Masefield illustrated many of his own works. *Reynard the Fox*, an epic poem about a fox hunt, contained more than a hundred of his own watercolor and pen-and-ink drawings.

By 1930, Masefield's work had become so popular that George V appointed him poet laureate. Masefield was awarded the Order of Merit in 1935 and remained poet laureate until his death in 1967.

SOME OTHER MASEFIELD WORKS

Poems: *The Widow in the Bye Street; The Daffodil Fields; Dauber; Lollingdon Downs; Right Royal; The Bluebells, and Other Verse.*

Plays: *The Tragedy of Nan, and Other Plays; The Tragedy of Pompey the Great; Good Friday; End and Beginning.*

Novels: *Multitude and Solitude; Sard Harker; The Bird of Dawning.*

Autobiographical Prose: *New Chum; So Long to Learn; Grace Before Ploughing, Fragments of Autobiography.*

LA SCALA: TWO CENTURIES OF OPERA

Italy is known as the birthplace of grand opera. And La Scala, in Milan, Italy, is considered by many to be the greatest opera house in the world. In 1978, La Scala celebrated its 200th anniversary.

Teatro alla Scala, better known as La Scala, opened its doors in 1778 on the former site of the church of Santa Maria alla Scala. For decades, elegant carriages brought beautifully dressed aristocrats and intellectuals to their boxes there. The theater was destroyed by Allied bombardment during World War II, but it re-opened in 1946. It was rebuilt according to the original designs and has lost none of its historic glory.

Opera is a spectacle, and it deserves a spectacular setting. La Scala—with its pink marble floors, glittering chandeliers, ornate boxes, and marble columns—gives it one. In the lobby are statues of four legendary Italian operatic composers who gained fame there in the 19th century—Guiseppe Verdi, Vincenzo Bellini, Gaetano Donizetti, and Gioacchino Rossini.

Among the many famous operas that had their first performances on La Scala's stage are Verdi's *Falstaff* and *Otello*, Bellini's *Norma*, and Giacomo Puccini's *Madama Butterfly* and *Turandot*.

Singers vie to perform at La Scala, with its rich history, perfect acoustics, and knowledgeable audiences. Italians from all walks of life know opera scores by heart and worship great voices. Almost every opera star of note has performed there, and the seats are usually sold out far in advance.

La Scala is also used for concerts, ballets, and recitals. Violinist Niccolò Paganini, pianist-composer Franz Liszt, and dancers Vaslav Nijinsky and Carla Fracci performed on its stage. The conductor Arturo Toscanini made his La Scala debut in 1896, and he conducted the gala re-opening in 1946.

In addition to the main auditorium, La Scala has a smaller theater for opera and chamber music. The building also houses a theatrical museum, to which a special Verdi museum is attached. After 200 years, La Scala remains a visible statement of Italy's rich musical heritage.

For decades, elegant carriages brought beautifully dressed people to the La Scala opera house (*at right*).

RUNAWAYS

Have you ever felt like running away from home? At one time or another, most of us have thought about doing it. And each year, more than 1,000,000 youngsters actually do run away from home.

A young woman named Elizabeth Swados wrote a musical show about boys and girls who run away from home. Its title is, simply, *Runaways*. The show opened in New York City in 1978 and it was praised by critics and general audiences alike. "*Runaways* seizes your heart," wrote one critic. "It makes me want to go home and kiss my kids," said a mother who saw the play.

There are 26 people in the cast. They range in age from 11 to the early 20's. They include blacks, whites, and Hispanics. Some are professional actors, others aren't. Some have a wonderful home life, with loving parents. But other cast members really were runaways or "problem" children.

In the play they represent children from many different backgrounds. There are poor kids and middle-class kids. One boy is a skateboard champ. Another is a graffiti artist. A third is a deaf-mute who speaks in sign language.

It's not a happy show. But then, it's not about a happy life. As one boy sings in the show, "When you're out there on the street you are all alone."

Swados talked to about 2,000 kids as she gathered information about runaways. She talked to them at schools, museums, community centers, and on the street. The world of the runaway, she found, is one of desperation, loneliness, and isolation.

In many of the play's songs, the youngsters tell why then ran away. They tell of parents who fight. They tell of parents who beat them—or perhaps even worse, ignore them. They tell of their fear of flunking classes.

But life on the street may be much, much worse. First, there is the struggle to survive. The runaways have to hunt for food. They often shoplift from supermarkets or eat food scraps they find in garbage cans. To get money, they beg or sell phony raffle tickets. Finding a place to stay is another problem.

So is keeping out of the hands of drug pushers and other criminals who prey on children.

The actors sing of these problems in songs set to a variety of music: rock, pop, blues, jazz, salsa. Occasionally, police sirens and other typical street noises are heard. All of the play's action takes place on a city basketball court. It is an unattractive place, surrounded by a high steel fence. There is no beauty there. But it is very much like the places where runaways actually do gather in big cities ... gather to search for friendliness, for love, for someone who will care for them.

Fantasy—the world of make-believe—is very important to runaways (and to children everywhere). Swados learned this as she worked with her young performers. "That's how a lot of them survive," she says. "It's for protection. Every single one of them, whether they were poor or middle-class, from an unhappy home or a well-adjusted home, had the most incredible imaginary world."

As she listened to the fantasies, Swados was reminded of the fantasies she herself had as a child. One of her fantasies became the basis of a song in the show. The song, "Appendectomy," is sung by a young girl who holds a limp cloth doll. The girl imagines that the doll needs to have its appendix removed. As she tends to the doll, she sings: "The rubber bands, please. It looks as if this child has also got a broken heart." Broken hearts are something that runaways seem to share.

Swados and the boys and girls who perform in *Runaways* tell us a very touching story. As people leave the theater, perhaps the thought that lingers in their minds is a plea made by children everywhere:

"Let me be a kid."

"Let me be young before I get old."

For runaways this isn't possible. On the streets, children grow up before their time.

Will the bird turn into a prince after she kisses it? fantasizes one of the runaways.

The runaways represent young people from many different backgrounds. One boy is a graffiti artist.

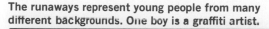

A TRIUMPH IN TRIANGLES

Many museums and art galleries are stern, dark buildings, where people go to view works of art. These buildings exist to house the great art works of the centuries—but not to give them "a home." In recent years, though, people who are responsible for commissioning new art centers have worked along with respected architects to break the mold of the past. And nowhere is this "home building" more apparent than in the brand new East Building of the National Gallery of Art in Washington, D.C.

▶PLANNING THE NEW BUILDING

The National Gallery of Art is the official museum for the people of the United States. The original structure, today called the West Building, was designed by John Russell Pope. When it was opened in 1941, the gallery contained fewer than 200 art works. Today the number has grown to 40,000.

About ten years ago, the people at the National Gallery of Art began to work on a project that was much larger than simply acquiring more works of art: the planning of the new east wing. There were two main reasons for its construction. First, more space was needed to house the gallery's ever-growing permanent collection. The second reason was the desire to build a study center for art scholars.

The architect of the East Building, I.M. Pei, had a puzzle to solve before he could even draw up a basic blueprint. The land on which the new wing was to be built was shaped like a trapezoid. A trapezoid is a shape that is something like a rectangle, but with slanting sides and a top and bottom of unequal lengths.

Pei began trying different sketches on paper. Nothing seemed workable for the oddly shaped piece of land. As Pei concentrated on the shape of the trapezoid, the answer to the puzzle emerged: two buildings in the shape of triangles—one large isosceles triangle for exhibition galleries, and one smaller right triangle for the study center. This simple sketch was to grow into a building so beautiful that many critics consider it a work of art in itself.

▶TRIANGLES AND GLASS

The East Building, which opened on June 1, 1978, is located on the Washington Mall, next to the West Building. A visitor approaching the building may first notice that it is made of the same pink marble as the older structure. In fact, the marble was taken from the same quarry in Tennessee that provided the original. Once inside, a world of marble, glass, and bold geometric shapes allows visitors to wander in an uncrowded atmosphere of space and light.

The plaza between the East building and the West Building is dotted with triangular glass structures. These are actually the skylights of the restaurants on the level below. From the restaurant area a visitor can board a "people mover"—a moving sidewalk running through a tunnel decorated with gleaming strips of metal. At the end of the tunnel is the spectacular central court that joins both triangles of the new building. The massive skylight over the court is composed of a repeated pattern of glass triangles, bathing the court in a prism of light. The most dominant artwork in the courtyard is the huge mobile created by Alexander Calder. It is the largest mobile ever designed by the artist and is made of aluminum to allow its dangling shapes to move freely in the air.

The exhibition space in the larger triangle will be used primarily for temporary exhibits. The space is so flexible that walls can be moved and ceilings raised or lowered to show each exhibit to its best advantage.

The smaller triangle of the East Building, which is the study center, will not open until 1979. But it already has an art library containing more than 300,000 books and a photographic file of over 1,000,000 prints.

The East Building of the National Gallery of Art provides a cheerful yet elegant home for the works that it contains. And, like any friendly host, it welcomes visitors warmly, inviting an inspection of its treasures. Perhaps its atmosphere has been best described by the gallery's director—"Lots of buildings seem to say, 'You're not good enough to enter me.' Our building says, 'Try it, you'll like it.'"

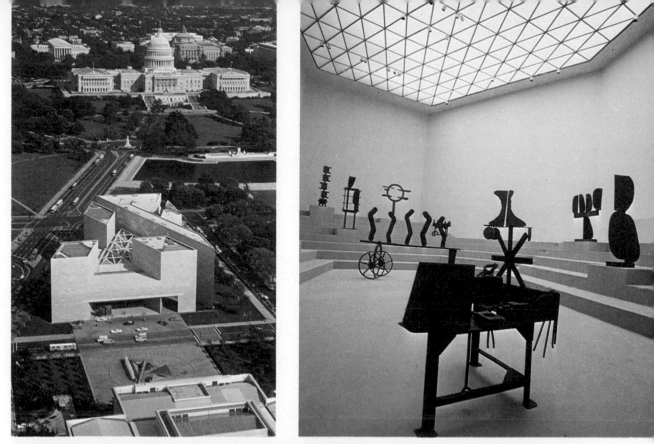

Inside and outside, the new East Building of the National Gallery of Art is truly a triumph in triangles!

FUN TO READ

An illustration from *Noah's Ark*, by Peter Spier. This beautiful picture story is told without words and was the winner of the 1978 Caldecott Award.

The Grocery Boat

Laura and Mark Lathrop lounged in the sun as they gazed wistfully at the twenty-two-foot cabin cruiser, rocking in the slip by their dock. It was there for the Lathrops to enjoy, because the use of the boat was included in the rent they were paying for the summer cottage at Lake Belvedere. But the beautiful craft might as well have been anchored in the Baltic Sea for the little bit of use Laura and Mark got out of it.

"If only that cruiser weren't such a 'gas hog,' we could drive it up to Miller's Point this morning," sighed Laura. "Oh, I just love riding in that boat! It's like skimming over the water on the back of a sea gull."

"With gas at sixty-five cents a gallon we can barely afford to circle our cove, let alone drive twenty miles to the point," Mark grumbled.

Just then a familiar car pulled up beside their cottage. "It's Dad!" cried Laura. "He's arrived for the weekend—already!"

"It's always good to see old Dad," gloated Mark as they raced across the beach. "But it's especially good today, because it's payday for us!"

Laura nodded. "With our combined allowances we can buy enough gas for a couple of cruiser rides this week, at least."

When they reached the car, Mr. Lathrop gave them each a playful left to the jaw and asked them to help carry in his suitcases and fishing gear. Then Mom whipped up a snack of milk and cookies and asked Dad about his week at his city office.

"It was a long, hot, busy week," he replied. "I can't wait to get into my old clothes and start fishing."

"Sure you don't want to go fishing in the cabin cruiser, Dad? We'll go along and help drive it," Laura coaxed.

Mr. Lathrop's eyes grew stern. "I thought we had that all settled," he said. "I told you that the rowboat was just right for the kind of fishing I like to do. I don't need to run an expensive cruiser to catch a few lake trout."

Laura and Mark groaned a bit, but put up no further argument. For, though Dad had taught them how to drive the cruiser at the beginning of the summer, it had been understood that Laura and Mark would have to provide the gas for any cruising they might wish to do on their own. Dad did not believe in pampering young people. The family vacation budget did not allow for the running and upkeep of a luxurious cabin cruiser. In fact, when they had rented the cottage, they had not realized that the use of the boat was part of the contract. Now its presence was a constant temptation, especially to Laura and Mark.

"Well, you know your mother and I have no objection if you wish to spend your own money on gas," said Dad, as he took some bills out of his wallet. "So it's up to you."

Happily they thanked him for their allowances. But then Laura commented ruefully, "Buying gas for the boat doesn't leave much for anything else. Skip Ballard's dad keeps their boat full of gas. Skip cruises all over the lake and doesn't have to spend a nickel."

"Well, I'm not Skip Ballard's dad," Mr. Lathrop replied. "And glad of it. I've observed that people who have things handed to them on a silver platter expect that silver platter to be handed to them for the rest of their lives."

"Even though we envy Skip, we don't expect constant handouts," Mark protested. "We'd just be content to find a way to earn more gas money. All the summer jobs here have been filled by older kids."

"It may seem so," Mrs. Lathrop spoke up, "but if one really wants to earn money bad enough, there's usually a way to do it. And when you find the way it can be very satisfying. Why, when I was a teenager, I made fifty dollars one summer, making rag dolls out of old socks."

"As a matter of fact," grinned Dad, "right now I'll offer a quarter to anyone who'll run up to Gruber's Grocery and bring me a quart of lime sherbet. It'll really hit the spot."

Both Laura and Mark jumped at the offer. They were planning to drive the cruiser to the store anyway. They wanted to buy boat fuel at Gruber's gas pump. And Dad's sherbet would stay firm in the boat's galley refrigerator until they returned.

Then Mom wrote something on a note pad. "Since you're driving up to the store anyway, you can bring home the things on this list, too," she said. "Just have Mr. Gruber charge them."

Laura and Mark raced down to the dock. Just then Mrs. Jansen from next door called to them, "If you two happen to stop at Gruber's Grocery, would you mind bringing me three pounds of hot dogs? We're having unexpected guests for a cookout."

"OK," Laura called back. "You can count on it."

"Do you think you could bring back a quart of milk and a loaf of bread for us?" Mr. Larkin called over from his dock.

"Sure thing," Mark nodded.

Laura and Mark quickly slipped on their life jackets, and soon they were chugging off toward Gruber's. Laura added the neighbors' requests to Mom's list. "If this sort of thing keeps on, we could set ourselves up in business," she giggled. "The Lathrop Delivery Service! It's lucky that the galley refrigerator and cupboards are big."

"That's the great thing about this boat," said Mark, as he navigated the cruiser along the cove. "It's so roomy we could carry half of Mr. Gruber's stock with us and some passengers besides."

"That's why it uses up so much gas," sighed Laura.

Soon they tied up at the dock in front of Gruber's Grocery.

First they asked Mr. Gruber to pump five gallons of gas into the cruiser's tank. Then they both hurried into the store with the list. As Mr. Gruber gathered the items together, Laura noticed that they were his only customers. "How come your store is so empty, Mr. Gruber?" she asked. "Your business is usually good on weekends."

"Haven't you heard? That new supermarket at Sunset End opened on Monday," he replied gloomily. "I hardly sold enough to break even this week."

"Oh, I'm sure your steady customers will stick by you," said Mark.

"Can't count on it," Mr. Gruber sighed. "It's mighty hard for us independent grocers to compete with big chain-store prices . . . oh, by the way, since you live near the Olcotts, would you mind dropping off these boxes of fresh strawberries? It will save them a trip up here."

"We'd be glad to," Laura laughed. "As you see, we're practically in the delivery business, anyway."

Then she noticed that Mark was gazing thoughtfully up at the shelves and jotting down prices on the pad. At last he said, "Mr. Gruber, your prices are about the same as chain-store prices."

"I know," he replied. "It's just that most people have the notion that big markets sell much more cheaply than small ones."

"Well, the way to compete with that new supermarket is to keep a couple of jumps ahead of them," Mark said. "You could offer your customers a special service. And Laura and I can supply that service."

"Just what would that be?" Mr. Gruber asked skeptically.

"A grocery boat!" cried Mark. Then he explained his plan.

Every morning he and Laura would drive the cabin cruiser up to Gruber's and load it with groceries. Besides canned goods and fresh produce, they would carry plenty of the kinds of foods that cottagers constantly need—bread, milk, eggs, snacks, and soft drinks, for example. Then they would drive their boat up and down Lake Belvedere, stopping frequently at various docks to make sales.

"Think how convenient it would be for shoppers!" Laura exclaimed, as Mark's idea captured her imagination. "Lots of people wouldn't bother to go to the supermarket if they knew a floating store would be docking nearby every day."

Mr. Gruber's eyes gleamed with excitement. "By Jove, I think you have something there! I've heard that some lake grocers provide floating stores. As for myself, I've never had enough money to invest in a boat. Now, how much would you two charge for this service?"

"Well, we love boating so much," said Mark, "that all we'd ask is that you'd supply the gas. Right Laura?"

"Right!" Laura agreed eagerly. "Why, the three of us will have the greatest summer ever!"

"I'll supply the gas you use between 9:00 a.m. and 4:00 p.m. daily and five dollars a day to boot," Mr. Gruber said. "Does that sound fair?"

"More than fair!" they shouted.

So it was that the first floating store made its appearance on Lake Belvedere. Each day Laura and Mark loaded the boat's galley with all the groceries it could hold. Mr. Gruber also installed a freezer aboard to carry ice cream, popsicles, and other frozen foods. On the side of the boat Mark hung a large sign which read, GRUBER'S GROCERY BOAT. The route they covered was from Miller's Point at the lake's north end to Hallman's Beach at the south. They anchored at twenty-four local docks daily, ringing a bell on their arrival. At each dock, housewives and children came running to browse and buy. And often Laura and Mark invited new friends that they made to ride the route with them.

The grocery boat became so popular that Mr. Gruber had no problem competing with the new supermarket. In fact, that summer was the most successful one he had ever had.

Needless to say, it was a fabulous summer for Laura and Mark, too. They had proved that there was always a way to earn money, if one used one's imagination and ingenuity. Furthermore, they never had to envy Skip Ballard again.

"This is such an exciting job!" Laura exclaimed one day, as they went around Miller's Point. "It's wonderful to be paid to do something you really love."

"Right," grinned Mark. "And somehow you feel mighty proud to be cruising along on gas you earned yourself. I'm really glad Dad doesn't believe in passing out silver platters!"

A Folletto

THE LITTLE PEOPLE

Are you someone who looks behind doors, under boxes and crates, and into the rose bushes in the garden, hoping to see just one elf? Do you hunt upstairs and down and stare at the windowsill, wishing for even a fleeting glimpse of the Little People? You needn't be ashamed to admit it, for many people are secretly on the lookout for elves.

There are many names for the Little People. Such words as sprite, goblin, and imp are often used to refer to them. They are also called the Fair Folk, the Good Folk, the Forgetful Folk, the Hidden Folk, the Good Neighbors from the Sunset Land, the Night Folk, Them, the Little Ones, the Little Darlings, Mother's Blessing, and the Lovers. The Faeries are a beautiful and powerful tribe of elves living in Ireland. But the word "Fairy," which belongs to a particular group of Little People in England, has been misused very often.

Elves are—probably—beings that spring from our imaginations, like the creatures we see in dreams. But many people wish that they were real, and so they keep their eyes peeled, just in case. Their hope is backed up by many stories of elf-sightings from every period of history. And every country in the world has a stock of lore on the history, habits, and appearance of its elves.

These stories tell us that elves have very likely been present in the world just as long as humans have. In those early days, they played a very important part in everyday life and were on good terms with people. There were house sprites, tree sprites, meadow sprites, sea sprites, ship sprites, barn sprites, and river sprites. In fact, almost every nook and cranny the world over had its resident elf. The elf protected its home spot and any animals or fish living in or near it.

In our time there seem to be fewer elves. But perhaps the reason we do not see them as often as our ancestors did is that we have forgotten how to look for them.

▶LOOKING FOR ELVES

According to folk tales, elves are very rarely "seen" with the eyes. They are able to become invisible or half-transparent. Elves are more often heard or felt. If they are seen, it will be at noon, at dusk, at midnight, on moonlit nights, or at dawn. Or they may be seen by someone with "the second sight" or "the seventh sense" (special mystical powers).

One old manuscript from 16th-century England gives a recipe for an ointment that was said to "enable one to see the fairies."

"Take a pint of sallet oyle (salad oil) and put it into a vial glasse; and first wash it with rose-water and marygolde water; the flowers to be gathered towards the east. Wash it till the oyle becomes white, then put it into the glasse, and then put thereto the budds of hollyhocke, the flowers of marygolde, the flowers or toppes of wild thyme, the budds of young hazle (hazel), and the thyme must be gathered near the side of a hill where fairies used to be; and take the grasse of a fairy throne; then all these put into the oyle in the glasse and sette it to dissolve three days in the sunne and then keep it for thy use."

Elves can take whatever form they want. They appear as beautiful women in rippling gowns, gnarled dwarves with red eyes, goats, butterflies, hooded old men, cats, saucers, stones, owls, and many other things. They can even appear in someone else's body.

Their height can vary, too. At times they are so tiny they can slip through keyholes. At other times, they grow until they are large enough to sweep through the forest with the storm winds and moan in the tree-tops. They can travel long distances in seconds, fly through the air, and swim through the ocean. They pop up unexpectedly and then vanish altogether—only to show themselves again, laughing, a minute later.

But elves have a few common characteristics that should help you recognize them. Some look like humans, except for one animal trait—a hoof, fish teeth, duck feet, seal skin, or pointed ears. Elves often have glittering eyes, and many have gray, brown, black, reddish, mossy, or furry skin. They usually wear dark, old-fashioned clothes or go naked. For festivals or dances, they wear the magic colors, red and green. They have a weakness for large buckles, shiny buttons, and colorful kerchiefs. Elves rarely wear shoes.

Look for elves in the countryside, in deserted houses, and in all pleasant, quiet places—on mountaintops, in rivers, and in the woods and open fields. Places where elves are *not* likely to be seen are in large cities or near factories and electric power plants. The elves move away from places that are polluted or noisy.

▶ELFIN ETIQUETTE

All elves are a little touchy and have quick tempers. It is best to act natural with them, but be polite. You should not speak to them first—wait until they say the first word. And always speak well of the elves, even when you think that you are alone.

It is a good idea to greet dust devils (small dust storms) and elder trees in a friendly manner because elves often travel or live in them. You should try not to walk on or into fairy rings—the circles of thick green grass or rings of mushrooms that spring up where the elves have danced—without the elves' permission.

If the elves try to give you a present, accept it and thank the Little People heartily. It isn't polite to tell anybody of your adventures with the elves, and you must never, never brag about knowing them. There are many stories of people who did not follow this advice and were blinded, maddened, or even tickled to death by angry elves.

Elves do not like salt, electricity, iron,

certain herbs, or crosses. If you want to avoid the elves, put a little salt in your pocket. The elves in each region have certain likes and dislikes. Some hate misers, others despise drunkards, and most dislike people who change their minds often.

▶ELFIN WORK

Elves have many jobs and duties. They know the healing powers of wild herbs and the magic of all natural things. If treated politely, they have been known to give humans never-ending balls of yarn or objects that turn into pure gold overnight.

The forest elves care for the wild animals and see that hunters do not harm their favorite pets. The forest women spin all the moss in the wood. The water elves herd schools of fish, love to drink, and are often bad-tempered. The field elves make the fields and meadows fruitful. They punish humans who trample the ripening grain. The mountain and mine elves know where veins of gold, precious stones, and lost treasure are hidden. They are master craftsmen.

The house sprites protect the house and barnyard. They also steal milk, grain, hay, wood, or money from the neighbors and warn their masters of fire, flood, or misfortune. They take care of the farm animals, rock the cradle, and help with the cleaning up. But they only do their jobs well if they are treated well. A little milk, porridge, black bread, beer, or something sweet should be silently set out for them. Elves should never be given clothing, shoes, or money or they will leave the house, never to return.

▶ELFIN PLAY

All elves love to dance, sing, and play musical instruments. The elves' singing, fiddling, and bagpipe playing are so enchanting that humans are often put under a spell by them.

Elves are mischievous. There are few truly "good" or completely "bad" elves: they are mixtures of good and bad. And they seldom pass up a chance to play a trick. Elves pull the covers off sleepers, tickle them with icy hands, pinch them, and roll them out of bed. They tug at braids, steal the laundry, hide keys, and mix the mustard and sugar together. They also give nightmares, tie cows together and tangle their tails, and let the pigs loose.

As long as their jokes are not cruel, it is best to humor them. If their play turns rough or dangerous, they can usually be scared off with the herbs dill, wormwood, vervain, Saint-John's-wort, marjoram, and centaury. Spells can be said against them, and priests can try to exorcise them. In Italy, the instructions for getting rid of a Folletto (a naughty wood sprite that sometimes drives people mad) are very complicated. One hundred and one eggs should be gathered from one hundred and one families. The person who has been driven mad by the Folletto must eat twenty-five to thirty eggs every day. The wood sprite will be gone in five days—but the person may never want to eat another egg!

▶ELF TALES

It is not only Italian elves that have some naughty traits. Here is a story of a not-so-nice elf in Scotland:

A man from Scotland captured a female sea elf, or mermaid, one day. She offered to grant him one wish if he would let her go free, and the man asked to be able to play the bagpipes. When the mermaid asked him if he wanted this gift for himself or for others, he answered, "I guess it's for myself." The mermaid was not happy with his answer and made him sorry that he had ever said those words. From that day on, he was able to play the bagpipes, but he was the only one who was able to enjoy the music. To everyone else, his piping sounded like the howling of a hundred lovesick alley cats.

But elves can be very generous to humans if they are treated well. Here is a story about a grateful English Pixy:

A Pixy once asked a farmer to lend him a cart and two horses. He told the farmer, "I'd want to take my good wife and littlings out of the noise of the ding-dongs." At first the farmer didn't know what the little red-headed fellow was talking about. Then he realized that the Pixy wanted to move away, and that the "ding-dongs" were the church bells in the village. The farmer wasn't very happy about lending his horses, but he agreed in order not to anger the little man. He was rewarded for his trust—when his horses were returned the next day, they were much healthier and could work twice as hard.

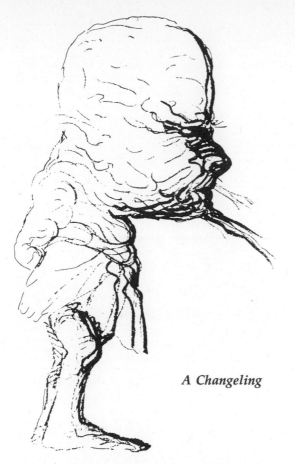

A Changeling

A Pixy

Changelings are creatures that elves substitute for human babies. They are usually ugly, loud, bad-tempered, always hungry, and always getting into trouble. It is no wonder that most families try to drive changelings away and get their own children back. The family in this story succeeded:

A Danish family once got rid of a bothersome changeling by serving it a pudding with a whole young pig baked into it. At first the changeling was delighted, for it was always hungry. But when the changeling saw the pig inside the pudding, its delight changed to disgust. "What is this?" it asked. "A pudding with hide? A pudding with hair? A pudding with eyes? And a pudding with legs in it? Three times have I seen a young wood growing by Tiis Lake, and never did I see such a pudding! The Devil himself can stay here now." And with those words, the changeling left, never to return, and the rightful child was restored to its family.

Some elves of the British Isles and Ireland deserve to be better known. The tiny English Portunes are among the few elves who are said to have died out. They used to

come to farmhouses and sit before the fire, roasting tiny frogs for their supper. Water ponies, such as the Shopiltee from the Shetland Islands, are very strange, rather nasty elves. They are the size of Shetland ponies, but their backs are completely covered with slimy seaweed. The Asrai are gentle lake women who can grow only in the moonlight. Once a century they come to the surface of the lake, on a night when the moon is full.

The Manx Sleigh Beggey and the Welsh Tylwyth Teg (the name means the Fair Family) are usually friendly towards humans. But the Scottish Red Caps throw rocks down onto travelers from their towers and then dye their caps red with the strangers' blood.

Elves—and the stories about them—are not about to die out. They are just as rambunctious, naughty, beautiful, and haunting as ever. Now is the time to find the elves, to ask them all sorts of questions, and to answer many of theirs. As one elf once cried out, "If you'd asked me that before, I would have told you lots more!" Good elfing!

The Saga of Two Trees

In a great forest deep in Finland's wilderness stood two pine trees. They were so old, so very old, that no one could remember when they had been young. It was just known that they had stood there, close together, since long, long ago. Their dark crowns reached high above all the other trees. In spring, the pine thrush sang his loveliest song on their boughs.

With tenderest of glances, the pale pink heather blossoms gazed up at the tall pines and asked one another, "Is it really possible to grow so high and become so great and so old in this world of ours?"

When summer's grasses had withered, when the heather slept deep in the ground, then the blizzard covered the whole region with deep snow, and the storm raced through the crowns of the pines, scattering snow from the evergreen branches. When the hurricane wrecked houses and crashed through the woods, the two pines remained unshaken, never wavering in their majesty and strength. Nor did they break when all things around them were breaking.

Not far from the two trees, on a slope in the woods, a cotter had built his home. The small house was thatched with turf and had only two small windows. The cotter and his wife owned only a potato patch and a small field. In the winter the cotter took his ax and went into the woods to cut down trees. Then he took them on a sled to the nearest sawmill, which lay a mile from the forest. In this way he earned enough to be able to enjoy bread, butter, milk, and potatoes. These the family thought quite enough, for they knew many who had to content themselves with bark bread, with no butter to spread on it.

The cotters had two small children, a boy named Sylvii and a girl named Sylvia. One winter's day the two children wandered out into the forest to look at the snares they had set to try to catch some small animal that could be used for food. When they reached the traps, they saw that each one held a prize: in Sylvii's was a white hare, and in Sylvia's, a snow grouse. Both creatures were still alive, for they had been caught only by the leg. The little animals cried so pitifully that the children, feeling sorry for them, opened the traps and let the animals go. The hare dashed off as fast as he could, and the grouse took quickly to her wings. But as they escaped, both creatures loudly cried out, "Ask Sky-High and Cloud-Beard! Ask Sky-High and Cloud-Beard!"

"I wonder what they mean by that," said the children, puzzled. "How ungrateful they were! They never even thanked us for their freedom."

"They told us to ask Sky-High and Cloud-Beard," repeated Sylvia. "Who can they be? I have never heard such strange names."

"Neither have I," said Sylvii.

At that very moment a sharp wind rushed through the two tall pines which rose high above their heads. There was whispering and rustling in the dark crowns of green needles; and in the rustling the children heard a very strange conversation.

"Are you still standing, Brother Sky-High?" asked one tree.

"Of course I am still standing," replied the other. "But how do you feel, Brother Cloud-Beard?"

"Alas, I am beginning to grow old," answered Cloud-Beard. "The wind has broken off a branch in my crown."

"Compared with me, you are but a child," said the tree named Sky-High. "You're only three hundred and fifty years old, whereas I have rounded out my three hundred and eighty-eighth year. You are a child! A mere child!"

"Listen, the storm is coming back again," sighed Cloud-

Beard. "We had better sing a little so our branches may have something to ponder."

Together the two tall pines sang this song:

> Hear our song,
> Loud and strong!
> Far in time and deep in mold,
> Grows our root,
> Stands our foot.
> This is how we face the storm!
> Dead leaves whirl;
> Petals curl;
> Aeons furl.
> Past our eyes
> Skies are drifting.
> Men are born.
> Hearts are torn.
> Here we stand, and ever will,
> Far in time, strong and still!

I think we should have a little talk with those children," murmured Sky-High.

"I wonder what they intend to tell us," whispered the boy to his sister.

"I want to go home!" Sylvia whispered back. "I feel afraid when I hear the strange song of the trees."

"Wait, there's Father coming with his ax!" cried Sylvii.

Sure enough, in a moment their father was standing beside them. He took a long look up at the trees and said, "These are just the trees I need for the mill." And he lifted his ax to cut a scar in the bark of Sky-High.

The children began to cry, "Oh, Father, please don't cut down that tree. His name is Sky-High! Father dear, I beg you, don't touch that other pine either; that's Cloud-Beard. They are so kind! They just sang us a song."

"What nonsense! Trees can't sing! But it's all the same to me. I'll go find two others," replied their father gruffly. So he went farther into the forest, while the children remained behind, hoping that Sky-High and Cloud-Beard would have something to tell them.

It was not long before the wind came back from the mill, where he had turned the millstones so that sparks had flown out like red hot flies. Again the wind began to whistle and cry in the pine trees. The children clearly heard the trees beginning to speak: "Together you have saved our lives; that was nobly done. Now, little ones, you can ask for gifts, and whatever you wish, that you will receive."

Though happy at this offer, the children were perplexed, for they believed they really had everything they needed or desired.

At last Sylvii said shyly, "I do wish we could get a little sunshine so we could trace the hare's footprints in the snow."

"Oh," added Sylvia, "I wish spring would come to melt the snowdrifts, for then the birds would sing again in the woods."

"What foolish children!" cried the trees. "You could have wished for anything in the world, and what do you wish for but what will happen anyway, even without your wishes. Since you have saved our lives, your wishes will be fulfilled, but in a more wonderful way than you can imagine. You, Sylvii, will receive this gift: wherever you go, and wherever you look, the light of the sun will shine around you. Sylvia, the drifts of snow will melt and spring will surround you wherever you go and whenever you speak. Are you both satisfied?"

"Oh, yes! Yes! You are wonderful! These gifts are more than we deserve. Many, many thanks, Sky-High and Cloud-Beard, for your great kindness to us!"

"Farewell, children. Good luck follow you both."

"Farewell, Sky-High and Cloud-Beard, and may you live forever and ever!"

So the children started on their way home. As they walked, Sylvii as usual glanced about him, looking for grouse in bush or tree. But what was really strange was that whenever his eyes turned, a beam of sunlight flew ahead of him. With no less astonishment Sylvia noticed that the snowdrifts beside their path melted as she passed.

"Look! Look!" she called to her brother. Scarcely had she opened her lips before green grass began to appear at her feet.

Trees began to bud, and the first lark was heard singing.

"How wonderfully good of Sky-High and Cloud-Beard to give us such presents!" they cried. They ran home to their mother, shouting, "I can see sunshine! I can melt snow!"

"Who can't do that?" answered their mother, laughing. But it was not long before her eyes grew wide with astonishment. Though the hour was late and the woods and field outside were growing dark, indoors it seemed that sunlight was shining. And this went on until Sylvii began to get sleepy and his lids fell slowly over his eyes. And though it was early winter, a perfume as of springtime hung in the air. The dry birch twigs on the table unfurled small green leaves.

In a tree outside, the family rooster began to crow cheerily, though it was early evening. And these strange changes went on until little Sylvia fell asleep.

"Listen, husband," said his wife when the woodsman came home. "There's something wrong with Sylvii and Sylvia. I'm afraid a troll got hold of them while they were playing in the forest today."

"Nonsense!" returned her husband. "But I have some news for you! None other than the King and the Queen are visiting our country, and will be driving past our church tomorrow. Shall we take the children and drive over there to catch a glimpse of the royal pair?"

"Wonderful!" replied his wife. "It isn't every day that we can get a look at a king and queen!"

The next morning the cotter, his wife, and their two children set out early on their way to church. They were so excited about the great people they were about to see that they seemed to have forgotten what had happened to their children on the previous day. They did not even notice how the sunlight leaped ahead of their sled, or how the birch trees came into bud as the family drove along.

When they arrived at the church they found a large crowd assembled. But men and women, even children, seemed frightened and anxious. It was rumored that the King had become angry because the countryside looked wild and uncultivated. Since he was a stern man, they feared he would blame his people, even punish them. As for the Queen, it was reported that she was cold whenever she traveled in Finland, and was bored and angered at the whole journey.

Everyone in the crowd had heard these rumors. Trembling and wretched, the people watched as the royal sleighs raced toward the church and came to a sudden stop before the church gate.

The King was frowning and the Queen looked sad, but they were forced to wait there for a change of horses. And since the hood of the sleigh had slipped down, they could not help being seen or looking around.

"Look how the sun is shining!" cried the King, and he smiled. "I don't understand why I feel so happy just now."

"Because Your Majesty ate such a good breakfast," said the Queen. "I feel happy, too."

"Because Your Majesty slept so well last night," remarked the King. "How lovely this part of Finland is. We always heard it was nothing but a wilderness. Look how the sunlight shines on those two tall pines over there in the forest. We ought to build a farm near this place!"

"Why not?" agreed the Queen. "The climate must be mild; look at the leaves bursting forth on the birch trees, even though it is still winter." And there was a happy tone in the Queen's voice.

Just then the royal pair caught sight of Sylvii and Sylvia, who had climbed the fence near the church to get a better view. As Sylvia chattered away, the fence she was on burst forth with many green leaves.

"Call those sweet children here," the Queen ordered her driver.

The driver obeyed and the two children came forward shyly, their fingers in their mouths, as was the custom.

"Children," began the King, "you both look so happy you have made us happy just looking at you. Climb up into our sleigh! When we go home you can live with us in our castle; there you will be dressed in silk and gold. Wherever you go, people will rejoice upon seeing you."

"Your Majesties, we thank you. But we really can't go away," answered Sylvii. "We have to stay home with our parents. And we can't leave our dear friends Sky-High and Cloud-Beard."

"Why can't you bring Sky-High and Cloud-Beard with you?" asked the Queen, for her heart felt strangely tender and yielding.

"Oh, thank you, Your Majesties, but we really cannot, because their roots are fast in the forest ground."

"What strange notions these children have," said the King and Queen to each other, and began to laugh so heartily that the sleigh shook with merriment.

The outcome of this curious meeting was that the royal pair ordered a farm to be built nearby. Their mood had changed so completely that people wondered what miracle had taken place.

To show their goodwill in a way that Sylvii and Sylvia could understand, they ordered the royal baker to bake a pretzel. But it was a pretzel so large that it took four horses to move it. The two children shared the pretzel with all the other children of the countryside. But even then, there was still so much left over that the cotter's horse could scarcely pull home a cart carrying the crumbs.

When the family drove home after seeing the King and Queen, the cotter's wife said to her husband, "Do you know why the royal pair were so terribly happy?"

"No," answered the man, keeping his eyes on the road, which was rough and treacherous.

"Because our two children were looking at them. Don't you remember what I told you yesterday?"

"Sh-sh!" warned her husband. "Don't let the children know, for it is better if they don't understand what marvelous gifts their friends in the forest gave them."

After that day, the region round the cotter's home slowly but surely changed into fertile and cultivated land, with pastures for grazing cattle. A beautiful castle was built near the church. And in that part of Finland, the birds sang all winter; the people had never heard the likes of their beautiful singing.

After some years, Sylvii became the royal forest ranger, and Sylvia was put in charge of the orchards. Everything under their care grew and flourished, and the gardens and fields and forest were a joy to behold.

One day Sylvii and Sylvia went once more to visit their old friends Sky-High and Cloud-Beard. A strong wind was blowing through their branches and a rustling and a rushing were heard in their dark crowns.

Again Sylvii and Sylvia understood the song of the two trees:

> We are so old, we are so gray,
> But tall and straight we stand today!
> In spring or fall
> When wild winds call;
> In summer shade
> Where dreams are made.
> In frost and snow,
> When young plants grow.
> In mist and night,
> Or morning's light—
> Aha, aha, aha, aha!
> We are so old, we are so gray,
> But tall and straight we stand today.

Just as the trees finished their song, the sounds of a cracking, a breaking, and a crash broke the forest stillness. When all was quiet again, there lay Sky-High and Cloud-Beard full length upon the ground. At that time, Sky-High was three hundred and ninety-three years old, and Cloud-Beard was three hundred and fifty-five. They had not been aware that their roots had rotted at last, giving the wind power over their fate.

Sylvii and Sylvia were grieved, and they both wept. They patted the moss-covered bark of their old friends to comfort them, and the snow began to melt around them. Pale pink heather blossoms grew up quickly over the fallen heroes.

"They will sleep in beds of heather and have sweet dreams," said Sylvii and Sylvia as they wiped their eyes, and then turned their steps toward home.

a Finnish story from *Scandinavian Stories*
by MARGARET SPERRY

POETRY

A POET THINKS

The rain is due to fall,
The wind blows softly.

The branches of the cinnamon are moving,
The begonias stir on the green mounds.

Bright are the flying leaves,
The falling flowers are many.

The wind lifted the dry dust,
And he is lifting the wet dust;
Here and there the wind moves everything.

He passes under light gauze
And touches me.

I am alone with the beating of my heart.

There are leagues of sky,
And the water is flowing very fast.

Why do the birds let their feathers
Fall among the clouds?

I would have them carry my letters,
But the sky is long.

The stream flows east
And not one wave comes back with news.

The scented magnolias are shining still,
But always a few are falling.

I close his box on my guitar of jasper
And lay aside my jade flute.

I am alone with the beating of my heart.

Stay with me to-night,
Old songs.

LUI CHI (1311–1375)

A CROWN OF WINDFLOWERS

"Twist me a crown of windflowers
    That I may fly away
To hear the singers at their song,
    And players at their play."

"Put on your crown of windflowers;
    But whither would you go?"
"Beyond the surging of the sea
    And the storms that blow."

"Alas! your crown of windflowers
    Can never make you fly;
I twist them in a crown today,
    And tonight they die."

CHRISTINA ROSSETTI (1830–1894)

THE CROCODILE

How doth the little crocodile
    Improve his shining tail,
And pour the waters of the Nile
    On every shining scale!

How cheerfully he seems to grin,
    How neatly spreads his claws,
And welcomes little fishes in
    With gently smiling jaws!

LEWIS CARROLL (1832–1898)

WINDY NIGHTS

Whenever the moon and stars are set,
  Whenever the wind is high,
All night long in the dark and wet,
  A man goes riding by.
Late in the night when the fires are out,
  Why does he gallop and gallop about?

Whenever the trees are crying aloud,
  And ships are tossed at sea,
By, on the highway, low and loud,
  By at the gallop goes he.
By at the gallop he goes, and then
  By he comes back at the gallop again.
                ROBERT LOUIS STEVENSON (1850–1894)

SYMPHONY IN YELLOW

An omnibus across the bridge
Crawls like a yellow butterfly,
And here and there, a passer-by
Shows like a little restless midge.

Big barges full of yellow hay
Are moored against a shadowy wharf,
And, like a yellow silken scarf,
The thick fog hangs along the quay.

The yellow leaves begin to fade
And flutter from the Temple elms,
And at my feet the pale green Thames
Lies like a rod of rippled jade.
                OSCAR WILDE (1856–1900)

I NEVER SAW A MOOR

I never saw a moor,
I never saw the sea;
Yet know I how the heather looks,
And what a wave must be.

I never spoke with God,
Nor visited in Heaven;
Yet certain am I of the spot
As if the chart were given.
                EMILY DICKINSON (1830–1886)

UNDER THE PONDWEED

Under the pondweed do the great fish go,
In the green darkness where the rushes grow.
  The King is in Hao.

Under the pondweed do the great fish lie;
Down in Hao the sunny hours go by.
  The King holds revelry.

Under the pondweed do the great fish sleep;
The dragon-flies are drowsy in the heat.
  The King is drinking deep.
                UNKNOWN, compiled by
                CONFUCIUS (c. 500 B.C.)

APARTMENT BUILDING

A giant with a thousand eyes,
Gazing down at passersby.
A box of crayons, accepting
Reds, whites, browns, and yellows.

SARA RANDELL
age 11
Clarendon Hills, Illinois

PURPLE

Grandpa dropped his glasses once
In a pot of dye—
And when he put them on again
He saw a purple sky!
Purple birds were rising up
From a purple hill;
Men were grinding purple grain
At a purple mill!
A purple baby was playing
With a purple doll.
Little purple dragon flies
Were climbing up the wall.
And grandpa ate his purple soup—
From a purple spoon!

MEGAN BALDERSON
age 9
Largo, Florida

HAIKU

A hungry rabbit
Hopping about happily
Forgot his hunger.

TODD SHAYS
age 8
Sandy Hook, Connecticut

AUTUMN

Rain is a time
when the sky turns on its water faucet.
The fog is a white linen sheet.
When most of the people in the world
turn on their dryers the wind blows.
The leaves that begin falling from trees
are brown snowflakes.
On the ground
they are the carpet for nature's palace,
At last comes night when the sun decides
to turn its light out.

JUDY WILKIE
age 10
Birmingham, Michigan

RACCOONS

Raccoons like to get into things.
And maybe take your valuable
    rings,
A bouncing ball, or even a bottle.
They like to snoop around the
    ground
for something with a mysterious
    sound.
Their food they wash before they
    taste.
They have a cute, mischievous face.
They hide behind a little black
    mask;
to love them is no difficult task.

BECKY VOTAW
age 12
Ft. Wayne, Indiana

BOOKS

A book is a place to learn something.
Some books teach you how to sing.
A book can be filled with joy.
A book can be better than any toy.
You shouldn't be shy about books.
Books have lots of good looks.
A book is your friend for all your life.
A book is comfort in all pain and strife.

ANDREA EADEH
age 11
North Wales, Pennsylvania

MY BROTHER

I have a little brother
Who has a thing about water—
One minute he's with me
The next, with trousers off,
He's disappeared into the sea.
He stands, he jumps, he runs
Watching the movement, the ripples
    of the sea.
Another day he may feel different—
Afraid of the bang, afraid of the spray,
Afraid of even being wet.
Maybe he's forgotten the happiness he
    had in the water.

SHÂN DAVIES
age 12
Cobham, Surrey, England

A SENSE OF MUSIC

I thought of glorious things
            as I stood on the
                    grassy hill.

The bird chirped in the
            willows.
Perched on a strong branch,
            chest puffed,
He would gurgle.
His lady would answer
Chirp,
        Gurgle,
                Laugh.

The stream below the hills
Trickled along its pebbles
        and rocks.
It sparkled and laughed.
It was music to my ears.

Music. What is music?
A violin solo,
        A piano concertino,
            A trumpet duet,
                A tune sung by a mortal
    voice?
No, music is none of these
        Music is a feeling
            Sad
                Happy
                    Determined
                        Mad
                            Unfeeling

Expressive
        Music is expressive
A feeling which no man can
        put into words
A sense which none but God
        can name.
Music is a brilliant light
        A helping hand
            Reassurance
                A feeling.

Music is life.

ALYSON SKABELUND
age 10
Albuquerque, New Mexico

Ferry to Freedom

In 1978, millions of Americans watched a television series called "Holocaust," which told the story of the persecution of the Jews by the Nazis. During the period when Adolf Hitler and his Nazi Party ruled Germany (1933–1945), an estimated 6,000,000 Jews were killed. Most of them died in concentration camps. Whenever the Nazis occupied a country, they rounded up the Jews and shipped them to these "death camps." It is a sad but true fact that in many of the European countries conquered by the Nazi German armies, there was little opposition to the campaign against the Jews. But there were exceptions. The most notable was the tiny nation of Denmark.

Unlike most other European countries, Denmark had no history of antisemitism. Danish Jews had full citizenship rights and were accepted by their fellow Danes. So when the Germans attacked and occupied Denmark in 1940, Danish Jews did not feel threatened. Because the Germans knew how the Danes felt, they left the Jews alone for three years.

But in 1943, special commando units were sent to Denmark to round up the Jews. The troops planned a lightning raid for October 1, 1943, the first day of Rosh Hashanah—the Jewish New Year. They knew that most Jews would be at home or in their houses of worship on that holy day. Fortunately, a high German official who opposed the plan tipped off a Danish political leader. Word of the raid was quickly passed on to the Jewish community.

In Copenhagen, Denmark's capital city, and throughout the rest of the country, Christian Danes pounded on the doors of Jewish neighbors and warned them of the danger. Postmen delivered the news with the morning mail; doctors called their Jewish patients; students raced about on bicycles spreading the alarm.

The Danes did more than just warn their Jewish countrymen. Christian Danes hid Jews in their own homes. Others were allowed to take refuge in Christian churches. The Danes worked so effectively that when the German troops staged their raid, they captured only a few hundred of Denmark's 8,000 Jews.

But the Jews could not stay in hiding indefinitely. They had to be smuggled out of the country to neutral Sweden—and to safety. And so Danish underground groups, working with local fishermen, organized a "ferry to freedom." The following is a dramatized account of the efforts of one of those groups. It is the story of Jens Lillelund, a Danish businessman turned resistance leader, and his fellow underground fighter Mogens Staffeldt, a bookstore owner. And it is also the story of many other Danes who risked their lives to save their Jewish friends.

The tall man in the trenchcoat moved quietly through the narrow side streets near Copenhagen's Town Hall Square. He walked as close to the brick buildings as he could so that their dark, broad shadows would conceal him. Although it was a cool night, beads of perspiration dotted his forehead. His deep-set blue eyes peered nervously from under thick eyebrows, anxiously searching for any sign of a German military patrol.

The man in the trenchcoat had every reason to be cautious. His name was Jens Lillelund and he was the leader of the *Holger Danske*—a group of Danish underground fighters that was waging a war of sabotage against the German occupation forces. It was well after curfew, and if he were caught it would mean prison or even a firing squad. But that wasn't what troubled Lillelund. He was more concerned about a group of Jewish refugees hiding in the back room of Mogens Staffeldt's bookstore.

That, in fact, was why Lillelund was wandering around the streets of Copenhagen at two o'clock in the morning. A few hours earlier, on this October day in 1943, Lillelund had brought the fugitive Jews to the bookstore, which was being used as a collection point. From there, they were to be taken to the coast and transported by fishing boat to neutral Sweden.

There were 20 Danish Jews in the group, and about half were young children. Naturally they were nervous and fearful. Lillelund and Staffeldt had tried to keep them calm. But at about 1 A.M. one of the children began crying and screaming hysterically. His mother tried to quiet him. But it was no use. The boy was in a state of terror.

Soon the panic spread. Within minutes, half a dozen children were screeching at the tops of their lungs. Lillelund and Staffeldt were close to panicking themselves. The bookstore was located directly opposite the headquarters of the German Gestapo—the dreaded Nazi secret police. When they had first decided to use Staffeldt's bookstore as a collection point, it had seemed a good joke to have a hiding place for Jews right under the noses of the Gestapo. But now the joke didn't seem so funny.

Something had to be done—and quickly. Lillelund figured the only way to quiet the children was to get a doctor to give them some sort of sedative. But at this hour, where could he find a doctor? His own physician, a Jew, was in Sweden—where he had fled after Lillelund warned him of the planned German roundup.

In desperation, Lillelund thumbed through the telephone book until he found the name of a doctor located just a few blocks away. Then he threw on his trenchcoat and rushed out into the darkness. Now he was stealthily making his way through the quiet, cobblestoned side streets.

He was only two blocks away from his destination when he heard a sound that sent a chill of fear up his back. It was the sound of a heavy engine—the steady, grinding roar of a German patrol car. Lillelund darted into a doorway and flattened himself against the wall.

The steady hum of the patrol car drew nearer. And then the vehicle was abreast of the doorway, the German insignia clearly visible on its gray chassis. Suddenly the engine sputtered and the car stopped. Had they spotted him? Lillelund wondered.

There were four heavily armed German soldiers in the car. Lillelund thrust his hand deep into the pocket of his trenchcoat and gripped the pistol he was carrying. He knew that one man with a pistol wouldn't be able to do much against four soldiers with rifles and submachine guns. But—if he had to—he could fire a few quick shots at them and then try to make his escape in the confusion.

But Lillelund didn't have to use his gun. The car was close enough so that he could hear the soldiers speaking. They were cursing the driver for having let the car stall. "You idiot," one of the Germans growled, "you pressed down on the clutch instead of the gas."

After some fumbling around, the driver got the vehicle started. With a lurch, the car sprang forward and soon disappeared from view. Lillelund sighed heavily and walked quickly in the opposite direction. Moments later he arrived at the doctor's house.

Lillelund rang the bell, a long, loud blast. No reponse. He rang it a second time. Finally, the door opened slightly and a gray-haired man in rumpled pajamas stuck his head out.

"Are you Dr. Pedersen?" Lillelund asked hurriedly.

"Yes, I am," the physician replied, eyeing him suspiciously.

"I'm sorry to disturb you, doctor, but I have a serious problem," Lillelund explained. "May I come in?"

The doctor hesitated briefly, then motioned Lillelund inside. The resistance leader understood the doctor's caution. After all, these were dangerous times. Perhaps the doctor was thinking that he was a Gestapo agent. On the other hand, Lillelund had every right to be worried, too. Although most Danes hated the Nazis and what they stood for, there were some who were collaborators—and others who were paid informers.

Lillelund decided that he had to risk the possibility that the doctor might be a German sympathizer. When they were seated in the doctor's office, he told the physician the whole story.

"I will be frank with you, doctor," he began. "I am a member of a Danish underground group that is hiding Jews and helping them to escape to Sweden. Right now there is a group including many children in a bookstore not far from here. The children are hysterical, and we need sedatives to calm them. Will you give me some medicine?"

The doctor's jaw tightened. "Don't be ridiculous," he replied after a long moment of silence. "You need a physician to handle this. I will go with you. Just give me a moment to dress."

"But doctor," Lillelund protested, "I don't want you to get in trouble. Besides, there is very little time."

The doctor smiled. "As long as the Germans are in Denmark, we are all in trouble, my friend."

The doctor hastily put some bottles and a hypodermic needle in his black bag and put on his coat. The two men then left and swiftly made their way back to Mogens Staffeldt's bookstore. There the scene was much the same as when Lillelund had left.

"My God, I'm glad you're back," the soft-spoken Staffeldt blurted. He held a shrieking child in his arms, gently rocking him back and forth in a vain effort to calm him.

The physician flung off his coat and began working feverishly. While Lillelund and Staffeldt held each of the struggling, screaming children, the doctor injected them with a sedative. The medicine had a fast effect and soon all the children were unconscious. In fact, they were completely motionless, and for a moment Lillelund feared that the youngsters were dead.

One of the mothers began to tremble. "They're so still. They're not breathing! Dear God, you've killed them!"

The other parents froze and turned pale. But the doctor quickly reassured them. "No, no, please don't worry. They're perfectly all right. I have just put them to sleep. Look, I will show you."

While Lillelund and the others watched, the physician walked over to one little girl, bent over her, and pinched her cheek. She moaned softly, and everyone breathed a sigh of relief.

As the doctor put his coat on and started to leave, Lillelund pulled a roll of bills from his pocket and said, "Please, Doctor, let me pay you. What is your fee?"

The doctor seemed startled, then a red flush of anger swept across his face. "Fee? There is no fee. I only did what any decent human being would do under the circumstances."

Lillelund was embarrassed. "I'm sorry, Doctor," he said. "Please accept my apology."

The doctor nodded, then walked out the door. The children were now resting quietly. Their parents had begun to regain their composure. One of the Jewish refugees, a slim, dark-haired man, walked over to his sleeping son and softly stroked the boy's hair. Suddenly, he turned to Lillelund, tears streaming down his face.

"Why are they doing this to us?" he asked. "We have lived in peace in this country. We've harmed no one. And these children—just small boys and girls. Why do the Nazis want to put them in concentration camps? I don't understand."

The man broke off, sobbing. Lillelund put his arm around the Jewish refugee's shoulder. "There is no reason," he said softly. "It is just blind hatred—the work of evil men."

Lillelund's self-control was breaking down. He walked out of the room, out of view of the others. Then the emotion of the night burst through, like a dam giving way before a flood. He covered his face with his hands and began to cry.

In the morning, Lillelund and Staffeldt gathered the refugees together and waited for the taxis to come and pick them up. Everything had been arranged in advance. The cabs drove up at intervals and stopped near a side door to the shop. One by one the families were placed in the taxis and then driven to an isolated spot on the Danish coast, just south of Copenhagen. There, the Jewish refugees boarded several small fishing boats that had been hired to carry them across the narrow strip of sea that separated Denmark from Sweden.

During the first days following the German attempt to round up the Jews, some Jewish families had tried to reach the coast on their own. Some were caught by the Nazis. Others managed to make it to the coast, only to be charged outrageously high fees by the fishermen who agreed to ferry them across to Sweden. A few refugees paid as much as 50,000 Danish kroner (about $6,000) to escape—although most of the fishermen charged fair prices, considering the risk they were taking.

Thanks to the efforts of Lillelund's resistance group, however, an agreement had been worked out. Reliable fishermen were recruited, and a flat price of 500 kroner (about $60) per passenger was set. So the Jews who left that morning didn't have to worry about being turned in by informers or cheated by greedy boat owners.

Because of the experience with that first group of Jewish children, Lillelund and Staffeldt added another procedure to their operation. All children were routinely given sedatives before being transported to the fishing boats.

Throughout October, several hundred Jewish refugees passed through Mogens Staffeldt's bookstore on their way to Sweden—so many that at times the shop looked more like a travel agency than a bookstore. Actually, Lillelund and Staffeldt were so busy with the refugees that they did everything they could to discourage customers. When a customer did come in, Staffeldt would curtly inform him, "Whatever it is you're looking for, we don't have it"—and then he would send him to another store.

During the day, small groups of Jews slipped into the store and were hidden in the back room. At night, under cover of darkness, they were taken in taxis or in ambulances to old warehouses in the city's waterfront section. Usually they left for Sweden that night. But sometimes, when there were German patrols in the area, they had to remain in drafty warehouses or shacks for several days. Lillelund and Staffeldt saw to it that they had food, as well as blankets to keep warm.

There were many dangerous incidents like the one with the panicky children. But there were also incidents that might have ended in disaster but instead were more amusing than dangerous. On one occasion, Lillelund had arranged for the escape of 14 Jewish fugitives on one of the larger fishing boats. But when he met with the ship's captain, the captain said he would have to back out. He explained that two new crewmen had signed on for this trip, and he wasn't sure about their loyalty. They might be German spies.

Finally, Lillelund and the captain came up with a clever scheme. The Jews would be given guns and told to hide in the ship's hold. When the boat was safely out to sea, they would break out of the hold and "force" the captain and his crew to take them to Sweden. The captain could then tell the authorities his ship had been hijacked.

"Just make sure there aren't any bullets in the guns," the captain insisted. "I don't want to get my head blown off if one of those refugees gets a little too nervous."

Lillelund returned to Staffeldt's bookstore, got several pistols, and gave the refugees a quick lesson in how to hold them. He instructed them to say "Hands up!" The refugees had never handled guns before, and they weren't happy about the plan. But Lillelund told them it was the only way to get the captain to sail his boat to Sweden.

The fishing boat left on schedule, with the refugees in the hold. Later, when the boat returned, the captain laughingly told Lillelund what had happened. "Everything went as planned. Except that when those refugees came out of the hold and pointed the guns at us, they forgot to say 'Hands up.' I guess they were too excited and scared. So I just said, 'Don't shoot. We'll take

you to Sweden.' And then they remembered what they were supposed to say, and they shouted, 'Hands up! You must take us to Sweden.' "

The captain also informed Lillelund that the two new crewmen were not German agents. In fact, they were anxious to help Danish Jews and had offered to sail on other such voyages.

Jens Lillelund and Mogens Staffeldt would not have been able to accomplish what they did without the help of many ordinary Danes. This was particularly true on one cold, bleak night at the end of October, when the rescue operation to save the Jews was in its final stages.

That night, Lillelund went to Copenhagen's Central Station to pick up a party of Jewish refugees. There had been no time to book a cab in advance. So Lillelund and the refugees had to wait on line at the taxi stand in front of the station. Several other people were ahead of them. Not far away, German soldiers stood guard and Lillelund was fearful his group might be spotted.

Finally, a cab pulled up. As a young man at the head of the line opened the door to get in, Lillelund motioned to the driver. The taxi driver saw the frightened looks on the faces of the Jewish refugees and understood the situation immediately. He turned to the man entering the cab and said softly, "Sir, you were first on line and you have a right to this cab. But I believe those people at the end of the line have more urgent business. Will you let them have the cab?"

The young man glanced over his shoulder. One look told him

the whole story. He stepped back and beckoned to Lillelund and his party to come forward.

"Go on," he said. "I'm in no hurry."

As the cab sped off, Lillelund told the driver, "That was a very nice thing you did. I'm very grateful."

"Think nothing of it," the driver replied. "I hate the Nazis for what they're doing. Just tell me where to go."

Lillelund instructed the man to drive to an isolated pier, where a fishing boat was waiting. The pier was deserted except for another small group of Jews and the fisherman who was to take them to Sweden. Lillelund asked the cab driver to wait while he made sure that everyone got into the boat.

However, the fisherman complained that there were too many people. "They won't all fit. My boat isn't that big," he exclaimed. "I thought there would be only six people. But you have eight."

Lillelund tried to reason with him. "Look, two more won't make a difference."

The fisherman waved him off. "I can't do it. Suppose we run into a German patrol boat. With all those people, the boat will be overloaded and they'll get us for sure."

One of the Jewish refugees stepped forward. "I'll stay behind. Let the others go."

A second refugee also offered to remain. Finally, an elderly Jewish man tapped Lillelund on the shoulder and said quietly: "I'm an old man. My life is almost over. Let the young people go. I have lived seventy years in this country and I might as well die here."

In desperation, Lillelund turned to the fisherman. "For God's sake, man, take them all."

The fisherman seemed embarrassed. He looked at the refugees and then at his boat. After a long pause, he said, "All right. Everyone into the boat. I'll probably regret this, but I'll take them all."

Moments later, the engine groaned and the boat sped across the inky black water, heading out to sea. In a few hours the refugees would be in Sweden. And another group of Jews would be spared the horrors of the concentration camps.

Lillelund got back into the taxi. "Where to?" asked the driver.

The resistance leader smiled. "The nearest cafe, my friend. I'd like to buy you a drink."

As the cab headed back to town, Lillelund thought of the hundreds of Jews he and Staffeldt had helped to escape. And he thought of the thousands of other Danes who had also worked to save the Jews. Jens Lillelund felt a great surge of pride in his people. He began to hum the opening bars of the Danish national anthem, *Der er et yndgit land*—"It is a lovely land."

HENRY I. KURTZ
Author, *John and Sebastian Cabot*

DON'T GLOP YOUR BELLYTIMBER!

Do the words in this title sound strange to you? You may not realize it, but you have probably been given just such a warning at the dinner table. The words mean "Don't gulp your food!"

The reason that "glop" and "bellytimber" are not familiar to you is because they are old English words that have become obsolete. Obsolete words are words that are no longer used. They are words that have died. At one time, "glop" and "bellytimber" were as common as our modern words "gulp" and "food." Now they are never used and cannot be found in current dictionaries.

How did these words die? Many words die when other words having the same meanings become more popular. And all of us contribute to the popularity of words by choosing some and rejecting others when we speak and write. "Glop" and "bellytimber" are only two of many words that were once alive but lost their popularity.

A word may also die if it describes a custom that has disappeared. For example, "flap-dragon" was a dangerous feat performed by medieval knights to impress their ladies. It meant drinking from a bowl filled with flaming brandy and bits of bread and raisins. When that custom died, so did the word "flap-dragon." When today's fads disappear, so will the words we use to describe them. In a few hundred years the words "skateboard," "yo-yo," and "bubble gum" may sound as strange as "flapdragon."

In 1978 we celebrated the 150th anniversary of the first American dictionary, *An American Dictionary of the English Language*. When Noah Webster (1758–1843) compiled this work in 1828, many words we use today—such as "radar," "motel," and "sweatshirt"—did not yet exist, and so they cannot be found in that dictionary. Similarly, many words that Webster included are no longer used today and, therefore, are not included in modern dictionaries. Because language changes rapidly, dictionaries are constantly being revised.

In the following story—"Who Stole Bartholomew-Pig?"—you will see obsolete and rare words used together with modern speech. All the strange words were once really alive and used in everyday conversations. "Bartholomew-pig" is one of those words that relate to a custom that became obsolete. From the 1100's through the 1850's, a fair was held in London on Saint Bartholomew's Day, August 24. There, a huge pig, called a bartholomew-pig, was roasted and shared among the townspeople.

After you have finished reading the story, try using a few of the obsolete words with friends or parents and see if they catch on. You'll be bringing an old word back to life again.

Noah Webster's dictionary of 1828 probably contained some of the words used in this story.

WHO STOLE BARTHOLOMEW-PIG?

The fair was at its height. <u>Thrings</u> of people strolled on the <u>wong</u> where <u>younghedes</u> announced games of skill and displayed <u>eyebiting</u> <u>trantles</u> for sale.

Roland Watson, the organizer of the fair, stepped out of the <u>cosh</u> he had set up as a temporary office to check on the fair. A multitude of sounds, smells, and sights made his ears, nose, and <u>wink-a-peeps</u> <u>quop</u> as he made his way through the <u>mung</u>. Cries of "Handmade <u>muckenders</u> and <u>snotter-clouts</u>!" and "Buy my <u>ringos</u>!" filled the air as Watson approached the main attraction—a platform that supported a huge <u>bartholomew-pig</u> roasting on a spit over a fire. Smiling confidently at the thought of sharing the pig with the townspeople at <u>cockshut</u>, as was the custom, Watson looked up at the platform and saw—nothing!

Where was bartholomew-pig?

Watson knew that Mr. Crawford had helped him set up the pig to roast earlier in the day. He tried to appear calm as he went over to a nearby booth to ask the younghede in charge if he knew what happened to the pig.

"Sorry, sir. I've been selling this <u>lubber-wort</u> so fast that I haven't had even a second to look up."

Then Watson questioned a <u>vecke</u> selling <u>tuzzy-muzzies</u>. "I wish that I could help you, sir, but I didn't even <u>snawk</u> it cooking. You see, I caught the <u>gwenders</u> a few days ago and my nose can't even tell the difference between these <u>pissabeds</u> and <u>bunnikins</u> I have right here."

"This calls for action," muttered Watson to himself. He rushed back to his cosh and summoned his <u>afterlings</u>.

"Now, don't make a <u>whoopubb</u>," he advised. "Something has happened to our bartholomew-pig. I don't know why some <u>greedigut</u> would steal it when there's plenty to share. But we've got to get it back by cockshut, as you know. So search every corner of this fair and go down to the <u>brooling</u> brook and even into the <u>voil</u>, if need be. Act quietly, don't get anyone alarmed by raising your <u>stevens</u>, and don't <u>dringle</u>. We'll all meet one hour from now at the platform. If you end up in a <u>brangle</u>, send an <u>erendrake</u>. We'll catch the <u>breedbate</u> who pulled this <u>reak</u> and give him a dose of his own <u>slibber-sauce</u>. <u>Whisterpoops</u> are too good for him!"

Roland Watson felt <u>carked.</u> He had one hour to search most of the fairgrounds on his own. "No time to indulge in <u>mubble-fubbles</u>," he said to himself. He walked over to the tent where <u>pancarts</u> announced the special events and called aside the <u>flatchet</u>-swallower. But he had no clues. Watson then questioned the animal trainer, whose <u>blonke</u> was drinking <u>Adam's ale</u> in the <u>boose</u>. But, again, no sign of bartholomew-pig. He talked to a <u>bugle-bearded</u> clown, a big man with <u>fardry</u> on his face who knew nothing but suggested that he wait and speak with two

Margin glossary:
- crowds
- field/youths
- bewitching trinkets
- hut
- eyes/throb/crowd
- bibs/handkerchiefs
- candies
- animal to be eaten at the fair
- twilight
- snack food
- old woman/bouquets of flowers
- smell
- a cold and the chills
- dandelions
- spring flowers
- subordinates
- hubbub
- glutton
- babbling
- town
- voices/waste time
- state of confusion
- messenger/mischief maker/prank
- medicine/slaps on the ear
- anxious
- melancholy
- posters
- sword
- horse/water
- stall
- shaggy-haired/white makeup

317

other clowns who were playfully yerding each other while the audience keaked and snirtled with delight. One clown with bright green painted murfles only shook his head when asked. The other clown, who was turngiddy from doing somersaults, only flerked his shoulders before running back into the ring.

Who stole bartholomew-pig?

Roland Watson had two more places to visit. The fairheaded bellibones at the farm-foods booth hadn't seen anyone sneak away in hudder-mudder with a cooked pig. They had enough to do just keeping the spiss crowd happy with nesh earthapples, homemade tipsycakes, and lulibubs. Watson's last stop was at the booth where poplollies were trying their skill at winning fartured dolls by chewing five dry crugs very fast and then whistling. Since most of them could barely wheeple, Watson found out no information from them.

"Barlafumble!" cried Watson as he walked toward the platform. The scrow was getting darker. A crowd had already gathered, getting ready for the bartholomew-pig feast. After Watson's afterlings reported no results from their efforts, Watson climbed atop the platform and announced, "My boonfellows, I have a merry-go-sorry tale to tell. Although this fair has been more iqueme than ever before, I am dretched to inform you that someone has stolen our bartholomew-pig. But don't be filled with ug. . . ."

Just at that moment, a woman cried out from a distance, "Mr. Watson! We have the breedbate!"

Mrs. Crawford hurried to the platform. "I was watching the sunset through our eyethurl when I heard strange slurping noises just a wurp away. I ran over to the ha-ha nearby and saw a large dog glopping huge pieces of the bartholomew-pig. My husband arrived soon after and told me what had happened. He was the one, you know, who had prepared the bartholomew-pig on the pudding-prick. The pig was roasting nicely when my husband noticed it was about to fall off. So he carefully eased the pig off the skewer. As he rested it on the platform, a dog jumped up and tore the pig apart. But, no need to quetch. There will still be enough bellytimber for all! When I realized that we couldn't eat the pig, I yarkened a lot of food from our farm as quick as a thrip. My husband is coming toward us now with all of it on a wagon."

"Mrs. Crawford! You are as precious to us as a bulse!" exclaimed Roland Watson, giving her a lip-clap. "This has been quite a darg for all of us. I am glad we have no magsmen among us. We are a voil of straight-fingered citizens! But a dog is a dog and we can't speak for it. If it wants to dig its flesh-spades into a roasted pig, we can't prevent it. But what we can do is cheer for the Crawfords who fellowfelt and helped us all!"

SUSAN KELZ SPERLING
Author, *Poplollies and Bellibones: A Celebration of Lost Words*

Glossary (marginal definitions):

- yerding — beating with a rod
- keaked/snirtled — cackled/chortled
- murfles — freckles
- turngiddy — dizzy
- flerked — shrugged
- fairheaded — pretty
- bellibones — girls
- hudder-mudder — secrecy
- spiss/nesh earthapples — dense/fresh cucumbers
- tipsycakes/lulibubs — rum cakes/lollipops
- poplollies — children (darlings)
- fartured/crugs — stuffed/crusts of bread
- wheeple — a whistle with no sound coming out
- Barlafumble — a cry meaning "I give up"
- scrow — sky
- boonfellows — good companions
- merry-go-sorry — story both happy and sad
- iqueme/dretched — pleasant/tormented
- ug — fear
- eyethurl — window
- wurp/ha-ha — stone's throw/ditch
- glopping — greedily swallowing
- pudding-prick — skewer
- quetch — moan
- bellytimber — food
- yarkened — prepared
- thrip — snap of the fingers
- bulse — purse of diamonds
- lip-clap — kiss
- darg/magsmen — day's work/swindlers
- straight-fingered — thoroughly honest
- flesh-spades — claws
- fellowfelt — sympathized

319

LOOKING AT BOOKS

Funny Feet!

Poor Priscilla! She's pigeon-toed. Her toes turn in and keep bumping into each other. She can't ski, she can't skate, and all the other penguins make fun of her. But this story by Leatie Weiss, with drawings by Ellen Weiss, has a happy ending. Following the doctor's orders, Priscilla wears a special pair of big clunky shoes and takes dancing lessons. Her feet get stronger and stronger. And, finally, she can waddle just like all the other penguins.

The View from the Oak

An ant hurries along a path. Suddenly, its antenna hits something. What does this feel like? Does bumping into a wall feel different from touching a dog or cat? Why not experiment—make a pair of antennae by attaching thin plastic rods to your head. Spend a few minutes trying to learn what it is like to be an ant. This is just one of the activities mentioned in this book by Judith and Herbert Kohl. Winner of the 1978 National Book Award for children's literature, it describes the strange but wonderful ways that animals sense time, experience space, and communicate with others of their kind. The book is based on ethology, a science that studies how animals behave in their habitats. You will learn how a blind rattlesnake can "see" its prey . . . how forest monkeys differ from city monkeys . . . why its nose is a dog's best friend . . . how two dolphins talk to each other even though they are 100 miles (160 kilometers) apart.

BRIDGE TO TERABITHIA

Jess Aarons wants to be the fastest runner at Lark Creek Elementary School. But Leslie Burke, a girl, runs faster than he does. Leslie and her parents are newcomers to the rural town where Jess lives. They are thought to be a bit odd. They don't even own a TV, though their house is filled with books. Somewhat to Jess's surprise, he and Leslie become friends. They create a secret kingdom in the woods, which they name Terabithia. Here, no enemy, not even Jess's fears or Leslie's imaginary foes, can defeat them. But a sudden, unexpected death ends their adventures in Terabithia. The strength that Leslie has brought to Jess enables him to cope with the tragedy. This touching novel by Katherine Paterson was awarded the 1978 John Newbery Medal, the highest award for a book for young people.

NOAH'S ARK

This delightful picture book, illustrated by Peter Spier, won the 1978 Caldecott Medal for excellence in illustration. It begins as Noah builds an ark and fills it with animals. Cow and moose, hare and goose, sheep and ox, bee and fox, and many other creatures climb aboard. With Noah and his family, they watch it rain for forty days and nights. When at last the flood subsides, they return to dry land and begin life all over again.

The Mystery of Corbin Lodge

Elaine Carter sat up in bed suddenly. Something strange had wakened her. The window near her bed overlooked the porch, from which the lawn below sloped down to a strip of white sand by the lake. The water gleamed faintly in the pale light from a thin moon. Everything was still in the dimness of midnight.

Elaine drew the bed covers around her shoulders. It was cold at night here in the north woods. Aunt Harriet had brought her an extra quilt and had taken another in to Elaine's brother, Ted. "I don't want my most special company to shiver," she had said, her eyes twinkling.

Elaine and Ted had come to stay with Uncle Frank and Aunt Harriet while Dad and Mother were on a business trip. They had spent weekends at Whispering Pines, Uncle Frank's cottage on Echo Lake, but this time they would stay for a month.

Elaine could hear the soft, rhythmic slap-slap from the lake as water lapped at the boat, nudging it gently against the dock. Then there was another sound, a soft, crunching sound—like cautious footsteps on sand. She leaned toward the window quickly.

The door behind her opened with a squeak and Elaine jumped. It was Ted, tousled and sleepy. "Say, did you hear something?"

Elaine pulled on her warm robe and got out of bed. She nodded in answer, shivering with the chill of the breeze through the open window.

Elaine and Ted crept to the window and peered through the dark night. They saw the bulky shadow of a man moving stealthily along the water's edge. He stopped by the boat and his dark figure was silhouetted against the dim sky for a moment; then he disappeared into the thick bushes beyond.

"He went toward the lodge," Ted whispered. "Old Corbin Lodge!"

Around the bend in the lake, visible in daytime from the porch of the cottage, was an old two-story inn. Worn by wind and spray to a bleak, bare grayness, old Corbin Lodge had not been used for several years. They'd asked about the old inn at the supper table.

"I've heard people say lately that it's haunted," Uncle Frank told them.

"Now Frank!" Aunt Harriet admonished. "Don't start that."

"Oh, boy!" Ted was enthusiastic. "Is there really a ghost there?"

"If there is, he keeps to himself," Uncle Frank said, winking.

"It used to be a great place for tourists, but no one goes there anymore."

Next morning during breakfast on the wide, screened porch, Ted and Elaine talked excitedly about the man they had seen the night before.

"Who do you think it was, Frank?" Aunt Harriet asked, with a bit of apprehension.

"I don't know." Uncle Frank looked thoughtfully down at the dock, and then in the direction of the old lodge. "Sure is queer."

"Maybe it was the ghost of Corbin Lodge," Ted laughed. He hurried through his pancakes. He would ask Danny Mason about it. Danny's father owned a little grocery store down at the village.

Ted and Elaine washed and dried the breakfast dishes and straightened their rooms. Then Aunt Harriet asked them to do some errands at the store.

"I hope Danny will be there. We haven't seen him since last summer," Ted said. "We'll ask him about that ghost!" Elaine ran to get her sweater, and they were off.

Danny grinned with pleasure as Ted and Elaine came up to the counter. He was packing groceries in a large bag for old Jud Peters. "Uncle Jud," a great fisherman, lived by the lake in a tiny house he called his "den." Sometimes he worked as a guide for tourists who came up to fish in the summer. What he couldn't tell about Echo Lake and the woods around it wasn't worth knowing. Ted, Elaine, and Danny liked his stories, his hearty laugh, and his thick gray beard.

"Well! Well! Elaine and Ted Carter!" Uncle Jud boomed. "Grew a mite since last summer. Reckon you've been busy with school and all. Books are mighty important, you know."

"Hello, Uncle Jud," Ted grinned. "How's the fishing?"

"Brought in a couple of good bass yesterday. Reckon the fish will all skitter clean to the bottom of the lake now that you're here," he joked.

"Guess that's where they are when I try," Ted mourned. "Sometimes I think there's nothing in that lake but minnows."

"They get away from me, too," Danny said, carefully putting a loaf of bread in the bag. "There you are, Uncle Jud."

"Say, we wanted to ask about the old lodge," Elaine said.

"Wouldn't go around that old place if I were you." Jud Peters pushed his worn billfold into the pocket of his vast fishing jacket. "Corbin Lodge hasn't been used for ten years or more."

"Has it been empty all that time?" Ted asked.

"Empty unless you call a haunted house occupied."

Elaine and Ted exchanged quick glances.

"Whole thing began quite a spell back," Mr. Peters said. "Mrs. Corbin, who lives next door to the store, is the only one left of that family. Old Thaddeus Corbin was her husband's uncle."

"Mrs. Corbin is a dandy neighbor," put in Danny. "She's always making cookies and doing things for people."

"Thaddeus Corbin was a queer old duck," Uncle Jud went on. "He made up riddles all the time. Even left a riddle in his will about the old lodge." Uncle Jud put on his wide-brimmed straw hat. "It was after he died that those yarns about the lodge being haunted started. It's said that someone went in and never came out. I know myself that there's something strange, because all the doors are hooked from the inside."

"And folks have heard queer things, too," said Danny.

"Like what?" Elaine asked, with wide-eyed interest.

"A downstairs door opens and closes all by itself. And footsteps on the stairs." Danny spoke slowly. "And the ringing bell——"

Elaine felt queer little prickles at the back of her neck.

"Spooky enough to make a fellow's hair stand on end," Uncle Jud said. "And with a bushy beard like mine, wouldn't I be a pretty sight?"

"Did you see the door that closes by itself? Or hear the bell?" Ted asked in growing excitement.

"There's folks that have. But not me. I'd shake hands with a grizzly before I'd tangle with a ghost!" Uncle Jud wagged his head. "You'd best stay away from Corbin Lodge."

Danny came over to Whispering Pines that afternoon, and the three talked of little else but the old lodge. "Mrs. Corbin doesn't want to sell it until the riddle is solved," Danny told them. "People think old Thaddeus Corbin must have hidden something valuable there."

"Boy! Maybe it's a treasure!" Ted said. "It sounds like a story out of a book!"

Aunt Harriet told them more about Mrs. Corbin.

"She needs money badly. If she can't sell the lodge soon, she may have to give up her home here."

"What is the riddle he left in his will?" Elaine asked.

Aunt Harriet had to laugh at their eager faces. "You two look ready to burst with curiosity. I don't remember the words, but I'm going to see Mrs. Corbin tomorrow. Come along if you like."

"We will!" Ted said.

The next afternoon Aunt Harriet and Ted and Elaine sat in the small living room of a brown house near the store. Mrs. Corbin, white-haired and cheery, brought in a plateful of spicy cookies and a pitcher of lemonade. The ice tinkled pleasantly against the cold glass. But Elaine and Ted were not very thirsty. The two were sitting closer and closer to the edge of their chairs, anxious for Aunt Harriet to ask the question.

"Elaine and Ted have been hearing about the riddle in your uncle's will," Aunt Harriet said at last. "Do you know any more about it?"

Mrs. Corbin sighed. "I've gone over it and over it. It seems so simple, but none of the places that seem to fit it *do*. Uncle Thaddeus has me really puzzled." She looked into space and said, "It's something like, 'Where flowers entwine, rare treasure you'll find.' "

Ted and Elaine looked at each other, perplexed.

"Would you like to see the original?" Mrs. Corbin asked. She went over to an old-fashioned rolltop desk and pulled out a narrow drawer.

"Here it is," she said, taking out a metal box. "Maybe fresh young minds can work it out. Perhaps that's what it needs."

Inside the box was a yellowed sheet of paper. They unfolded it carefully and read the scrawled message:

Look carefully where flowers entwine
And golden treasure you may find.

"All I can think of," Elaine said slowly, "is a garden with flowers."

"There was a small one back of the lodge," said Mrs. Corbin. "Uncle Thaddeus loved flowers. But it's been searched about a dozen times. It's all overgrown now, like a wilderness."

"Would you mind if we looked around?" Ted asked. The whole thing grew more challenging with each moment that passed.

"Look all you want, outside or inside." She smiled at their eagerness. "But don't get into any danger."

Elaine and Ted could hardly wait to start. They planned to begin their search in the old flower garden. Perhaps they might spot something that previous searchers had overlooked. They asked Uncle Frank for permission to use the shovels in the tool shed if they decided to do any digging at the lodge.

The sun was warm the next morning as the two hurried off. But when they stepped from the sunlit road into the shadows of the tall pines that surrounded the gloomy lodge, there seemed to be a sudden chill in the air. They went quickly along a narrow cement walk that led around to the backyard. Shrubbery had grown high beside the lodge, and the yard in front and back was tangled and dense with undergrowth.

"Do you hear anything?" Elaine whispered as they came to the back. They stood for a moment, listening. Then Ted pushed a sagging gate, which opened into a garden. A short length of chain, once used to hook the gate, now hung loose and clanged dismally against the rusty metal hinge.

"What did you expect?" Ted asked, with a forced laugh. "Groans and moans, maybe?"

"I was thinking about that ringing bell people have heard. There's something weird about a bell, isn't there?"

"This whole place is weird. I suppose it was great when lots of folks were here." Ted stopped. " 'Where flowers entwine.' There's a vine around that old gatepost. *That* has flowers, and it entwines. Let's start there and go over the gatepost inch by inch."

"I hope we can find it. Wouldn't Mrs. Corbin be pleased!"

They searched for more than an hour; at the end they were tired and hot, and a little discouraged. They had found nothing at all.

"Maybe we'd better go now. But we'll come every day until we've gone over this whole garden." Ted was determined.

Their vacation days passed quickly. They swam in the lake and went fishing; they took long rides in the boat with Uncle Frank and Aunt Harriet and saw cottages tucked away in pleasant coves or built on high banks, nearly hidden by trees. They took long walks, visited Uncle Jud, and came back with tremendous appetites. And every day they went to the old garden and searched——with no success. At last they decided in desperation to dig in the garden. It didn't seem very promising, but they could think of nothing else to do.

Then late one night Elaine saw that hulking black figure again. It moved slowly along the water's edge, stopped for a moment, then vanished into the bushes in the direction of the lodge.

When the two went over to the old garden the next morning they felt very hesitant. They stopped at the gate and stood silently for a few moments. Then they started digging again. They were digging a deep hole just inside the gate. Perhaps the people who had dug earlier hadn't gone deep enough. It was hot and very wearing work.

At last Elaine straightened and said, "I keep wondering. Do you suppose the answer is *inside* the lodge, not outside?"

"Mrs. Corbin said we could go inside any time." Ted leaned his shovel against the gate. "We're certainly not getting anywhere here. Come on."

They crossed the yard and went up the crumbly steps to the narrow back porch. "All the doors are locked *from the inside,*" Elaine said, in a low, insistent voice.

"Mrs. Corbin told me one kitchen window can be opened," Ted said. They went to a low window near the back door. Ted slid his fingers along the bottom until he found a catch. It was loose and moved easily, but it took him three or four strong tugs to raise the window enough for them to squeeze through.

The kitchen was large. A huge stove, rusty with disuse, stood at one end of the room. A table was near it, and many cupboards lined the walls.

They moved softly into a large dining room. Tables and chairs had been stacked against the walls. The house seemed to threaten them.

"Must have been nice in here," Ted said jauntily.

"I don't see any flowers," said Elaine; her voice sounded edgy. "Do you hear anything?"

"Just you," Ted grinned.

Next was what seemed to have been a living room with a massive stone fireplace at one end. The room was now bare of furniture. The floor was laid with old-fashioned wide boards, and dust from the cracks went up with little puffs as they walked across the room.

They stopped again. It was very still. "I don't see any flowers here," Elaine whispered.

"Did you think they would be growing out of the floor?" Ted's voice was strangely hollow. "Let's see what else there is."

They looked into the other rooms and peered through the front door to the wide screened porch on the front, facing the lake. The screening was rusty and torn; here and there it hung in strips that flapped drearily in the wind.

"I——I expect Aunt Harriet needs me to help with supper," Elaine broke the eerie stillness.

"Uncle Frank wanted me to mow the lawn," Ted said. "We'd better be going. Maybe we'll come in again tomorrow."

"Mrs. Corbin will have to sell her place soon," Aunt Harriet told them that evening. "I saw her today, and she said she can't wait any longer for the treasure."

Elaine and Ted listened with dismay. That night they talked it over and decided they had been silly. They would go inside again tomorrow, and look upstairs and down.

All morning they were busy with errands, and it was late afternoon before they started out. As they went up the back steps Elaine said, "When I get this far, I begin to feel cold and funny; it's as if someone—or something—were *watching*."

"We won't have to climb in the window this time." Ted sounded more cheerful. "We left the back door unlocked." He pulled at the screen door. "Guess it's stuck." He gave a more vigorous yank. But something in his sister's expression made him stop dead.

"The door is locked—from the inside!" said Elaine.

Ted swallowed quickly. "But we left it unlocked. Aw, the lock slipped or something. Come on."

In a moment they were through the window, but somehow something seemed different. What was it? As they tiptoed through the dining room, Elaine kept one hand tightly on Ted's sweater. At the foot of the broad stairway, they stood still and looked into the dimness above.

"Come on," Ted said.

The creaking stairs were covered with faded carpet. At the top was a long hallway with rooms on each side. They could see the lake from the dusty windows of the front bedrooms. They had just started down the hall when there was a distinct sound of a door closing somewhere in the dim downstairs.

"The—closing—door, Ted!" Elaine clutched her brother's sleeve.

"Probably just the wind," Ted said. "Come on."

The wind was blowing harder. They hadn't noticed it before, but now the clouds were gathering swiftly over the lake. Elaine wished she were somewhere else.

Ted went ahead along the hall. They peered into the open doors of the rooms, empty now and musty with dampness. The last room at the end of the hall was smaller, and an old chest of drawers stood at one side. One of the drawers had been left half open.

"There are *clothes* in there. Look!" whispered Elaine.

Ted went into the room. "There's something strange. Something *different* about this room."

Elaine looked from the one narrow window to the other side of the room. In the gathering darkness it was hard to see clearly. "The walls are different," she said at last. "The others are plain, and this room is papered."

"That's all it is," Ted sounded regretful. "Just wallpaper. It's awfully faded, but the pattern was roses or something."

Elaine gave a quick exclamation, "Roses are flowers!"

"Now *that* is really brilliant!" Ted exclaimed.

"You stop that, Ted Carter. Think a minute."

"Say! Flowers—*entwined*!" Ted looked closely at the faded wallpaper.

"It's just separate roses, though. They don't entwine," Elaine said.

"Look!" Ted shouted. "Look here! Right here. There's a seam in the paper." Ted ran a hand up the wall.

"Of course there are seams," Elaine remarked. "*Now* who's being brilliant?"

"Feel. Right here," Ted insisted. "See this spot where those stems come together?"

Ted put Elaine's fingers on the wall. Her eyes opened wide. "It feels like a frame, or a little door."

Ted carefully pulled at the paper. It came loose easily.

"It's a cupboard! It is!" Elaine whispered. "Hurry, Ted!"

Ted pulled the paper away; underneath was a wooden door about two feet square, with a tiny knob recessed at one side. Ted got his fingers on the knob and tugged the door open. On a single shelf in the small opening was a tin box just like the one Mrs. Corbin had showed them. They stared at each other in jubilation. Then Ted reached for the box.

"Ted!" Elaine grabbed his arm. "Wait! Listen!"

There were footsteps outside the door. The silence that followed was more terrifying than sound. Ted moved in front of Elaine. As they stared, the door opened. Elaine pressed herself hard against the wall and tried to scream, but no sound came. There in the doorway stood a tall dark figure. It was the man by the lake!

"I'll take that box."

The man took a step forward. The collar of his black coat was

turned up around his face. Dark hair drooped over his forehead, but his lips were twisted in a smile of triumph. His dark eyes were fixed on the box in Ted's hand, and his right hand held a gun that left them no choice in the matter.

Keeping the gun steady, the man moved toward them and snatched the box from Ted's hand. It rattled heavily as he shook it, and he smiled. "I figured a couple of smart kids might find it, when older heads had failed," he said appreciatively. "It's too bad, though; you're too smart for your own good. I can't leave you to spread the alarm. I'll have to take you along. Don't make any noise, or it will be the last noise you'll ever make."

He motioned with his weapon for them to go in front of him. Elaine hung on to Ted's hand in total hopelessness as they moved quietly through the dark hall and down the stairs. Ted was trying desperately to think of something he could do, but the swift, muscular man was more than he could cope with.

At the back door the man said menacingly, "Don't try anything. Turn left and go through the garden toward the beach, so we won't be seen."

The garden! Ted's heart leaped and he pressed Elaine's hand, hoping that the same thought had occurred to her. She squeezed his hand in return, but he could not be sure she had understood. In any case, it was a desperate chance——but their only one.

The man stood close behind them as the gate swung open. In the growing darkness, and with his attention fixed on Ted and Elaine, he did not see the hole they had dug beyond the gate. Just as they went through the opening, Ted jerked Elaine's arm, and they leaped nimbly to the side. The man lunged after them, stepped into the hole, and fell headlong.

"Run, Elaine!" Ted yelled, as he brought his foot down heavily on the hand that held the gun. The ruffian howled in pain and his grip loosened. Ted grabbed the gun and tossed it far into the undergrowth. The man struggled to his feet and lunged for Ted, who tried to dodge. Just then a big form moved through the gate behind them, and a big voice boomed, "Oh, no you don't!"

It was Uncle Jud Peters. He caught the collar of the man and spun him around, pulling the collar tightly against his throat. The man gave one amazed gasp, struggling to free himself; but he was no match for Uncle Jud, and he finally gave up even trying to get away.

Behind Uncle Jud was Danny, who was trying to get through the gateway. As the man gave up the struggle in a series of strangled coughs, Danny moved into the garden. "Are you all right?" he asked.

"Sure," Ted grinned.

"Know who this guy is, Danny?" Uncle Jud asked. "Sam Rhoades. Used to work for old Thaddeus Corbin years back. Orneriest man that ever lived." He gave his captive a shake. "Looking for that stuff Thaddeus hid, were you, Sam?"

"Almost had it, too," Sam Rhoades snarled. He glared at Ted. "If I get my hands on you again, I'll break your neck."

"You won't be bothering anybody for quite a spell," Jud Peters said. "And you won't be doing any more haunting. I figured you might be causing all these spooky goings-on. You with your locked doors and footsteps and ringing bells, trying to scare people away till you could find the treasure."

What a celebration they had! Sam Rhoades was soon "properly taken care of," as Uncle Jud put it, by the authorities. Then they went first to Whispering Pines, and they all hurried to the small brown house by the store. Ted carried the mysterious box. It was only right that Mrs. Corbin should open it, but they could hardly bear the waiting.

Uncle Frank and Aunt Harriet, Danny and Uncle Jud, Ted and Elaine stood by the table as Mrs. Corbin looked at the box.

"You found it in the old lodge? Where was it?"

Then everyone was talking at once. Ted and Elaine told how they had dug and searched in the old garden, looking for "entwined flowers," and how they explored the old lodge with its mysterious locked doors.

They couldn't talk fast enough when they came to the part about finding the flowered wallpaper and the little cupboard; then the creaking footsteps and that awful, frightful moment when the man stood in the doorway.

"But how did you get there, Uncle Jud?" Ted asked. "Say, you were great! And you said you wouldn't tangle with a ghost!"

"When my friends were there? And besides, Sam Rhoades is no ghost. Anyway, Danny and I had been keeping an eye on the old place and saw you go in. We were in the backyard when Sam brought you out, holding that gun on you. We had to wait for a clear moment. That was mighty good thinking, Ted."

Mrs. Corbin lifted the lid of the tin box.

"Wow!" Ted exclaimed. "Gold coins!"

"Uncle Thaddeus collected these years ago," Mrs. Corbin said, slowly. "I'd forgotton all about his interest, or his collecting. So this was his 'golden treasure.' "

It was a rare collection. Some of the curious, odd-shaped coins were very old and worth a great deal of money.

"Now I can stay here." Mrs. Corbin looked around at her home with loving eyes. "And you must all stay for supper."

What an evening it was! Mrs. Corbin and Aunt Harriet fixed a delicious supper in celebration. It seemed to Ted and Elaine that they had never been so happy, or so hungry, before.

"But my legs still feel like cooked macaroni," Elaine said later. "I'll never forget this vacation."

"I certainly won't either," Ted grinned at his sister. "Remember how you kept pulling and pulling on my arm? When we get home, I'll have the only sweater in town with one sleeve that reaches the floor!"

THE NEW BOOK OF KNOWLEDGE
1979

The following articles are from the 1979 edition of *The New Book of Knowledge*. They are included here to help you keep your encyclopedia up to date.

MARGARET MEAD (1901—1978)

By the time she was 10 years old, Margaret Mead was studying her two younger sisters. Her grandmother had encouraged her to take notes about how each child grew and developed within the family circle. This interest in her own family led to an interest in cultural anthropology—the study of the human family, especially peoples of different cultures or ways of life. In time, Margaret Mead became one of the world's best-known and most respected anthropologists.

Margaret Mead was born in Philadelphia, Pennsylvania, on December 16, 1901. Her mother was a sociologist, and her father a professor of economics. They hoped she would be a social scientist, too. She thought of becoming an artist or a writer but then studied psychology at Barnard College, in New York City. In her senior year, a course in anthropology turned her to the study of people who still lived in age-old ways.

Her first field trip, in 1925, took her to the Samoan islands in the Pacific Ocean, to study adolescent girls. After returning to New York in 1926, she wrote *Coming of Age in Samoa* (1928). The book became a best seller, and it established her as a major anthropologist. She joined the American Museum of Natural History as a curator of ethnology (the study of races and cultures) and remained associated with the museum throughout her career. Columbia University granted her a doctorate in 1929.

In 1928, Margaret Mead returned to the Pacific to study the Manus tribe in Papua New Guinea. Her research led to another book, *Growing Up in New Guinea* (1930). She then studied several other Pacific island cultures and an American Indian tribe.

Later, she became interested in modern cultures. In *Male and Female* (1949), she drew on her studies of primitive societies to explain relationships between men and women. She also studied such subjects as the generation gap, race, and the relation of culture to education and personality.

Margaret Mead lectured, wrote many books and articles, and taught at several universities. Whatever her topic, she always received wide attention.

Margaret Mead speaks with villagers on the Pacific island of Bali.

336

PELÉ

As a boy, Edson Arantes do Nascimento shined shoes and ran errands. But on days when his father played soccer, Edson watched his father play and dreamed of being a player himself. Eventually, he became—in the opinion of many people—the greatest soccer player in the world.

Pelé, as Edson was nicknamed, was born on October 23, 1940, in Três Corações, Brazil. He left school after the fourth grade and was apprenticed to a shoemaker. But he continued to think of playing soccer. His father coached him at first and then placed him with more accomplished players.

When Pelé was 15, his coach took him to São Paulo to join a professional team. But the team there turned him down. The coach took him to another team, in Santos. Pelé made a poor showing, but the Santos coach accepted him for the second team. In his first game, Pele scored four goals. He soon moved to the first team and became a

sports hero. He could kick with either foot, "head" the ball with accuracy, and put a curve on it as well.

In 1958, Pelé helped the Brazilian national team win the World Cup. He was a legend in world play while still in his teens. And not surprisingly, he became the target of other players. In self-defense, he became a rougher player, and he began to lose some of his enthusiasm for the game. But before he stopped playing in international games in 1971, he led Brazilian teams to three World Cup, two World Club, and five South American championships. He continued to play for Santos until 1974.

Partly because of Pelé, people in the United States became enthusiastic about soccer. He was lured out of retirement in 1975 to play for the New York Cosmos. In 1977, Pelé led his team to the North American Soccer League championship. He then retired from the game.

PELICANS

"A wonderful bird is the pelican!" says the old rhyme; "its bill will hold more than its belly can." And indeed, the bill of a pelican is remarkable: attached to its bottom half is a large skin pouch. People sometimes think pelicans store food in their pouches, but this is not so. Pelicans live on fish. When a pelican catches a fish it uses the pouch like a dip net, scooping up the fish, letting the water drain out, and then swallowing the fish.

▶THE PELICAN FAMILY

Pelicans are large water birds; some kinds may reach a length of 180 centimeters (6 feet), weigh 10 kilograms (25 pounds), or more and have a wingspread of up to 300 centimeters (10 feet). Although they are large, they are good swimmers and graceful flyers. They form a family all to themselves, with some six to eight species (kinds). Most are white or grayish, sometimes with pink tints or darker wingtips. One of the American species is brown or blackish gray. A variety of this species, the Eastern brown pelican, is the state bird of Louisiana. A few other families of water birds, such as the tropic birds, gannets, and cormorants, share certain characteristics with the pelicans. Together they make up the bird order Pelecaniformes, or "pelican-shaped."

"A wonderful bird is the pelican! its bill will hold more than its belly can," says the old rhyme.

▶WHERE AND HOW PELICANS LIVE

Pelicans are found in lakes, swamps, lagoons, and coastal waters of all the continents except Antarctica. The American species range farther north than do the Old World ones. Those that live in cooler climates migrate to warmer areas in the winter. In Europe, pelicans are now found only in the areas around the Black and Caspian seas and in the Balkans, where the Danube delta is a favorite breeding ground.

Pelicans are sociable birds: they feed and nest in large groups. Some species even engage in co-operative fishing. They form lines or semicircles and swim toward the shore, driving the fish before them. When the fish reach the shallower water near the shore, they are easily scooped up by the pelicans.

The American brown pelican, however, has a fishing method unlike that of other pelicans. It flys above the water, then dives or spirals down, plunges under the water to seize a fish, and bobs back to the surface.

Pelicans build simple nests, always near water and sometimes floating on it. They lay one to four eggs, and sit on them for four or five weeks. The young hatch naked and blind, but are soon covered with down. The parents feed them on predigested fish, which the chicks take from the parents' pouches. The young leave the nest for good after about four months, but do not get their adult plumage (feathers) for a couple of years, and do not breed until they are three or four years old.

Pelicans are long-lived birds. They may live for over 30 years. The adults have few natural enemies (sea lions and sharks catch a few). But they are easily disturbed when nesting, and may then abandon their eggs or chicks. Many animals prey on chicks and fledgling pelicans. And pelicans share two problems with many other birds and animals: their habitats (the places where they live, which for pelicans are wetlands) are being destroyed by human building projects, and the pelicans are being poisoned by pesticides (weed- and insect-killing chemicals) in the environment.

Reviewed by JOHN BULL
American Museum of Natural History

A Peace Corps volunteer trains local workers for the building trades in Gaborone, Botswana.

PEACE CORPS

The Peace Corps is an organization of volunteers, sponsored by the United States Government. Its goal is to promote world peace and friendship. To achieve this goal, members of the Peace Corps go to interested countries to help them meet their needs for trained workers. Through their work, Peace Corps volunteers help promote understanding between many peoples of the world and the people of the United States.

President John F. Kennedy established the Peace Corps by executive order in March, 1961. It was approved by Congress later that year. Originally the Peace Corps was an independent agency. But since 1971 it has been a part of ACTION—the U.S. Government agency for volunteer activities at home and abroad.

▶WHO THE MEMBERS ARE AND WHAT THEY DO

The women and men in the Peace Corps represent a cross section of the population. They come from every state in the Union and from Puerto Rico, the Virgin Islands, and Guam. They must be U.S. citizens and at least 18 years old—many are over 60. Most members are unmarried, but there are many married couples serving together.

In the early days of the Peace Corps, most volunteers were teachers who staffed the classrooms of emerging nations around the world. Today many of these nations have trained their own classroom teachers. And volunteers are asked to serve in new roles. They may help a country improve its health care, food production, or water supply, especially in rural areas.

Some volunteers come to the Peace Corps already trained in particular fields, such as nursing, forestry, and agriculture. But most volunteers are trained by the Peace Corps. Host countries explain what help they need, and volunteers are trained to do a specific job. They may be trained, for example, to develop fish ponds to increase the food supply or to teach disease prevention to the people of a village.

One interesting project is the Peace Corps Partnership. Schools, civic groups, and neighborhood and youth organizations

This Peace Corps volunteer acts as a business adviser for a group of artisans on a co-operative in Zunil, Guatemala.

in the United States take part in this project. They provide funds that communities overseas—helped by Peace Corps workers—use to build classrooms or clinics where once there were none.

No matter what their jobs, all volunteers are still involved in teaching, although they are no longer mainly in classrooms. Their aim is to work themselves out of a job by training local people to take their place.

Selection

Volunteers for the Peace Corps are selected on merit. No applicant is refused for reasons of race, religion, or political affiliation. But some applicants may be turned down because they offer no skills or show little ability to learn a foreign language. Others may not possess the kind of attitude that a successful volunteer must have.

Candidates first fill out a questionnaire and list references, as well as the names of teachers or employers who may be contacted. Candidates who have the needed skills are invited to train for a project in a certain country. They may accept or refuse the invitation, state a preference for another country, or ask to be invited for another

project at a later date. Medical standards are very high. But blindness and similar disabilities do not automatically bar candidates if their skills and abilities match the needs of a particular project.

Success depends on the ability to perform the assigned job satisfactorily, after training, and the ability to adjust to life overseas. Volunteers for the Peace Corps must be dedicated to their jobs—whether they are teaching in a school, helping to improve local farming methods, working in a hospital, or surveying for mineral resources. They must be prepared to work hard, and they must always show understanding. Peace Corps members are a new kind of ambassador. They have won praise in every country where they have served.

Training

During the eight to twelve weeks of training, the Peace Corps makes sure that candidates are prepared for the jobs to which they will be assigned. There is a training program for each country and project. Training is given at colleges and universities in the United States and at other training sites. Emphasis is placed on training within

College students in Western Samoa enjoy a science class conducted by a volunteer (right).

Farmers in an agricultural co-operative in western Belize work with a Peace Corps volunteer.

the host countries so that trainees have experience in the culture in which they will work. They spend 60 or more hours a week in study. Their programs include the language of the particular country, as well as its history, geography, economy, traditions, and customs. A review of United States history, culture, and institutions is also included in the program.

Conditions of Service

The term of service is about 24 months, not including the training period. Volunteers receive no salary, but they are given allowances that cover clothing and living costs. The living allowance is designed to let volunteers live at a level similar to that of the people with whom they work. A health worker in Colombia, for example, receives an allowance equal to what a local health worker earns. When members leave the Peace Corps, they receive $125 a month for each month of satisfactory service including the training period. While overseas, leave is limited to two days for every month of service. All necessary transportation between a member's home, training station, and overseas post is provided.

▶WHERE VOLUNTEERS ARE AT WORK

Peace Corps members are sent only to those countries whose governments have made definite requests for their help. Today volunteers are serving in more than 60 countries in Africa, Asia, and Latin America. The success of the Peace Corps program can be measured by the fact that most countries where members are at work ask that more be sent.

▶WHAT SERVICE MEANS TO VOLUNTEERS

For many members, service in the Peace Corps provides a great adventure. This is heightened by the Peace Corps ideal of service to people in the developing nations of the world. When members go back to the United States, they return with a knowledge of the people of a particular country, as well as their language, culture, and traditions. Many new opportunities are open to them in a variety of fields. Former volunteers include Lillian Carter, mother of President James E. Carter, U.S. representative Christopher Dodd, Jr., of Connecticut, and Senator Paul Tsongas of Massachusetts.

CAROLYN R. PAYTON
Director, Peace Corps

341

CHARLIE CHAPLIN (1889–1977)

Did you ever think about what makes you laugh? Charlie Chaplin found the secret to making people laugh, and it worked wherever his films were shown. With his funny little derby hat, cane, baggy pants, and tiny mustache, Chaplin created the famed Little Tramp of silent films. No movie character has ever been more widely enjoyed. Chaplin portrayed his tramp as an insecure fellow, constantly running into trouble but always coming out of each situation with his pride intact. People still laugh at the little man's struggles with authority or with people bigger than he. Chaplin also knew how to bring a tear to the eye with just the right amount of sadness.

Charles Spencer Chaplin was born on April 16, 1889, in London. His childhood was one of extreme poverty. But Charlie showed an early gift for performing and longed to be an actor. He went to the United States for the first time in 1910 as part of a vaudeville troupe. In 1913 the troupe toured the United States, and Chaplin came in contact with film producer Mack Sennett. His first short film, *Making a Living*, was made in 1914 for Sennett. By 1915, Chaplin was internationally famous and was earning $1,250 a week.

His talent was extraordinary. He wrote, directed, and produced most of the films in which he appeared. He even composed the music for those with sound. A short man, he could move with amazing quickness and ease. Chaplin's comic ideas were brilliant, and some have become classics. In *Modern Times* (1936), a worker is fed by machine to save time on the assembly line, but the machine goes out of control and the worker is unable to stop it. In *The Gold Rush* (1925), the starving tramp makes an enjoyable meal of his shoe.

Of the 80 films that Chaplin made, the best known include *The Kid* (1921), *City Lights* (1931), and *The Great Dictator* (1940). In *The Great Dictator,* Chaplin

Charlie Chaplin as the starving tramp in *The Gold Rush*.

In *The Great Dictator*, Chaplin satirized the political views of Adolf Hitler.

used his first speaking role to satirize the political views of Adolf Hitler.

After World War II, Chaplin was determined not to rest on his previous successes. He abandoned the Little Tramp character and tried to grow as an artist. He made *Monsieur Verdoux* (1947), about a man who murders women for their money, and *Limelight* (1952), about an aging vaudeville performer. *A King in New York* (1957) criticized a time in U.S. history when many people were unjustly accused of being Communists. His last film, *A Countess from Hong Kong* (1967), was a love story. A rediscovered masterpiece, *Woman of Paris* (1923), which Chaplin directed but did not act in, was released again in 1978.

Chaplin had good business sense and became quite wealthy. But controversy surrounded him. He was criticized for not becoming an American citizen and for his political views, which some people thought leaned toward Communism. In 1952, when Chaplin sailed for England, the U.S. attorney general ordered that he not be allowed back into the United States without an investigation of his political views.

Chaplin settled in Switzerland with his fourth wife, Oona O'Neill, daughter of playwright Eugene O'Neill. They had been married in 1943 and had a large family—five daughters and three sons. (Chaplin also had two sons from a previous marriage.) In 1972, Chaplin revisited the United States, for the first time, to accept honors from the film community. He was knighted by Queen Elizabeth II in 1975. When he died in Switzerland on December 25, 1977, the world mourned one of the greatest creative artists of the 20th century.

WILLIAM WOLF
Film Critic, *Cue* magazine

CONSERVATION

Have you ever saved aluminum cans, bottles, or old newspapers and taken them to a collection point? Or turned off the water while brushing your teeth? If so, you have practiced conservation.

The word conservation comes from a Latin word meaning "to keep" or "to guard." It once meant careful preservation and protection chiefly of forests and wildlife. Now we know that we must apply conservation to everything in our environment. We must include all the natural resources that our planet provides—air, water, soil, forests, and grasslands, wildlife, minerals, and the like—as well as the many products that are made from these resources.

The practice of conservation is really a way of life that avoids waste of our natural resources and finds ways to share the limited supplies. It means that we must not pollute the environment—or must clean up areas that are already polluted. Individuals, businesses, governments, and entire nations must learn to follow this way of life.

The challenge of conservation is perhaps the greatest challenge that people have ever faced. The world's population is growing faster than the supplies of food, drinking water, housing, and other necessities of life. We must plan now so that people of our generation and those of future generations will have the resources they need. People are a resource, too. If people lack food, housing, health care, and the chance to become productive members of society, there is great suffering, and human resources are wasted.

▶METHODS OF CONSERVATION

There are many methods of conservation, and all of them are related. This is so because all of Earth's resources—all the living and nonliving things in our surroundings—are linked together. For this reason the conservation—or waste—of one resource directly affects another.

Water. Water is essential to life. But water must be clean to be of use. Often we use our lakes and rivers—and even the oceans—as sewers and dumping places for wastes of many kinds, some of them poisonous. Most bodies of water can absorb and recycle some wastes. But many have been overloaded, or polluted. Sewage treatment plants have helped in some cases, as have measures taken by industries to clean up waters that they have polluted. Accidental pollution from oil spills at sea is an increasing problem, too.

The best hope for conserving our lakes, rivers, and oceans seems to be informed and concerned citizens. They must take the lead, first in seeing that the waters of the world are protected by laws and then in seeing that the laws are obeyed.

There are many simple things that we as individuals can do to conserve water. We can turn off the tap while brushing our teeth. We can water lawns and gardens in the evening, when less moisture will evaporate. We can keep drinking water in the refrigerator so we will not have to run the faucet to get cold water. And we can fix leaky faucets. Untold quantities of water could be saved each year in these ways.

Soil. Perhaps our most important resource is soil. Topsoil, the uppermost layer of fertile soil, is the only type of soil that will produce high yields of food crops. It forms very slowly. As many as 100 years of careful management are needed to make 1 inch (2.5 centimeters) of good topsoil. Yet it can be quickly lost—eroded away by wind, rain, or flood. During the 1930's, overgrazing, poor farming practices, and years of drought stripped the grass from vast areas of the Great Plains in the United States. With no grass to hold it in place, precious topsoil was blown away. The area was known as the Dust Bowl until grass and trees were planted and reservoirs were built to hold water for irrigating the land.

Farmers can preserve soil in a number of ways. Contour plowing—plowing horizontally across slopes—helps prevent erosion by water. Planting of trees or bushes (hedgerows) between fields prevents erosion by wind. Planting different kinds of crops, rather than the same crop year after year, slows the loss of nutrients from soil.

Forests and Grasslands. Forests provide timber for building houses and making furni-

Three methods of conserving our resources. Above: Children sort metal cans that were collected for recycling. Right: Giant sequoia trees are protected in Sequoia National Park, California. Below: Contour plowing on hillsides helps to prevent soil erosion.

Here, an oil spill at sea is being sprayed with chemically treated sand. The oil and sand mixture then sinks to the seafloor.

ture, as well as wood for paper, chemicals, and many other products. As the population grows and demand for these things increases, forests are in danger.

Perhaps the most important forest conservation method is selective cutting. In selective cutting, only mature trees are cut down. Younger ones are left to grow, so that the forest can provide a continuous supply of timber. And individual large trees remain as homes for wildlife.

Grasslands provide food for livestock, which are an important part of the world's food supply. When too many animals are permitted to graze in one area, the grass is devoured or trampled and never gets a chance to grow back. In the United States, federal agencies control the number of animals that are allowed to graze on public lands. In other parts of the world—particularly in Africa near the Sahara—the combination of overgrazing and drought has led to severe famine. The United Nations is helping African nations with conservation methods, including reseeding and land management.

Wildlife. The earth has more than 1,500,000 kinds, or species, of plants and animals. Part of the wildlife kingdom has already been lost, and a great many species are threatened. The Endangered Species List, started by the U.S. Government in 1969, contains about 600 animal species that are in danger of becoming extinct, or dying off. Once an animal or plant species is gone, it cannot be re-created. And we may never know what value it might have had in the web of life.

Uncontrolled killing, for profit or sport, was once the chief cause of extinction. Today laws regulate hunting and fishing in many countries. But other dangers to wildlife exist. As the population grows, more forests are cleared, and wildlife habitats are lost. New dams may threaten the existence of certain kinds of fish. A highway may cut some animals off from sources of food.

Conserving other natural resources helps to protect wildlife. If we use less paper, fewer trees will be cut down. If we use less electricity, fewer dams will be built. We can help to conserve wildlife directly, too—by obeying hunting and fishing laws, planting bushes and shrubs to provide food and shelter for wildlife, and putting out birdseed in winter.

Minerals. Many of the things we use—cars, bicycles, appliances—are made from metals. These metallic minerals took ages to form, and they are limited in supply.

In some cases, substitutes have been found for metals. For example, plastics are now used to make many things that were once made only of metal. Scientists are seeking ways to reduce waste in the processing of ores. Recycling also conserves minerals. If the metal in aluminum cans can be used again, less new ore will be mined.

The chief mineral fuels are the coal, oil, and gas that we burn to heat our homes, run our cars and factories, and provide electricity. Like the metals, they took millions of years to form, and supplies are limited. Some scientists think the world will run out of oil before alternate sources of energy can be developed. And as the population grows, the demand for energy increases.

There are many things that we can do to conserve energy. We can insulate our homes and regulate our thermostats to use less fuel. We can walk or bicycle to the store rather than ride in an automobile, and we can use trains and buses for longer trips.

Threatened species. Above: The cheetah is nearly extinct in Asia. Below: Whooping cranes have become a symbol of the save-the-wildlife movement in North America.

We can use fewer electric lights and no electric can openers or other gadgets. Such measures save energy without harming the quality of life.

Manufactured Goods. Think of all the manufactured items you use each day—furniture, baseballs, television sets, toys, books, clothes. It takes only a minute to make a long list. Manufactured goods must be conserved because they are the products of natural resources and energy. These resources are wasted when manufacturers make things that wear out quickly. Many containers, such as disposable soft drink bottles, are meant to be used once and then thrown away. In the United States, some states have banned disposable containers.

By repairing worn or broken articles, we could conserve the energy and resources needed to make new ones. We would also reduce the amount of garbage. Large cities create mountains of garbage each day, much of it unnecessarily. Many towns and cities have set up recycling centers where people bring bottles, aluminum cans, and newspapers, so that the materials they are made from can be reprocessed and used again.

▶CONSERVATION IN THE PAST

Conservation is not a new concern of society. It has been an important part of civilization for many centuries. The farmers of China and Southeast Asia have used methods such as terrace farming for thousands of years to prevent soil erosion. The Romans realized that their coastal fisheries would be endangered if they drained the nearby wetlands where young fish were bred.

In North America, the first conservationists were the Indians. They killed only the animals that they needed, and they wasted nothing. When European settlers came to North America, they found a continent of seemingly endless resources. They set out to use those resources to the fullest, and the new population grew and prospered. But many resources were overused and wasted.

Uncontrolled killing wiped out the Carolina parakeet, the passenger pigeon, and the Atlantic gray whale. By 1889 only a few hundred bison were left, compared to the millions a hundred years earlier. As cities and industries grew in the late 1800's, streams and rivers were dammed for waterpower or polluted by wastes.

By the early 1900's, many people in the United States were concerned about the waste of resources and the destruction of forests and places of scenic beauty or scientific or historic interest. Some conservationists and naturalists who were greatly concerned laid the foundations for the present system of national parks, forests, and wildlife refuges.

In the years that followed, many other countries established national parks. And conservation efforts of many kinds continued quietly until the 1960's and 1970's, when the growing population strained resources all over the world. The publicity given to massive oil spills from supertankers and to reports of the diminishing numbers of such animals as the tigers of India helped to increase interest in conservation.

▶CONSERVATION TODAY

In spite of public concern about conservation, waste and pollution have continued. Population growth is only partly to blame. Technology has also played a part by enabling manufacturers to turn out an almost endless stream of products, from electric carving knives to snowmobiles. More wood, minerals, and energy are needed for increased production of manufactured goods. As a result, many countries have passed laws to conserve natural resources and protect the environment.

In the United States. The National Environmental Policy Act of 1969 requires the U.S. Government to prepare a study, called an environmental impact statement, before it begins any project. If the government wants to build a highway, for example, it must first study the effect that the highway will have on wildlife, soil, water, and the like. Many state and local governments have passed similar laws. In 1977, Congress passed a law requiring strip-mine operators to restore the land that they mine to its original state.

These are only examples of specific governmental actions. Both the nation and the states long have had many special departments or agencies dealing with conservation. More recently, they have established environmental protection agencies to end or control pollution in the areas of air, water, solid wastes, noise, radiation, and poisonous substances.

There are also many private organizations that work to save threatened areas and conserve natural resources. One of the largest of these organizations is the National Audubon Society, with over 400,000 members. Other private organizations include the Sierra Club, the American Forestry Association, Friends of the Earth, and the National Wildlife Federation.

Around the World. A number of United Nations agencies are co-ordinating conservation programs on a worldwide basis, and private conservation groups are active in many countries. The International Union for Conservation of Nature and Natural Resources is the oldest such private organization. Its scientists research environmental problems in over a hundred countries.

Canada, like the United States, has a wide range of programs, agencies, and laws dealing with the management of natural resources and protection of the environment.

Many areas of special beauty or interest are preserved in national and provincial parks.

Early settlers in Latin America wasted natural resources. But serious environmental problems did not occur until after World War II, when a tremendous growth in population strained natural resources. Many countries have since built irrigation projects to redevelop overused land. Countries in the Amazon region have agreed to protect the tropical jungle by establishing several parks.

Conservation treaties have been signed by many European countries. Nations that border the Mediterranean Sea have agreed to work together to clean up the water and prevent oil spills. Members of the European Economic Community have established pollution guidelines, and many countries have wildlife refuges. The countries of southern Europe, where many resources have been overused, are starting extensive conservation programs.

In southern Africa, several countries have developed programs to protect natural resources. South Africa and Kenya have sys-

People create mountains of garbage, much of it unnecessarily.

Elephants have long been prized for their ivory tusks. They are protected in Kenya, where big-game hunting is forbidden by law.

tems of national parks, and Kenya has banned big-game hunting. In 1977 a U.N. conference on the spread of desert areas brought attention to Northern Africa. Programs to stop this spread—including the planting of a "green belt" of trees in the northern Sahara—have been started. Egypt has begun developing a series of national parks along the Nile River.

In Asia, overgrazing, the cutting down of entire forests, and the killing of wildlife have left many countries with serious environmental problems. Conservation programs are difficult to enforce in some of these countries because the basic needs of their vast populations must often be met first. Some countries, such as Japan and India, have established national parks and wildlife refuges and are acting to conserve resources in various ways. In others, such as Cambodia and Vietnam, less has been done.

▶CAREERS IN CONSERVATION

In the past, young people interested in ca-reers in conservation were limited to forest, park, and wildlife management. Jobs in these fields are still available. But there are many other possibilities as well. There is a tremendous need for specialists in all forms of energy. Sanitary engineers are needed to develop new methods of recycling manufactured goods and using wastes. Soil conservationists are needed to study how soils are formed and how they can be made more productive. Lawyers are needed to help with the growing number of conservation regulations. Urban planners and landscape architects also contribute to conservation efforts.

A person who plans a career in conservation will find courses in basic science, mathematics, and ecology especially useful. A solid education is necessary because many conservation problems are very complex and highly technical.

GERARD A. BERTRAND
Chief, International Affairs
U.S. Fish and Wildlife Service

ENERGY SUPPLY

Only a few centuries ago, people's energy supply was made up almost entirely of wood and water. Wood was burned to heat homes and to cook food. Water was used to turn grinding stones. People had not yet discovered the vast underground reserves of petroleum. They had not discovered electricity. There were no air conditioners or refrigerators, no automobiles or airplanes, no plastics or nylon.

Today our energy supply consists mostly of coal, petroleum, and natural gas. These, in turn, produce electricity, which runs machines, heats and cools buildings, and does many other jobs for us.

We are rapidly using up these fuels. Petroleum is being used up so fast that some experts predict we may run out of it early in the 21st century. What will take its place? What will produce the energy needed in tomorrow's world?

▶WHAT DETERMINES ENERGY SUPPLY?

Several factors are important in determining energy supply. These factors also influence how much energy people use. Often one factor influences another.

Availability. Obviously, people tend to use the sources of energy that are most plentiful and easiest to obtain. Coal and petroleum became important sources of energy because people found huge deposits of these substances—deposits that were easy to remove, or recover, from the ground. In contrast, the nuclear energy stored in hydrogen is not used because it is not available. Scientists have not yet been able to control the release of this energy.

Economics. When there is a large supply of something people need and it is easy to obtain, it is cheap. For example, until recently the United States had a great deal of easy-to-recover petroleum. It was sold for low prices, and people used it without thinking of cost.

As the costs of a resource such as petroleum increase, people are impelled to study, develop, and use other resources. For example, efficient solar heating systems that did not even exist ten years ago are now available at prices that make them seem good investments to many people, at least over the long term.

Politics. Much of the money used to study energy sources comes from the government. If the government puts money into one area—nuclear energy, for instance—more research and development will be done there than in other areas.

Government laws and regulations also influence how we use energy. For example, cars and trucks use much more fuel to carry people and goods from one place to another than do railroads. But laws and government practices sometimes have encouraged the building and use of roads while doing little to encourage the building and upkeep of railbeds.

Local groups exert political pressure, too. People may protest the building of a power plant in their community or the drilling of an oil well in their offshore waters. A city may want to burn its garbage to produce electricity. The technology exists. It would actually save money. It would cause little pollution. But people who live where the plant could be built may fight its construction. They want and need energy, but they do not want a big plant and lots of garbage trucks in their neighborhood.

Environmental Issues. The energy sources most used today have a variety of bad effects on our environment. The mining of coal destroys land. Transporting oil across oceans has resulted in oil spills that kill ocean life. The burning of coal and petroleum produces air pollution. Nuclear fission creates dangerous radioactive wastes.

Laws have been passed to limit pollution. Coal mine operators, for example, must replace strip-mined soil. But restoring the land costs money. The cost is added to the price that people pay for coal. If the cost rises enough, another source of energy may become more economical.

▶MAJOR ENERGY SOURCES

Today more than 90 percent of the world's energy supply comes from the burning of fossil fuels—coal, petroleum, and natural gas. A small amount comes from nuclear fission and waterpower.

This is an oil rig in the North Sea. The North Sea also supplies natural gas.

Coal. Coal supplies about 30 percent of the world's energy and just under 20 percent of the energy used in the United States. Coal will continue to be an important fuel resource in the years to come.

Coal is obtained from either underground or surface mines, depending on the depth of the coal. Burning coal creates serious air pollution. In places where great amounts of coal are burned, as in power plants, antipollution devices can be used. These are expensive and not completely effective.

A better way to use coal would be to convert it first to a liquid or a gas. Either of these produces more heat than can be produced by burning the coal. They can also be used in fuel cells, which change the chemical energy of a fuel directly into electrical energy. At present, the making of liquid and gas fuels from coal is very expensive. Making gas from coal also requires great amounts of water, which is not always available near coal fields.

Petroleum. The most widely used source of energy is petroleum. It supplies about 45 percent of the world's requirements and

somewhat more of the United States' requirements. Much petroleum is also used for the chemicals it contains. These chemicals are used to make fertilizers, drugs, synthetic fibers, plastics, and many other products.

Like coal, petroleum creates environmental problems. Removing large quantities of petroleum from under the ground may cause the land to sink. Transporting petroleum may result in oil spills. Burning causes air pollution.

Some people say there is a great deal of oil left in the ground. That is true. But much of it is difficult or impossible to remove from the rocks. It is there but it is not available with present technology or at a price people are willing to pay.

Known reserves of petroleum that can be recovered are being used up rapidly. Oil companies are searching for new reserves, particularly in offshore waters, and testing ways to remove hard-to-recover resources.

In the western United States—especially in Colorado, Utah, and Wyoming—there are immense deposits of rock called oil shale. The world's largest deposits of tar sands, re-

Power plants like this one use nuclear fission to generate electricity.

sembling sandstone, are found in Alberta, Canada. Oil can be extracted from these materials. But at present the process is very costly. Huge amounts of water also are needed and great mountains of waste rock are produced.

Natural Gas. Natural gas supplies nearly 20 percent of the energy used by the world and more than 25 percent of the United States' energy. Deposits are usually found in the same areas as petroleum deposits. Like petroleum, natural gas is a rapidly disappearing resource.

Nuclear Fission. The breakdown, or fission, of uranium atoms supplies about 2 percent of the world's and 4 percent of the United States' energy requirements. Fission releases a tremendous amount of heat, which can be used to make steam to drive electric generators.

Early supporters of nuclear power believed that it would provide plenty of energy at low cost. But many problems have developed. The cost of building nuclear power plants has soared. And there is great public concern about the possibility of a spread of radiation following an accident in a nuclear plant. As yet there is also no sure, safe way to dispose of the burned-out fuel, which is radioactive. And the supply of uranium on the earth, like the supply of fossil fuels, is limited.

Waterpower. About 6 percent of the world's and 3 percent of the United States' energy requirements are met by falling water that is used to generate electricity. There is no pollution, and the resource—water—is not used up. But there are not many places left where suitable dams can be built. For this reason we cannot expect waterpower to meet a large portion of our energy requirements.

▶**ALTERNATE ENERGY SOURCES**

Some sources of energy either are not being used at present or are used only in a limited way. How useful they might be still must be proved. The following are brief descriptions of some promising sources:

Solar Energy. Energy radiated by the sun is free, nonpolluting, and limitless. The problem is to collect, use, and store this energy efficiently and economically.

Solar energy shows growing promise as a major source of energy for the future. Already, some 2,000,000 Japanese buildings and thousands of buildings in the United States are using solar systems to heat rooms and water supplies. Some large-scale systems that concentrate enough energy to make steam to drive electric generators are also in operation.

Geothermal Energy. The interior of the earth is hot. Water seeping down deep into the earth is turned to steam. The steam can be piped to homes for heating or to generating plants. Electricity produced in this way costs less than electricity from other sources. No air or water pollution results.

Geothermal heat is now used in Iceland, Italy, New Zealand, and northern California, where natural reservoirs of hot water and steam are located. Efforts to drill deep holes and pump water down into the earth are being made in several places.

Wind Energy. Windmills have been used for hundreds of years to grind grain and pump water. More recently, they have powered small electric generators. Researchers are developing and testing large windmills—called wind generators—that could produce electric power on a large scale.

Wind generators could be used in places that have fairly strong and fairly constant winds. At present, costs are high. Some of the equipment also needs to be improved.

Nuclear Fusion. Once scientists solve the problems with nuclear fusion, this may be a source of energy for thousands of years. Fusion is the union of hydrogen atoms to produce helium atoms. In the process, enormous amounts of energy are released. Fusion does not produce radioactive wastes, and the oceans are an almost endless source of hydrogen atoms. But scientists have not been able to build a system that can contain and control the fusion process. Even optimists do not expect fusion to be available for energy needs until after the year 2000.

Garbage Power. Trash and garbage can be processed to make gas and oil. Or they can be burned to heat buildings or to make steam for generating electricity. European cities have been turning wastes into electricity for many years. This technology has par-

ticular appeal for big cities that produce large amounts of wastes. Such cities are running out of places to put all their garbage.

Tidal Energy. The daily rise and fall of the tides can be used to drive turbines for generating electricity. Tidal plants are hard to build because they must be in deep water. They also must be strong enough to withstand the pressure of enormous amounts of rushing water. These dams are very costly.

Ocean Thermal Energy Conversion (OTEC). Heat from the sun is absorbed by surface ocean waters. In tropical waters, there may be a 25°C (45°F) difference between surface and deep waters. An offshore power plant can use this difference to generate electricity. Warm surface water is pumped around tubes containing ammonia or another liquid with a low boiling point. The ammonia vaporizes and passes through a turbine that is connected to a generator. The ammonia is then chilled back to its liquid state by cold water pumped up from ocean depths, and the process can be repeated. The electricity can be sent to shore by cable, or it can be used on board a floating ocean platform for various industrial processes. If experimental programs are successful, OTEC may be commercially available by the year 2000.

▶WHICH WILL WE USE?

The field of energy supply is one of rapid change. New predictions of available supplies and of probable demands are continually being made. New ideas for developing alternate sources are continually being proposed. As these are tested, some prove to be unusable. Others need changes. Others may work—if the economics, politics, and environmental aspects are acceptable.

Probably we will depend on a variety of energy sources in the future. People in some places may use the wind as their primary energy source. In some coastal areas, tidal power may dominate. In some places, coal or petroleum will be used, and so on. Until then, it is important that we conserve the supplies we have—to make them last as long as possible.

▶CONSERVING ENERGY

Everyone can help conserve energy. Some actions may not come easily. They

A wall of mirrors, focusing the sun's rays, provides energy for this solar furnace in France.

will demand new habits and attitudes from government, industry, and every individual —whether young or old.

One way to conserve energy is to increase the efficiency with which we use our energy supplies. For example, it would be more efficient to gasify coal and use the gas to operate fuel cells than it is to burn coal directly. Car engines, appliances, and many other items can be designed so that they would operate on less energy.

The people of the United States use more energy than any other people on earth. Some conservationists believe that they could cut personal (including home) energy use by one third without serious inconvenience. The following are some suggestions they offer for saving energy (and money as well):

Heating. Set home thermostats to 19°C (67°F) for heating and to 25°C (77°F) for cooling. Be sure all windows and doors are closed when heating or cooling a room or a house. In regions where winter temperatures are low, install storm doors and windows, as well as attic and wall insulation.

Appliances. Use washing machines, clothes dryers, and dishwashers only with full loads. An empty machine uses nearly as much energy as a full one. Turn off lights and appliances in empty rooms or when they are not needed. Install fluorescent lights. A 50-watt fluorescent light gives three times as much light as a standard 50-watt bulb.

Transportation. Keep in mind that a bus or train uses less energy per person than does a car. A carpool is a more efficient use of energy than is driving alone. Small cars are better energy savers than large ones. Bicycles are better than cars.

Everyone needs to ask: What am I doing to conserve energy? What more can I do—starting today?

MORRIS K. UDALL
Chairman, Committee on Interior
and Insular Affairs
U.S. House of Representatives

INTERNATIONAL STATISTICAL SUPPLEMENT
(as of December 31, 1978)

NATION	CAPITAL	AREA (in sq mi)	POPULATION (estimate)	GOVERNMENT
Afghanistan	Kabul	250,000	20,300,000	Noor Mohammed Taraki—president
Albania	Tirana	11,100	2,600,000	Enver Hoxha—communist party secretary Mehmet Shehu—premier
Algeria	Algiers	919,593	17,900,000	Rabah Bitat—interim president
Angola	Luanda	481,351	6,800,000	Agostinho Neto—president
Argentina	Buenos Aires	1,072,158	26,100,000	Jorge Rafael Videla—president
Australia	Canberra	2,967,900	14,200,000	Malcolm Fraser—prime minister
Austria	Vienna	32,374	7,500,000	Rudolf Kirchschläger—president Bruno Kreisky—chancellor
Bahamas	Nassau	5,380	220,000	Lynden O. Pindling—prime minister
Bahrain	Manama	240	270,000	Isa ibn Sulman al-Khalifa—head of government
Bangladesh	Dacca	55,126	81,000,000	Ziaur Rahman—president
Barbados	Bridgetown	166	250,000	J. M. G. Adams—prime minister
Belgium	Brussels	11,781	9,900,000	Baudouin I—king Paul Vanden Boeynants—premier
Benin (Dahomey)	Porto-Novo	43,483	3,300,000	Mathieu Kerekou—president
Bhutan	Thimbu	18,147	1,200,000	Jigme Singye Wangchuk—king
Bolivia	La Paz Sucre	424,163	6,000,000	David Padilla Arancibia—head of government
Botswana	Gaborone	231,804	710,000	Sir Seretse Khama—president
Brazil	Brasília	3,286,478	112,000,000	Ernesto Geisel—president
Bulgaria	Sofia	42,823	8,800,000	Todor Zhivkov—communist party secretary Stanko Todorov—premier
Burma	Rangoon	261,789	31,500,000	U Ne Win—president U Maung Maung Kha—prime minister
Burundi	Bujumbura	10,747	4,000,000	Jean-Baptiste Bagaza—president
Cambodia (Kampuchea)	Pnompenh	69,898	8,600,000	Pol Pot—communist party chairman Khieu Samphan—head of state
Cameroon	Yaoundé	183,569	6,700,000	Ahmadou Ahidjo—president
Canada	Ottawa	3,851,809	23,500,000	Pierre Elliott Trudeau—prime minister
Cape Verde	Praia	1,557	310,000	Aristides Pereira—president
Central African Empire	Bangui	240,535	3,000,000	Bokassa I—emperor

NATION	CAPITAL	AREA (in sq mi)	POPULATION (estimate)	GOVERNMENT
Chad	N'Djemena	495,754	4,200,000	Félix Malloum—head of government
Chile	Santiago	292,257	10,700,000	Augusto Pinochet Ugarte—president
China	Peking	3,705,396	866,000,000	Hua Kuo-feng—communist party chairman and premier
Colombia	Bogotá	439,736	25,000,000	Julio Cesar Turbay Ayala—president
Comoros	Moroni	838	370,000	Ahmed Abdallah—president
Congo	Brazzaville	132,047	1,400,000	Joachim Yombi Opango—president
Costa Rica	San José	19,575	2,100,000	Rodrigo Carazo Odio—president
Cuba	Havana	44,218	9,500,000	Osvaldo Dorticós Torrado—president Fidel Castro—premier
Cyprus	Nicosia	3,572	640,000	Spyros Kyprianou—president
Czechoslovakia	Prague	49,370	15,100,000	Gustáv Husák—communist party secretary and president Lubomír Štrougal—premier
Denmark	Copenhagen	16,629	5,100,000	Margrethe II—queen Anker Jorgensen—premier
Djibouti	Djibouti	8,800	110,000	Hassan Gouled—president
Dominica	Roseau	290	80,000	Patrick R. John—prime minister
Dominican Republic	Santo Domingo	18,816	5,000,000	Antonio Guzmán—president
Ecuador	Quito	109,483	7,600,000	Alfredo Poveda Burbano—president
Egypt	Cairo	386,660	38,800,000	Anwar el-Sadat—president Mustafa Khalil—premier
El Salvador	San Salvador	8,260	4,100,000	Carlos Humberto Romero—president
Equatorial Guinea	Malabo	10,830	320,000	Macie Nguema Biyogo—president
Ethiopia	Addis Ababa	471,777	29,000,000	Mengistu Haile Mariam—head of state
Fiji	Suva	7,055	600,000	Ratu Sir Kamisese Mara—prime minister
Finland	Helsinki	130,120	4,700,000	Urho K. Kekkonen—president Kalevi Sorsa—premier
France	Paris	211,207	53,200,000	Valéry Giscard d'Estaing—president Raymond Barre—premier
Gabon	Libreville	103,346	530,000	Albert B. Bongo—president
Gambia	Banjul	4,361	550,000	Sir Dauda K. Jawara—president
Germany (East)	East Berlin	41,768	16,800,000	Erich Honecker—communist party secretary Willi Stoph—premier
Germany (West)	Bonn	95,976	61,400,000	Walter Scheel—president Helmut Schmidt—chancellor
Ghana	Accra	92,099	10,500,000	Fred W. K. Akuffo—head of government
Greece	Athens	50,944	9,300,000	Constantine Tsatsos—president Constantine Caramanlis—premier
Grenada	St. George's	133	100,000	Eric M. Gairy—prime minister

NATION	CAPITAL	AREA (in sq mi)	POPULATION (estimate)	GOVERNMENT
Guatemala	Guatemala City	42,042	6,400,000	Romeo Lucas García—president
Guinea	Conakry	94,926	4,600,000	Sékou Touré—president Lansana Beavogui—premier
Guinea-Bissau	Bissau	13,948	540,000	Luiz de Almeida Cabral—president
Guyana	Georgetown	83,000	830,000	Arthur Chung—president Forbes Burnham—prime minister
Haiti	Port-au-Prince	10,714	4,800,000	Jean-Claude Duvalier—president
Honduras	Tegucigalpa	43,277	2,800,000	Policarpo Paz García—head of state
Hungary	Budapest	35,919	10,700,000	János Kádár—communist party secretary György Lazar—premier
Iceland	Reykjavik	39,768	220,000	Kristján Eldjárn—president Ólafur Jóhannesson—prime minister
India	New Delhi	1,266,598	626,000,000	Neelam Sanjiva Reddy—president Morarji R. Desai—prime minister
Indonesia	Jakarta	735,269	143,000,000	Suharto—president
Iran	Teheran	636,294	34,300,000	Mohammed Reza Pahlavi—shah Shahpur Bakhtiar—premier
Iraq	Baghdad	167,925	12,000,000	Ahmed Hassan al-Bakr—president
Ireland	Dublin	27,136	3,200,000	Patrick Hillery—president Jack Lynch—prime minister
Israel	Jerusalem	7,992	3,600,000	Yitzhak Navon—president Menahem Begin—prime minister
Italy	Rome	116,303	56,600,000	Alessandro Pertini—president Giulio Andreotti—premier
Ivory Coast	Abidjan	124,503	6,700,000	Félix Houphouët-Boigny—president
Jamaica	Kingston	4,232	2,100,000	Michael N. Manley—prime minister
Japan	Tokyo	143,750	114,000,000	Hirohito—emperor Masayoshi Ohira—premier
Jordan	Amman	37,738	2,800,000	Hussein I—king Mudar Badran—premier
Kenya	Nairobi	224,959	14,300,000	Daniel Arap Moi—president
Korea (North)	Pyongyang	46,540	16,700,000	Kim Il Sung—president Li Jong-ok—premier
Korea (South)	Seoul	38,022	36,400,000	Park Chung Hee—president Choi Kyu Hah—premier
Kuwait	Kuwait	6,880	1,100,000	Jaber al-Ahmed al-Sabah—head of state
Laos	Vientiane	91,429	3,500,000	Souphanouvong—president Kaysone Phomvihan—premier
Lebanon	Beirut	4,015	3,100,000	Elias Sarkis—president Selim al-Hoss—premier
Lesotho	Maseru	11,720	1,200,000	Moshoeshoe II—king Leabua Jonathan—prime minister

NATION	CAPITAL	AREA (in sq mi)	POPULATION (estimate)	GOVERNMENT
Liberia	Monrovia	43,000	1,800,000	William R. Tolbert—president
Libya	Tripoli	679,360	2,500,000	Muammar el-Qaddafi—president
Liechtenstein	Vaduz	61	23,000	Francis Joseph II—prince
Luxembourg	Luxembourg	999	360,000	Jean—grand duke Gaston Thorn—premier
Madagascar	Antananarivo	226,657	8,500,000	Didier Ratsiraka—president
Malawi	Lilongwe	45,747	5,600,000	H. Kamuzu Banda—president
Malaysia	Kuala Lumpur	127,316	12,600,000	Yahaya Putra ibn al-Marhum—paramount ruler Hussein Onn—prime minister
Maldives	Male	115	140,000	Ibrahim Nasir—president
Mali	Bamako	478,765	6,000,000	Moussa Traoré—president
Malta	Valletta	122	330,000	Sir Anthony Mamo—president Dom Mintoff—prime minister
Mauritania	Nouakchott	397,954	1,500,000	Mustapha Ould Salek—president
Mauritius	Port Louis	720	910,000	Sir Seewoosagur Ramgoolam—prime minister
Mexico	Mexico City	761,602	64,600,000	José López Portillo—president
Monaco	Monaco-Ville	0.4	25,000	Rainier III—prince
Mongolia	Ulan Bator	604,248	1,500,000	Yumzhagiyn Tsedenbal—communist party secretary
Morocco	Rabat	172,413	18,300,000	Hassan II—king Ahmed Osman—premier
Mozambique	Maputo	302,329	9,700,000	Samora Machel—president
Nauru	—	8	8,000	Hammer DeRoburt—president
Nepal	Katmandu	54,362	13,100,000	Birendra Bir Bikram Shah Deva—king Kirtinidhi Bista—prime minister
Netherlands	Amsterdam	15,770	13,900,000	Juliana—queen Andreas A. M. Van Agt—premier
New Zealand	Wellington	103,736	3,200,000	Robert D. Muldoon—prime minister
Nicaragua	Managua	50,193	2,300,000	Anastasio Somoza Debayle—president
Niger	Niamey	489,190	4,900,000	Seyni Kountche—head of government
Nigeria	Lagos	356,668	66,700,000	Olusegun Obasanjo—head of government
Norway	Oslo	125,181	4,100,000	Olav V—king Odvar Nordli—prime minister
Oman	Muscat	82,030	820,000	Qabus ibn Said—sultan
Pakistan	Islamabad	310,403	75,300,000	Mohammed Zia ul-Haq—president

NATION	CAPITAL	AREA (in sq mi)	POPULATION (estimate)	GOVERNMENT
Panama	Panama City	29,209	1,800,000	Aristides Royo—president
Papua New Guinea	Port Moresby	178,260	2,900,000	Michael Somare—prime minister
Paraguay	Asunción	157,047	2,800,000	Alfredo Stroessner—president
Peru	Lima	496,223	16,400,000	Francisco Morales Bermúdez—president
Philippines	Manila	115,830	45,000,000	Ferdinand E. Marcos—president
Poland	Warsaw	120,724	35,000,000	Edward Gierek—communist party secretary Piotr Jaroszewicz—premier
Portugal	Lisbon	35,553	9,000,000	António Ramalho Eanes—president Carlos Mota Pinto—premier
Qatar	Doha	4,000	100,000	Khalifa ibn Hamad al-Thani—head of government
Rhodesia	Salisbury	150,803	6,700,000	John Wrathall—president Ian D. Smith—prime minister
Rumania	Bucharest	91,700	21,700,000	Nicolae Ceauşescu—communist party secretary Manea Manescu—premier
Rwanda	Kigali	10,169	4,400,000	Juvénal Habyalimana—president
São Tomé and Príncipe	São Tomé	372	82,000	Manuel Pinto da Costa—president
Saudi Arabia	Riyadh	829,997	9,500,000	Khalid ibn Abdul-Aziz—king
Senegal	Dakar	75,750	5,100,000	Léopold Senghor—president
Seychelles	Victoria	107	62,000	France Albert René—president
Sierre Leone	Freetown	27,700	3,500,000	Siaka P. Stevens—president
Singapore	Singapore	224	2,300,000	Benjamin H. Sheares—president Lee Kuan Yew—prime minister
Solomon Islands	Honiara	10,983	210,000	Peter Kenilorea—prime minister
Somalia	Mogadishu	246,200	3,400,000	Mohammed Siad Barre—head of government
South Africa	Pretoria Cape Town	471,444	26,100,000	John Vorster—president Pieter W. Botha—prime minister
Spain	Madrid	194,897	36,700,000	Juan Carlos I—king Adolfo Suárez González—premier
Sri Lanka (Ceylon)	Colombo	25,332	14,000,000	Junius R. Jayewardene—president Ranasinghe Premadasa—prime minister
Sudan	Khartoum	967,497	17,000,000	Gaafar al-Numeiry—president
Surinam	Paramaribo	63,037	450,000	Henck A. E. Arron—prime minister
Swaziland	Mbabane	6,704	500,000	Sobhuza II—king
Sweden	Stockholm	173,732	8,300,000	Carl XVI Gustaf—king Ola Ullsten—prime minister

NATION	CAPITAL	AREA (in sq mi)	POPULATION (estimate)	GOVERNMENT
Switzerland	Bern	15,941	6,300,000	Hans Hürlimann—president
Syria	Damascus	71,586	7,800,000	Hafez al-Assad—president Mohammed Ali al-Halabi—premier
Taiwan	Taipei	13,885	16,800,000	Chiang Ching-kuo—president Sun Yun-suan—premier
Tanzania	Dar es Salaam	364,898	16,100,000	Julius K. Nyerere—president
Thailand	Bangkok	198,456	44,000,000	Bhumibol Adulyadej—king Kriangsak Chamanand—premier
Togo	Lomé	21,622	2,400,000	Gnassingbe Eyadema—president
Tonga	Nuku'alofa	270	91,000	Taufa'ahau Tupou IV—king Prince Tu'ipelehake—prime minister
Trinidad & Tobago	Port of Spain	1,980	1,100,000	Sir Ellis Clarke—president Eric Williams—prime minister
Tunisia	Tunis	63,170	6,100,000	Habib Bourguiba—president
Turkey	Ankara	301,381	42,000,000	Fahri Korutürk—president Bulent Ecevit—president
Tuvalu	Funafuti	10	10,000	Toalipi Lauti—prime minister
Uganda	Kampala	91,134	12,400,000	Idi Amin—president
U.S.S.R.	Moscow	8,649,512	259,000,000	Leonid I. Brezhnev—communist party secretary and president Aleksei N. Kosygin—premier
United Arab Emirates	Abu Dhabi	32,278	240,000	Zayd ibn Sultan—president
United Kingdom	London	94,226	55,900,000	Elizabeth II—queen James Callaghan—prime minister
United States	Washington, D.C.	3,615,123	219,000,000	James Earl Carter, Jr.—president Walter F. Mondale—vice-president
Upper Volta	Ouagadougou	105,869	6,300,000	Sangoulé Lamizana—president
Uruguay	Montevideo	68,536	2,800,000	Aparicio Méndez—president
Venezuela	Caracas	352,143	12,700,000	Luis Herrera Campins—president-elect
Vietnam	Hanoi	128,402	48,000,000	Le Duan—communist party secretary Ton Duc Thang—president Pham Van Dong—premier
Western Samoa	Apia	1,097	150,000	Malietoa Tanumafili II—head of state
Yemen (Aden)	Madinat al-Shaab	112,000	1,800,000	Abdul Fatah Ismail—president
Yemen (Sana)	Sana	75,290	7,100,000	Ali Abdullah Saleh—president
Yugoslavia	Belgrade	98,766	21,900,000	Josip Broz Tito—president Veselin Djuranovic—premier
Zaïre	Kinshasa	905,565	26,400,000	Mobutu Sese Seko—president
Zambia	Lusaka	290,585	5,300,000	Kenneth D. Kaunda—president

INDEX

A

B

D

E

F

H

I

J

K

L

M

Q

R

S

T

V

W

ILLUSTRATION CREDITS AND ACKNOWLEDGMENTS

The following list credits or acknowledges, by page, the source of illustrations and text excerpts used in THE NEW BOOK OF KNOWLEDGE ANNUAL. Illustration credits are listed illustration by illustration—left to right, top to bottom. When two or more illustrations appear on one page, their credits are separated by semicolons. When both the photographer or artist and an agency or other source are given for an illustration, they are usually separated by a dash. Excerpts from previously published works are listed by inclusive page numbers.

14 Oliphant, *The Washington Star,* Los Angeles Times Syndicate
15 UPI
16 UPI
17 Wide World
18 Paterson—Liason
19 UPI
20 UPI
21 Wide World
22 Tass From Sovfoto
23 UPI
24 Wide World
25 Wide World
26 Wide World
27 UPI
28 Hans Namuth
29 Sebastiao Salgado—Liason
30 UPI
31 Wide World
32 Wide World
35 Reprinted from *The Saturday Evening Post* © 1943 The Curtis Publishing Company
36 UPI
37 UPI
38 Bettmann Archive
39 Wide World
41 Wide World
42 Wide World
43 UPI
44 Sipa Press/Black Star
45 Mike Norcia—Photoreporters
46 Sipa Press/Black Star
47 Courtesy Copley News Service
48 UPI
49 Wide World
50– Stan Wayman—Photo Researchers
51
52 Courtesy Peabody Museum of Natural History, Yale University; UPI
53 Steve Northrup—*The New York Times;* Larry Morris—*The New York Times*
54– Peter D. Capen
55
56 Bob Campbell—Bruce Coleman
57 Peter Ward—Bruce Coleman; Bob Campbell—Bruce Coleman
58 Zoological Society of San Diego, Inc.
59 © Beth Bergman 1978
60 Harry Engels
61 Peter D. Capen; C. A. Morgan; C. A. Morgan
62 Harry Engels; Charlie Ott—National Audubon Society/Photo Researchers; Roman Vishniac
63 Charlie Ott—National Audubon Society/Photo Researchers; Larry West
64– Courtesy the American Museum of Natural
65 History
66– Text reprinted from *Ranger Rick's Nature*
67 *Magazine,* © September, 1977. By permission of the publisher, the National Wildlife Federation
66 R.D. Estes—Photo Researchers; © John M. Burnley—National Audubon Society/Photo Researchers
67 Tom Bledsoe—Photo Researchers; Tom McHugh—Photo Researchers
68 Dr. Norman E. Gary
70– Dr. Norman E. Gary
71
72– Tom & Michele Grimm
73
74– Courtesy Mobil Oil Corporation
75
76 Prologue adapted from *Transportation in the World of the Future,* by Hal Hellman. © 1968, 1974 by Hal Hellman. Adaptation by permission of the publisher, M. Evans and Company, Inc., New York
77 Vought Corp.
78 Drawn by Christopher Kitrick, based on a design by R. Buckminster Fuller
79 Vought Corp.
80 Paul W. Bower—Vought Corp.
81 Rohr Marine, Inc.
82 Van Bucher—Photo Researchers
83 Marvin E. Newman—Woodfin Camp
84 Courtesy Hansen Planetarium/Celestron International
85 Courtesy Smithsonian Institution
86 Jonathan Rawle—Stock, Boston
87 Courtesy National Oceanic and Atmospheric Administration
88 UPI
89 Tass from Sovfoto
90 NASA
91 NASA; UPI
92 Wide World
93 *The New York Times*
94 The Museum of Modern Art Film Stills Archive. © 1977, 20th Century-Fox Film Corp.
95 Courtesy Dr. John F. Asmus
96 Bettmann Archive
97 NASA
98 Emil Schulthess—Black Star
99 Animals Animals/ © Oxford Scientific Films
100– Manny Rodriguez
101
102 Courtesy Regis McKenna
103 Nelson Morris—Photo Researchers
104 Abbie Carroll Wilson
105 *The New York Times*
106 Musée d'Art et d'Histoire Neuchâtel, Suisse
107 UPI
108 Queen's Devices, Inc.
109 NASA; Westinghouse Science Talent Search
110 Bettmann Archive
111 Francois Bota—Liason
112 Paolo Koch—Photo Researchers
113 Thomas D. W. Friedmann—Photo Researchers
114 James Pollock—National Audubon Society/Photo Researchers
115 John Wheatley
116 Wide World
117 UPI
118 UPI; Wide World
119 Wide World
120 Wide World
121 Ann Hagen Griffiths—DPI
122– Jan Braunle
123
128– From *Many Hands Cooking: An International*
129 *Cookbook for Girls and Boys.* Cooked and written by Terry Touff Cooper and Marilyn Ratner. Illustrated by Tony Chen. Thomas Y. Crowell Company in cooperation with the U.S. Committee for UNICEF New York. © 1974. By permission
130– *Owl Magazine.* **Answers:** The early flowers
131 have disappeared and tulips and dandelions are blooming in green grass. The yellow forsythia bush now has green leaves, as have the birch and maple trees. Butterflies have appeared. The cat is lying in the sun. The robin eggs have hatched. The geese are no longer migrating. The rosebush is uncovered. The window is open. The dog now lives outside in its kennel. The leaves are raked up. The wash is on the line. The swing is back on the tree. The children are dressed in light clothes.
132 Alexandra Stoddard
134– Alexandra Stoddard
136
137 Ann Hagen Griffiths—DPI
140– Jan Braunle
141
142– Courtesy *Creative Crafts Magazine*
145
146 Jenny Tesar
147 Jacques Chazaud

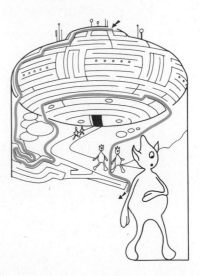

148– Courtesy Krause Publications, Inc.
149
150– Courtesy Binney & Smith
153
154 Jan Braunle
155 Judith Hoffman Corwin
156– John V.A.F. Neal—Photo Researchers
157
158 Focus On Sports
159 Mitchell B. Reibel—Focus on Sports
161 Vannucci Foto Services
162 Jerry Wachter—Focus On Sports
163 Wide World
164 *The Toronto Star*
165 Wide World; *The Toronto Star*
166 UPI
167– Wide World
168
169 UPI
170 Manny Millan—*Sports Illustrated* © Time Inc.
171 Courtesy Winnipeg Jets
172 UPI
173 Mitchell B. Reibel—Focus On Sports; J. DiMaggio, J. Kalish—Peter Arnold
174 UPI; Wide World
175 UPI
176 Bruce Curtis—Peter Arnold
177 UPI
178 George Tiedemann—*Sports Illustrated* © 1978 Time Inc.
179 Villalobos—Liason
180– Wide World
182
183 Wide World; UPI
184 Ann Hagen Griffiths—DPI
185 Mimi Forsyth—Monkmeyer
186 Run For Life/Connecticut Mutual Life Insurance Co. via Authenticated News International
187 Michael Philip Manheim—Photo Researchers
189 Focus on Sports
190– Courtesy Australian Information Service
191
192 John G. Ross—Photo Researchers
193– British Crown Copyright: Reproduced with
195 the permission of the Controller of Her Majesty's Stationery Office
196– Courtesy Old Fort William
197
198 Russ Kinne—Photo Researchers
199 Courtesy Florida Department of Commerce
200 D. R. Bridge—Woodfin Camp
201 S. L. Waterman—Photo Researchers
202 Courtesy Australian Information Service (Painting by J. Dance)
203 George Buctel
204 Mike Wells
205– BBC Copyright Photos
206
207 Mike Wells
208 Courtesy British Tourist Authority
209 Copyright the Frick Collection, New York
210 William C. Blizzard
212 William C. Blizzard; William C. Blizzard; Dolly Sherwood
213 Courtesy State of West Virginia, Department of Culture and History

214– Jenny Tesar
215
216 B & C Alexander—Bruce Coleman
217 Fred Baldwin—Photo Researchers; B & C Alexander—Bruce Coleman
218 Pål-Nils Nilsson—Tiofoto
219 Isabel Brito—DPI
220 Andy Bernhaut—Photo Researchers
221 Courtesy AMARC, Pavillion du Canada
222– Courtesy the Children's Theatre Company and
223 School
224– Courtesy of Scholastic Photography Awards,
227 conducted by Scholastic Magazines, Inc., and sponsored by Eastman Kodak Company
228– Courtesy Harry Goldsmith
229
230 Boy Scouts of Canada; Boy Scouts of America
231– Boy Scouts of America
233
234– Courtesy the Children's Theatre Company and
235 School
236– Girl Scouts of the USA
239
240 Jenny Tesar
241 NBC
242 UPI; Martha Cooper—New York Post
243 Wide World; Maddy Miller—*U.S. Magazine*
244 Michael Putland—Retna
245 Wide World
246– Jonathan Atkin
249
250– Presented by Pentel of America, Ltd.
253
254– United States–China People's Friendship
255 Association and Environmental Communications
256 Lobl—Shostal
257– Courtesy Xerox Corporation
259
260– Cooper-Hewitt Museum
261
262– United States–China People's Friendship
263 Association and Environmental Communications
264– Robert R. McElroy—*Newsweek*
265
266 UPI
267 UPI; © 1977, 20th Century Fox Film Corp. All rights reserved
268 Fin Costello—Retna
269 Alan Pappé—Lee Gross
270 Michael Putland—Retna
271 Redferns: Photo Tony Russell—Retna
272 Michael Putland—Retna; Paul Canty—LFI/Retna; Richard E. Aaron—Retna
274– © Walt Disney Productions
275
276 Comic strip: © 1935 Walt Disney Productions; © Walt Disney Productions; © Walt Disney Productions
277 © Walt Disney Productions
279 EPA
280 Masefield Collection, Rare Book and Manuscript Library, Columbia University
281 EPA
282– Martha Swope
283

285 R. C. Lautman; Dennis Brack—Black Star; R. C. Lautman
286– Excerpted from *Noah's Ark* by Peter Spier.
287 Illustration copyright © 1977 by Peter Spier. Reprinted by permission of Doubleday & Company, Inc.
288– Text by Frances B. Watts, from *Easy*
291 *Economics Stories,* © 1977 by The Saturday Evening Post Company, Indianapolis, Indiana; Artist, Charles McVicker
292 Heinz Edelman
295 Heinz Edelman
296– From *Scandinavian Stories,* by Margaret
303 Sperry. Illustrations by Jenny Williams. Illustrations © 1971 by Franklin Watts, Inc. used by permission.
306– Reprinted by permission from *The Christian*
307 *Science Monitor,* © 1977 and © 1978. The Christian Science Publishing Society. All rights reserved
308 Allan Eitzen
311 Allan Eitzen
314 Allan Eitzen
316 Bettmann Archive
318 Allan Eitzen
320 *Funny Feet!* by Leatie Weiss. Illustrated by Ellen Weiss. © 1978 by Franklin Watts, used by permission.
321 From *The View From the Oak,* © 1977 Judith and Herbert Kohl. Used with the permission of Charles Scribner's Sons and Sierra Club Books.
322 Illustration by Donna Diamond from *Bridge to Terabithia* by Katherine Paterson, © 1977 by Katherine Paterson. By permission of Thomas Y. Crowell.
323 Excerpted from *Noah's Ark* by Peter Spier. Illustration © 1977 by Peter Spier. Reprinted by permission of Doubleday & Company, Inc.
324– Text by Christine Scott, from *Jack and Jill*
334 magazine, © 1968 by the Curtis Publishing Company; Artist, Charles McVicker
336 Ken Heyman
337 Syndication International
338 John Foster—U.S. Fish & Wildlife Service
339 Peace Corps Photo by Sklarewitz
340 Peace Corps Photo by Emma Rivera
341 Peace Corps Photos by Carolyn Redenios
342 The Museum of Modern Art—Film Stills Archive
343 Culver
345 Alcoa; A. Devaney; A. Devaney
346 Shell Oil
347 Jarrold; Mark N. Boulton—National Audubon Society
349 Paolo Koch—Rapho Guillumette
350 Byron Crader—Lenstour